POVERTY AND THE LAW

OÑATI INTERNATIONAL SERIES IN LAW AND SOCIETY

A SERIES PUBLISHED FOR THE OÑATI INSTITUTE
FOR THE SOCIOLOGY OF LAW

Titles in this Series

Emerging Legal Certainty: Empirical Studies on the Globalization of Law
Edited by Volkmar Gessner and Ali Cem Budak

Totalitarian and Post-Totalitarian Law
Edited by Adam Podgorecki and Vittorio Olgiati

Family Law and Family Policy in the New Europe
Edited by Jacek Kurczewski and Mavis Maclean

Foreign Courts: Civil Litigation in Foreign Legal Cultures
Edited by Volkmar Gessner

Procedural Justice
Edited by Klaus F. Röhl and Stefan Machura

Prison Labour: Salvation or Slavery
Edited by Dirk van Zyl Smit and Frieder Düntel

(ALL THE ABOVE TITLES PUBLISHED BY ASHGATE)

Criminal Policy in Transition
Edited by Penny Green and Andrew Rutherford

Social Dynamics of Crime and Control
New Theories for a World in Transition
Edited by Susanne Karstedt and Kai-D Bussmann

Making Law for Families
Edited by Mavis Maclean

(PUBLISHED BY HART PUBLISHING)

Poverty and the Law

Edited by
PETER ROBSON
and
ASBJØRN KJØNSTAD

OÑATI INTERNATIONAL SERIES IN LAW AND SOCIETY

A SERIES PUBLISHED FOR THE OÑATI INSTITUTE
FOR THE SOCIOLOGY OF LAW

·HART·
PUBLISHING
OXFORD – PORTLAND OREGON
2001

Hart Publishing
Oxford and Portland, Oregon

Published in North America (US and Canada) by
Hart Publishing c/o
International Specialized Book Services
5804 NE Hassalo Street
Portland, Oregon
97213-3644
USA

Distributed in the Netherlands, Belgium and Luxembourg by
Intersentia, Churchillaan 108
B2900 Schoten
Antwerpen
Belgium

Hart Publishing is a specialist legal publisher based in Oxford, England. To order further copies of this book or to request a list of other publications please write to:

Hart Publishing, Salter's Boatyard,
Folly Bridge, Abingdon Road, Oxford OX1 4LB
Telephone: +44 (0)1865 245533 or Fax: +44 (0)1865 794882
e-mail: mail@hartpub.co.uk
WEBSITE: http//www.hartpub.co.uk

British Library Cataloguing in Publication Data
Data Available
ISBN 1–84113–190–3 (cloth)
ISBN 1–84113–191–1 (paperback)

Typeset by Hope Services (Abingdon) Ltd.
Printed and bound in Great Britain by
Lightning Source UK Ltd

Series Editors' Foreword

Poverty is one of the great problems facing individuals, families, organisations, states and international agencies at the dawn of the new millennium. Law is one among all too few tools to combat world poverty. This book explores some of the ways that law is, or might, combat poverty by focusing on the protection afforded the poor by constitutional rights, the legal ability of interest organisations to improve the living standards of their members, new kinds of unemployment, social movements of the landless and indigenous, legal services for the poor, and the defense of human rights.

This book is the product of a workshop held in 1997 at the International Institute for the Sociology of Law (IISL) in Oñati, Spain. The IISL is a partnership between the Research Committee on the Sociology of Law and the Basque Government. For more than a decade it has conducted an international master's programme in the sociology of law and hosted hundreds of workshops devoted to sociolegal studies. It maintains an extensive sociolegal library open to scholars from any country and any relevant discipline. Detailed information about the IISL can be found at www.iisj.es. This book is the most recent publication in the Oñati International Series in Law and Society, a series that publishes the best manuscripts produced from Oñati workshops conducted in English. A similar series, Coleccion Oñati: Derecho Y Sociedad, is published in Spanish.

The workshop itself was organized by the Comparative Research Programme on Poverty (CROP). CROP is a response of the academic community to the problem of poverty. Initiated in 1992, the CROP network of scholars provides research-based information to policy-makers and others responsible for poverty reduction. Researchers from more than one hundred countries have joined the CROP network. Nearly half come from the so-called developing countries and countries in transition. With the aim of providing sound and reliable knowledge that can serve as a basis for poverty reduction, CROP brings together researchers for workshops, coordinated research projects and publications, and offers educational courses for the international community of policy-makers. Detailed information about CROP can be found at www.crop.org.

William L. F. Felstiner
Eve Darian-Smith

About the Editors

Peter Robson is Professor of Social Welfare Law in the Law School, University of Strathclyde, Glasgow, Scotland. He has taught Housing Law at the Universities of Stirling, Glasgow and Heriot-Watt, Edinburgh. He is Chair of the campaigning housing charity SHELTER and Chair of the East End Advice Centre, Glasgow. His books include *Justice, Lord Denning and the Constitution; Residential Tenancies; Welfare Law;* and *Homeless People and the Law*. He has carried out empirical research into the impact of legislation on landlords' letting practices and on the effectiveness of the law dealing with the rights of abused women. His recent work covers the representation of law and the legal profession in popular culture. He is currently expanding the brief observations outlined in his chapter on the ways in which progressive lawyers can impact upon the economic and political scene to the benefit of the poor and the disadvantaged.

Asbjørn Kjønstad, born in Norway; Professor Dr. Juris at University of Oslo since 1978; Dean at the Faculty of Law, University of Oslo 1986–88; Vice President in the European Institute of Social Security 1993–97; visiting scholar at Boston University Law School and Boston College Law School 1995–96; Juris Doctor Honoris Causa at Lund University, Sweden, May 1996; Visiting Professor at University of Leuven March and April 1997. He has written 32 books and about 120 articles on social security law, medical law, welfare law, tort law and family law.

About the Contributors

Michael Adler is Professor of Socio-Legal Studies at the University of Edinburgh in Scotland. His main interests are in the socio-legal aspects of welfare policy, with special reference to the legal problems experienced by low-income households; the implications of individual rights for collective policies; and the relationship between administrative decision-making and administrative justice.

Hélène Grandvoinnet wrote this chapter for the OECD Development Centre, where she worked for three years on poverty and corruption issues. After collaborating with the World Bank World Development Report 2000 on poverty, she is now a Public Sector Specialist in the World Bank (Africa Region).

Ross Hastings is a Professor of Criminology at the University of Ottawa (Canada). He graduated from the Faculty of Law at the University of Colombo. He teaches in the areas of crime prevention, community policing and criminal justice policy. He is the former Chair of the National Crime Prevention Council of Canada, and has worked extensively with both police and government agencies in the areas of organisational change in support of new directions in justice policy.

Ajith Hettihewage is an attorney at law, practising in Kandy, Sri Lanka.

Yuri Kazepov holds a Ph.D. in sociology. He teaches sociology at the University of Urbino, Italy. In 1995–96 he was a Jean Monet Fellow at the European University Institute (Fiesole, Italy). Since 1990 he has been a member of the editorial board of *Inchiesta (Dedalo)* and since 1992 a co-ordinator of the *Observatory on Urban Poverty* at the University of Milan. He is also an expert of the EU Commission (DG Research). He has published extensively on poverty, social policies and citizenship from a comparative perspective.

Nicola Loughran is preparing her doctoral thesis on the socio-legal effects of welfare-to-work policies. She also teaches legal theory to law undergraduates. She has co-authored *Children & Young Offenders in Scotland – A Review, Evaluation of Parties' Experience of Mediation, Edinburgh Mediation Project Report* and *Edinburgh Mediation Project, Final Report.*

Antonella Mameli received her legal education at the University of Cagliari, Italy (*Laurea in Giurisprudenza*) and graduated from Yale Law School with a masters degree (LL.M—Master of Laws) and a doctorate (JSD—Juris Science Doctor). She is a member of the Italian Bar, the New York Bar and the Washington DC Bar and is now in private practice in Milan.

Camilo Perez-Bustillo is Research Professor at the State of Mexico campus of the *Instituto Tecnologico y de Estudios Superiores de Monterrey* (ITESM) where he teaches media studies, law and international relations. He is also a resident scholar at the Permanent Seminar on Chicano and Border Studies of the Social Anthropology Division of Mexico's National Institute of Anthropology and History (DEAS-INAH), and the representative in Mexico of the US-based National Lawyers' Guild.

R.P. Saunders is a Professor in the Department of Law at Carleton University in Ottawa (Canada). He teaches criminal justice policy and reform, and has written extensively on the criminal law and interdisciplinary approaches to legal reform.

Kalinga Tudor Silva is Professor of Sociology at the University of Peradeniya, Sri Lanka. He is the author of several books including *Watta-Dwellers: A Sociological Study of Selected Urban Low-income Communities in Sri Lanka* (Lanham: University Press of America, 1992) and *Towards a Healthy Society.* (Manila: de Lasalle University, Social Development Center, 1996). He is currently engaged in research on the impact of economic liberalisation on poverty in Sri Lanka.

Paul Spicker is a Senior Lecturer in Social Policy at the University of Dundee. He is the author of several books on related subjects, including *Stigma and Social Welfare* (1984), *Poverty and Social Security: Concepts and Principles* (1993), *Social Policy* (1995), *The Welfare State: A General Theory* (2000) and a range of academic papers.

Introduction

ASBJØRN KJØNSTAD and PETER ROBSON

This collection of essays represents the second stage in a programme developed by CROP to focus attention on the global impact of legal policies on levels of poverty. They stem from a Conference/Workshop on Law and Poverty held at the Institute for the Sociology of Law in Oñati in 1997. The papers collected here illustrate the distinct dimensions of poverty in a range of different political and cultural settings. They also show how poverty is exacerbated by quite discrete local cultural factors in some instances. There is nonetheless a universal element which runs through all the contributions. The fate of those who are disadvantaged in society depends crucially on their access to the goods through the world of work. Access to the fruits of people's labours may be restricted by accidents of birth. Thus gender, ethnic background or disability can result in individuals having a much higher chance of experiencing poverty than those outwith these groups. The success of these unprivileged groups in achieving a measure of prosperity is bound up with geographical and political factors.

The papers presented here represent both broad themes and specific policy developments. Most address the experiences within one particular political culture and concentrate on current experience rather than historical developments. This focus is quite deliberate at this stage in the CROP Law and Poverty Workshop. We are concerned to build up a picture of the interface of law and poverty in a range of distinct cultures so that we can develop comparative perspectives. From the particular we seek to make links between successful strategies operated in individual struggles and to identify the factors which appeared to bring success. Perhaps in the era dominated by unrestrained free market capitalism across the world it is more frequent that we have to identify the setbacks and problems encountered by the poor and those working with them on poverty issues. The lessons to be learned in this process, however, are invaluable.

INTRODUCTION

The Workshop was concerned to explore the effectiveness of programmes of poverty eradication. We were particularly interested in the role of legislative and other rights under law in this process. In order for us to conduct an informed debate we need to give some thought to both our definitions of poverty and our notions of rights. Paul Spicker's contribution to this book reminds us of the range of meanings which poverty connotes. He then explores an area with which this debate is intimately connected, namely the complex nature and status of rights. The problems which arise from attempts to deal with poverty through the mechanism of individual rights are a central theme of this paper.

THE EXPERIENCE OF POVERTY

Over the years studies, from the first observational reports in the nineteenth century through to the statistical compilations and ethnographic studies of the twentieth century, have delved into the lives of the poor. Their experiences have informed the nature and extent of social reforms. The additional stresses and problems of existing with restricted choices about how and where to live have resulted in programmes designed to overcome these limitations. What also need to be noted are the arcane areas which have been accorded limited attention. These range from the difficulties and humiliations which the poor have been required to undergo before they receive help to the side effects of the lack of power that is the mark of poverty.

In relation to the first of these themes Yuri Kazepov provides a brief guide to the complex patchwork of entitlements and claims of poor individuals in Italy. With its decentralised system of administration we can see how the accidents of local geography play a major part in determining the level of provision for those outwith the world of waged work. This provides an even more fragmented picture than we receive from studies of poverty provision in the United States and is in interesting contrast to national poverty alleviation programmes found in Britain and Scandinavia.

In "Strategies for Police Accountability and Community Empowerment" Ross Hastings and Ron Saunders examine an aspect of the powerlessness of the poor overlooked in the traditional literature on poverty. They discuss the ways in which policing impacts on poor communities in the often overlooked context of Canada. This theme is examined in the specific context of the policing strategies and the accountability of the police. The lack of control experienced by poor communities in respect of policing adds to their overall disempowerment. The authors discuss developments in the province of Ontario and explore a range of alternatives to the traditional models of developing police strategies and ensuring accountability .

STRATEGIES TO CONFRONT POVERTY

The political processes operating in different countries have produced a range of different accommodations to the threat from the dispossessed over the years. Organised labour has been successful in many industrialised nations in securing rights for poor workers through political action. Mass class parties have directly and indirectly sought to address the questions of low wages and inadequate benefits for times of sickness and unemployment. Whilst this has transformed the political face of modern Europe in the twentieth century, some groups have been ignored in this political process.

One such group are the untouchables in southern Asia. Kalinga Tudor Silva concentrates on how in Ceylon the impact of caste has traditionally affected those at the bottom of the pyramid, the untouchables. He draws attention to developments in the political power of this group and how they have sought, as a group, to develop a credible strategy to deal with the structural inequality which is the essence of a caste system. He points out the tensions and problems experienced in operating an affirmative action programme as a method of confronting caste oppression.

A more subtle form of unequal treatment is considered by Peter Robson and Nicola Loughran. They examine the impact of neglect and absence of policies in relation to a group marginalised by social prejudice, namely disabled people. They trace efforts here to combat their exclusion from the world of work, and efforts to deal with the additional costs of disability. They suggest that there is a paradoxical situation wherein paper rights have expanded whilst the resources devoted to disability issues have kept no pace with the real costs of disability. In this area there has not been overt ideological retrenchment. The impact of the new rights on the lives of disabled people has, however, been disappointing. This is directly connected to their limited industrial and political influence.

ACCESS TO JUSTICE FOR THE POOR

The development of political and social rights for the powerless in society has occurred at the behest of those suspicious of the significance of justice systems. The significance of procedural rights and justice through the court system serving the interests of the rich has only recently been recognised. The importance of ensuring not only that rights are secured but that their effectiveness is guaranteed has become as a focus for the concerns of those in poverty.

In contrasting the very different socio-political contexts in the United States and Italy Antonella Mameli addresses the impact of using constitutional equal protection provisions on the success of the poor in mobilising to counter exclusion. She compares the United States and Italian experiences on this issue. The evidence suggests that the familiar division of the deserving from the undeserving which has informed poverty policies in many cultures provides the key to understanding how some groups have made advances in the twentieth century in these two political systems.

As far as the United Kingdom is concerned Mike Adler takes a detailed look at the way in which the rights of poor people to challenge those making decisions about their entitlement to benefits from the state has been steadily eroded over the past twenty years in Britain. This issue has been neglected but it is of crucial significance for those seeking to provide a sound grounding for protecting the social claims of the poor from the vagaries of party politics.

OVERVIEWS

The collection concludes with two quite distinct overviews. First, Helene Grandvoinnet provides a wide-ranging geographical overview in "The Rule of Law and Poverty Reduction: a Comparative Perspective". She traces the nature of the experience of poverty in a representative selection of developing countries, and shows how strategies have been developed to engage with the poverty encountered by a range of disadvantaged groups. She notes that one of the problems they encounter is how to make effective those rights which they manage to secure from their more affluent compatriots. In contrast, Camillo Perez-Bustillo concludes this volume by considering all its themes as they affect one country. He examines the context of the uprisings of the poor in Mexico in the 1990s. He outlines the impact of the experience of poverty on indigenous people and suggests that the Chiapas actions reveal not only strategies for confronting the experience of poverty but also the relationship to access to justice of the oppressed.

These essays point the way to further work. CROP has encouraged this with a further Workshop, which evaluated the use of law as a tool to combat poverty and was held in Oñati in May 1999.

Introduction

1

The Rights of the Poor: Conceptual Issues

PAUL SPICKER

SUMMARY

BEFORE WE CAN talk about the rights of the poor, we need to address two deceptively simple questions. First, who are the poor? Secondly, what are rights?

Definitions of poverty include:

- concepts which refer to material status, including need, multiple deprivation, lack of security and lack of resources;
- those which refer to moral status, including entitlement and serious hardship; and
- those which refer to social relationships, including relationships of inequality, class, dependency and exclusion.

Rights for the poor can be legal or moral; they can concern claim-rights or liberties; they can be particular, contingent or universal; and they can be individual or collective. Different definitions of poverty imply different strategies for the development of rights. Although the concepts of poverty overlap, and strategies based on rights are not exclusive, there are dangers in ignoring the multifaceted nature of the problems, and there are circumstances in which rights which alleviate poverty in one sense may aggravate it in others.

WHO ARE THE POOR?

Poverty is not a straightforward concept with a single unambiguous definition. In *The International Glossary on Poverty*, I outlined eleven overlapping but discrete meanings of poverty.[1]

1. *Need*. Poverty refers, in the first place, to need: a shortage or lack of basic goods. People are said to be poor when they lack basic or essential items,

[1] See Spicker, P. (1999), "Definitions of poverty: eleven clusters of meaning", in Gordon, D. and P. Spicker (eds.), *The International Glossary on Poverty*, CROP International Studies in Poverty Research, Zed Books, London.

such as food, clothing, fuel or shelter. The idea of "basic needs" has been extended in debates on development to include essential facilities (like sanitation and a water supply) and communal services (like roads and cultural activities).

2. *Resources*. It may refer to a lack of resources, a shortage of income or wealth. Poverty is often defined simply in terms of lack of income, though it may also be taken to refer to a limited possession of money or marketable resources which can be used to obtain necessities.
3. *Standard of living*. Poverty may refer to a low standard of living. People have a low standard of living because of lack of resources, but neither the lack of resources nor the needs which arise need to be permanent for the level of living to be low overall. An important element is duration: people who experience problems for only a brief period, for example as a result of a natural disaster, are not generally considered to be poor.
4. *Multiple deprivation*. It may refer specifically to a constellation of problems associated with lack of resources and experienced over time. Baratz and Grigsby, for example, point to the characteristic problems of poverty as including a lack of physical comfort, a severe lack of health, a severe lack of safety and security, a lack of "welfare values" relating to status and social position, and a lack of "deference values" relating to the structure of power.[2]
5. *Inequality*. Inequality is disadvantage within a social context; definitions of poverty which describe it in those terms are equivalent to definitions of poverty as inequality. "There is an inescapable connection between poverty and inequality: certain degrees or dimensions of inequality . . . will lead to people being below the minimum standards acceptable in that society. It is this 'economic distance' aspect of inequality that is poverty." [3]
6. *Class*. Poverty may refer to a common economic position, or class. In Marxian analyses, classes are defined in terms of their relationship to the means of production, and in developed countries poor people are primarily those who are marginalised in relation to the economic system. In the Weberian sense, classes refer to people in distinct economic categories: poverty constitutes a class either when it establishes distinct categories of social relationship (like exclusion or dependency) or when the situation of poor people is identifiably distinguishable from others. Occupation of a position in the class depends not only on resources or needs, but on status, opportunities, and the duration of the experience.
7. *Dependency*. Dependency is the state of reliance on others for resources. The sociologist Georg Simmel argued that "poverty", in sociological terms,

[2] Baratz, M. and W. Grigsby (1971), "Thoughts on poverty and its elimination", in *Journal of Social Policy* 1(2), 119–34.

[3] O'Higgins, M. and S. Jenkins (1990), "Poverty in the European Community", in Teekens, R. and B. van Praag (eds.), *Analysing Poverty in the European Community*, Eurostat News Special Edition, Luxembourg: EC.

referred not to all people on low incomes but to those who were dependent.[4] This reflected a widespread use of that time, which identified poverty with the existing Poor Laws, and which still survives in modern usage.

8. *Lack of security*. Poverty refers to lack of security or vulnerability. Charles Booth referred to poor people as "living under a struggle to obtain the necessaries of life and make both ends meet; while the "very poor" live in a state of chronic want".[5]
9. *Exclusion*. People who are excluded are unable to participate in the society of which they form part. This extends beyond the experience of deprivation to include problems resulting from stigmatisation and social rejection. The European Community has defined poverty as exclusion resulting from limited resources:

   > "The poor shall be taken as to mean persons, families and groups of persons whose resources (material, cultural and social) are so limited as to exclude them from the minimum acceptable way of life in the Member State in which they live."[6]

10. *Lack of entitlement*. Poverty can be seen as a lack of entitlement. Drèze and Sen argue that poverty must be understood in terms, not of need or lack of resources, but of lack of entitlement. People starve, not because there is no food, but because they are not entitled to use the food which exists.[7] By extension, we can argue that people are not homeless because of lack of housing, but because they do not have the right of access to the housing which exists, or to land on which housing can be constructed.
11. *Unacceptable hardship*. Finally, poverty can be seen as a morally unacceptable state of serious hardship or suffering. Piachaud writes: "the term "poverty" carries with it an implication and moral imperative that something should be done about it. Its definition is a value judgement and should be clearly seen to be so . . ."[8]

These definitions of poverty are closely inter-related, and it is possible for someone to be poor in several, or even all, of those senses at the same time; but they are conceptually distinct, and may refer to different sets of circumstances.

The Poor

Who, then, are "the poor"? Evidently, there are at least eleven answers; people can be classified as poor when they meet any of these criteria. It should be noted

[4] Simmel, G. (1908), "The poor", in *Social Problems* 1965 13, 118–39.

[5] Booth, Charles (1902), *Life and Labour of the People in London*, Macmillan, First Series: Poverty, vol. 1, 33.

[6] Council Decision of 19.2.84, cited by Ramprakesh, D. (1994), "Poverty in the Countries of the European Union", in *Journal of European Social Policy* 4(2), 117–28.

[7] Dreze, J. and A. Sen (1989), *Hunger and Public Action*, Oxford, Clarendon Press.

[8] Piachaud, D. (1981), "Peter Townsend and the Holy Grail", in *New Society* 10.9.81, 421.

that a supplementary criterion may be applied: even if some people fit the criteria for poverty, they may not be considered poor if they fall within categories of people who are conventionally classified in different terms (for example students, people with disabilities resident in long-stay institutions, or people undertaking military service).

There is also a further dimension to consider. Poor people are generally thought of as individuals, households or families: this is certainly the focus of most serious research on poverty. The claim that groups, areas, or nations can be "poor" has been attacked as an "ecological fallacy"[9] which assumes that aggregate statistics based on individuals can be attributed to groups. However, any element in any of the definitions of poverty could apply to a collectivity: even if some people in the collectivity are not poor as individuals, they can be affected by the poverty of the group, because of the implications of this poverty for the physical environment, social relationships and the structure of services.[10]

Consideration of the position of the poor is incomplete unless it includes discussion of communities, areas and peoples.

RIGHTS

Claim-rights and liberties

Rights are rules which govern social relationships.[11] The nature of these rules varies, but what is special about them is that, whether or not they affect the behaviour of the people who hold the rights, they affect the way that others behave towards them. Many rights imply correlative duties, and the relationship between rights and the behaviour of others is sometimes misrepresented in the argument that rights and duties are necessarily correlated.[12] However, some rights imply no direct obligation on others; freedom does not mean that others should act in a particular way, but only that they should refrain from acting in certain circumstances. Hohfield distinguishes four categories of rights: claim-rights, immunities, powers and liberties.[13] Claim-rights imply duties on other people; many rights to the receipt of social services fall into this category. Liberties prevent actions by other people. Powers are a restricted form of liberty, which allow some people to do things which others cannot; a driving licence is an example. Immunities are also a form of liberty, which exempt people from

[9] Bulmer, M. (1986), *Social Science and Social Policy*, London, Allen and Unwin, ch. 11.

[10] See e.g. Jencks, C. and P. Peterson (eds.) (1991), *The Urban Underclass*, Brookings, Washington D.C.; Evans, D., N. Fyfe and D. Herbert (eds.) (1992), *Crime, Policing and Place: Essays in environmental criminology*, Routledge, London.

[11] Spicker, P. (1988), *Principles of Social Welfare*, Routledge, London, 58.

[12] Benn, S. and R. Peters (1959), *Social Principles and the Democratic State*, Allen and Unwin, London, ch. 4.

[13] Fundamental legal conceptions, 1923; cited by Weale, A. (1983), *Political Theory and Social Policy*, Macmillan, London, ch. 7.

obligations applying to others; an example is a tax relief, though this might also be seen as a claim-right.

Claim-rights tend to be more important in the discussion of poverty, but liberties are not negligible. The basic claim-rights most often referred to in discussions of poverty are: claims for social security (that is, poor relief or income maintenance); rights to housing, in the sense both of access to decent housing and avoidance of deprivation; access to health care; and the right to be educated. The basic liberties include: protection from crime; protection from unsafe or unhealthy environments; the avoidance of discrimination; and legal security, in the protection of citizens from arrest or legal harassment, and the avoidance of injustice. Some rights hover ambiguously between categories: the right to raise a family may be seen either as a claim for support or as a presumption against intervention, while the right to work is sometimes represented as a claim-right to be provided with work, and sometimes as a liberty to pursue work in the market-place.

Moral and legal rights

Some rights are moral, based in social norms (or, some would argue, universal codes of behaviour); some are legal, and legal rights may or may not have a moral basis. The term "welfare rights" is mainly used to refer to legal rights for people. The primary test of legal rights is the existence of a positive sanction, and consequently the scope for the redress of grievances. Some declarative legal rights have no apparent sanction attached: in the US and Japan, for example, elderly people have a right to be respected.[14] There is a legal argument that such rights are not in fact without sanction; they become operative in law, in conjunction with other principles, if they can be shown to be breached. The "right to be respected", though it may appear meaningless, may still be relevant, for example in tort cases which hinge on the nature of the duty of care owed by one person to another.

On the face of it, moral rights which lack the force of law seem to be of limited relevance to the debate about poverty. There are three important arguments to the contrary. The first is that where such rights are affirmed—for example in the Universal Declaration of Human Rights, or the UN Declaration of the Rights of the Child—they may still have a persuasive effect. This is particularly important in determining the role of actors within key organisations, both national and international. Secondly, in cases where legal rights exist but are not approved morally, there may be profound problems in enforcing the right. The term "stigma" has been used to refer to the position of people who are reluctant to claim benefits or services to which they are entitled.[15] Although the scope and

[14] International Council on Social Welfare (1969), *Social Welfare and Human Rights*, Columbia University Press, New York.

[15] Spicker, P. (1984), *Stigma and Social Welfare*, Croom Helm, Beckenham.

effects of stigma are disputed, there are certainly general problems of low utilisation and limited access which become aggravated in relation to the poorest claimants. "Where morality is at issue", Joel Handler argues, "welfare is conditioned, regardless of any notional entitlement."[16] By contrast, legal rights which are ill defined but morally approved of, like the universal right to (discretionary) medical care in the UK, may carry considerable weight in practice.

The focus of rights

Rights are commonly classified as either particular or general. A person has a particular right if someone else has undertaken a personal obligation specifically towards them (for example as the result of a promise, a contract, or an injurious action); a general right applies to everyone else in similar circumstances (for example to all such children, old people or mentally ill people).

There is an analogous distinction to be made between rights which are dependent on personal circumstances (the circumstances in which people have become poor, like old age, disability and sickness), which properly speaking are contingent general rights, and general rights which are available to anyone in the category, usually referred to as "universal" rights. Contingent general rights—I shall shorten this to "contingent rights", for convenience—are determined on two bases. Some are intended to define the categories of people who are eligible: for example, old people, children, disabled people and so on. Others are intended to exclude those who are ineligible: the first Old Age Pensions in Britain excluded people who had been dependent on the Poor Law, and current means-tested provision excludes people who otherwise fit the criteria for benefit but are not available for full-time work. Inclusion and exclusion seem to amount to the same thing: both define in-groups and out-groups simultaneously. The primary difference lies in the presumption of entitlement, which is important in practice; the key question is whether a person has to prove entitlement or whether another party must prove non-entitlement.

The question of whether people have contingent or universal rights when they are in need is usually represented in terms of the arguments on "selectivity" and "universality"—whether people have general rights as citizens or human beings, or whether they have rights only when they are in need. The discussion of universality and selectivity clearly overlaps with the distinction between contingent, general and universal rights; any general right to benefit based on need must, by definition, be selective. The nature of contingent rights complicates the situation: some benefits which are contingent on personal circumstances (for example, benefits for orphans or war pensions) are presented as universal in form, in the sense that they apply to everyone within a category, even if that category is very narrowly defined.

[16] Handler, J. (1972), *Reforming the Poor*, Basic Books, New York.

Individual and collective rights

A further issue to be considered is the nature of collective rights. Although most discussions of rights are based on the position of individuals, arguments have been made for a different emphasis, establishing rights for disadvantaged groups or peoples.[17] This is a complex subject, but has been scarcely examined because of the absence of appropriate mechanisms in many legal systems for redressing the situation of groups. (The main exception is found in the US: not the existence of "class actions", because class actions are still taken by and on behalf of identifiable individuals, but rather the Brandeis brief, which allows consideration of the consequences for a wider society of the actions under review). If collective rights exist, they can presumably be particular, contingent or universal, in the same way as individual rights. A focus on the group or community may be especially appropriate and enforceable in circumstances where rights are enshrined in the obligations of states towards their citizens.

RIGHTS FOR THE POOR

When we talk about rights for the poor, we need to establish what we mean by the poor, and what kind of rights they might have. For the purposes of this chapter, the different definitions of the poor can be grouped into three main categories, which have very different implications for discussions about rights. These are:

- definitions of poverty which refer to material status, including need, multiple deprivation, lack of security and lack of resources;
- those which refer to moral status, including entitlement and serious hardship; and
- those which refer to social relationships, including relationships of inequality, class, dependency and exclusion.

Similarly, although rights have several dimensions, it should again be possible to simplify the terms of the discussion for the purposes of analysis. Powers and immunities can be seen as contingent forms of liberty. Rights for the poor can therefore be legal or moral; they can concern claim-rights or liberties; they can be particular, contingent or universal; and they can be individual or collective.

[17] See e.g. Edwards, J. (1994), "Group rights versus individual rights: The case of race-conscious policies", in *Journal of Social Policy* 23(1), 55–70; Crawford, J. (ed.) (1988), *The Rights of Peoples*, Clarendon Press, Oxford.

Improving material status

If poverty is seen in terms of material status, it seems to follow that claim-rights are probably more important than liberties. Liberties are primarily concerned with preventing negative action towards people, which means that although they can stop negative consequences they cannot meet material needs in their own right. Some liberties are basic to continued existence, like the right not to be killed, while others are necessary to social life, like the right to form a family. Their assertion is an important precondition for the operation of other rights. They are necessary, but they are not sufficient for improvements in material statements. Claim-rights, by contrast, are not always necessary, because there may be other routes by which material welfare can be improved, but they may be sufficient; they can be used directly to meet material needs, for example rights to education, health, sanitary provision, housing and income maintenance.

Although some critics have represented the debate on the focus of rights as a matter of principle—for example, Townsend associates selectivity with discrimination against the poor, and universality with the acceptance of basic rights[18]—the arguments about particular, contingent, general and universal rights tend to be more concerned with the effectiveness of the methods used than with the principles concerned. The basic argument for selectivity—a general right for the poor—is that it is an efficient means of relief, offering maximum benefit at least cost. Offering benefits to people who are not poor is seen as wasteful. The arguments against selectivity are: cost (it is expensive to administer), the creation of perverse incentives, the problems of setting borderlines and the failure of selective benefits to reach many of the people for whom they are intended. Contingent benefits have similar problems. The arguments for universal benefits are that they are simple to understand and effective, but that they are expensive, and have limited flexibility.

Any claim-right, whether particular, contingent or universal, will improve material status, and consequently might serve to reduce the extent and scope of poverty to some degree. There is an argument that the extension of rights to some will lead to material improvement for others; the "trickle-down effect" in developing countries is supposed to lead to more people benefiting from a developing economy than those directly involved in economic activity. (The argument is not entirely persuasive; the effect can also be to increase inequality and to exclude those who are not part of the developing economy).

The issue of enforcement—whether rights are positive—is crucial, but its relative importance is different in relation to liberties and claim-rights. A moral right to a liberty may be respected even when it is not associated with a particular sanction, because compliance is possible without positive action. The state-

[18] Townsend, P. (1976), *Sociology and Social Policy*, Penguin, Harmondsworth, 126.

ment that "no-one shall be subjected to torture or to cruel, inhuman or degrading treatment or punishment"[19] is not difficult to respect; the main direct action it requires is some criminal sanction against transgressors, and it is possible for a state to assert that it is complying even when no such sanctions are actually imposed. In relation to claim-rights, by contrast, the actions which have to be taken are frequent and prolonged. The right of each person to "a standard of living adequate for health and well-being of himself and his family, including food, clothing, housing and medical care and necessary social services"[20] cannot be ensured without significant intervention in the social structure. The European Convention of Human Rights therefore guarantees a right to education, but only in the sense of guaranteeing access to such education as exists, not by requiring states to provide education or to ensure its provision.[21] Claim-rights are generally established through the creation of specific duties against which a claim can be made (even if the claim is moral rather than legal). The approach taken in the International Covenant on Economic, Social and Cultural Rights, or the European Social Charter, is for contracting states to bind themselves by accepting duties to their citizens: the International Covenant includes obligations on states, for example, to provide for the reduction of infant mortality, the improvement of environmental health, the control of infectious disease and medical care.[22]

Asserting moral status

The term "moral status" is vague, because it depends on a shifting range of moral perceptions of the circumstances of the poor. It is tempting to assume that entitlements are definable in legal terms, because so many of them are focused on property, and the law determines the procedures through which property is held or transferred. If that were true, it would be possible to redefine entitlements by redefining legal status; famines could be avoided by laws which redefined the ownership of food. This is clearly not how things work.

The discussion of rights in terms of moral status and entitlement is usually expressed in terms of "citizenship", in the sense used by T.H. Marshall.[23] Citizenship can be seen both as a set of rights in itself—social, economic and civil—and as a status which offers "the right to have rights".[24] The key to the establishment of citizenship is moral and political, rather than legal; law is the means by which entitlements are expressed, but it is not necessarily the source

19 Article 5 of the UN Declaration of Human Rights.

20 Ibid., article 25(1).

21 Jacobs, F. and R. White (1996), *The European Convention on Human Rights*, Clarendon, Oxford, ch. 15.

22 In Sieghart, P. (1983), *The International Law of Human Rights*, Clarendon, Oxford, 195.

23 Marshall, T.H. (1981), *The Right to Welfare*, Heinemann, London.

24 Earl Warren, cited in Goodin, R. (1982), *Political Theory and Public Policy*, University of Chicago Press, Chicago, 77.

of them. It is morality which defines which circumstances are acceptable and which are not, which determines who is entitled and which determines what forms of transfer of property are permissible. There is, of course, a close relationship between law and morality, which is a well established topic in the study of jurisprudence; changes in law can anticipate changes in morality, by defining some conduct as acceptable or unacceptable, while in other cases the law lags behind changes in moral conduct.

Both liberties and claim-rights are part of a framework of entitlements, and the development of new forms of rights must be understood in the context of that framework. Neither liberties nor claim-rights can be established and made workable unless their establishment is compatible with the terms on which a society operates. The moral status of the poor is different in a society devoted to the principles of *laissez-faire* and the market than in a society which stands for collective effort and solidarity. The point is fairly obvious, and it usually leads to the conclusion that a different kind of society is needed: the basic argument is for change, revolutionary or otherwise.

There are, though, alternative ways of establishing rights. Both universal and contingent rights depend on a prior moral acceptance of donative rights, which might not apply. This is where particular rights come into their own, because their acceptance does not rely on external moral intervention. The strategy followed in French social policy, which has been influential in Europe, has been to build on solidaristic social networks, progressively extending the scope of solidarity to include those who were previously excluded. The original basis of these networks was a combination of pre-existing solidarities, like the solidarities of family and community, with contractual rights gained through the development of mutual aid. In the same way, arguments about the development of rights in the Third World have relied on economic development, and on the progressive integration of people into the network of relationships built on the formal economy, as the primary route through which entitlements can be established. Particular rights, because of their individualised and quasi-contractual nature, are distinctively enforceable: the European Court of Human Rights, while rejecting the general principle that rights to social security can be seen as a form of property, seemed to accept that a particular interest established through contribution would establish a property right,[25] which in principle would be protected on the same basis as other property rights.

Changing social relationships

Seeing poverty in relational terms tends to alter the nature of the arguments made about both poverty and rights. On the face of it, rights are concerned with

[25] App. 4288/69, X v. *United Kingdom*, 17.3.1970 13 Yearbook 892, cited by Jacobs, F. and R. White (1996), *The European Convention on Human Rights*, Clarendon, Oxford, 248–9.

social behaviour, and social relationships should be amenable to change through the establishment of rights. Both moral and legal rights are necessary to redress disadvantage and to foster integration. There is a potential problem here: rights which can alter social relationships positively can also alter them negatively. There may be a problem, for example, where the effect of a liberty (such as independence for the family) is to reinforce non-intervention, and so to entrench disadvantage. The issue is most acute in discussions of citizenship and solidarity, concepts which have the potential to be exclusive as well as inclusive. If defining rights simultaneously defines those who do not have rights, the alteration of social relationships may lead to the exacerbation of inequality and exclusion.

The position of claim-rights is ambiguous. Some, like rights to housing and employment, may be fundamental to social integration, but there is a risk that an emphasis on claim-rights may reinforce the status of dependency, and with it the problems of poverty. (This is not intended as an endorsement of the idea of the "dependency culture", an ancient idea which has been repeatedly disproved by empirical research; it refers to the simpler and more basic proposition that people who are treated as paupers do not cease to be paupers because they are treated more intensively.) Some liberties are fundamental: non-discrimination, equality of treatment and the avoidance of stigma are basic aims of any strategy to deal with poverty without exclusion.

The emphasis on non-discrimination has also been a powerful argument for universal benefits and services. Contingent rights may be accepted on the same basis, but selectivity, or general rights for the poor, can be seen as socially divisive. (This is why, in debates on universality and selectivity, universalists have tended to assume that contingent rights belong to their camp.) Particular rights present a paradox. On the face of it, particular rights are individualised, and so intrinsically unequal; pension rights based on an individual's contributions, for example, reflect that person's work record, and might be seen as perpetuating the inequalities of which the work record forms part. However, the French approach to welfare has taken such rights as the basis for a strategy against exclusion, through the combination of the extension of solidarity and special measures for integration (or "insertion"). Particular measures are intrinsically exclusive, which must mean that exclusion cannot be avoided in a system which relies on them.[26] But this does not mean that such measures are ineffective in relation to poverty; it only means that they cannot be completely effective, and the benefits which are on offer may serve the population better than alternative systems.

[26] Spicker, P. (1993), "Can European social policy be universalist?", in Page, R. and J. Baldock (eds.), *Social Policy Review 5*, Social Policy Association.

CONCLUSION

None of the definitions of poverty which I have considered is genuinely exclusive: all of them could apply to the same person simultaneously. This means that, although I have distinguished between the approaches for the purposes of analysis, in practice the debates are rarely distinct. This is particularly apparent in the discussion of universality versus selectivity, usually treated as a single debate despite the very different implications of considering poverty in material or in relational terms.

For the same reason, the approaches taken are not mutually exclusive. Although approaches which are useful in one respect may be of little value in others—and that includes important principles like universality, liberties and legal enforcement—they are all of value in certain respects. There is sometimes a naïve belief that human rights must be good things. There are, however, some potential contradictions, which point to associated dangers. One is that claim-rights, which may be constructive from the point of view of material status, may foster exclusion by reinforcing an inferior or dependent social position. Secondly, particular or contingent rights can reinforce the position of some while excluding others. Thirdly, liberties can be used to obstruct intervention in areas where it may be desirable. Attempts to assert rights for the poor can be constructed in different ways, and the interpretation of key issues, like the defence of liberties or the development of a structure of particular rights, may not always work for the benefit of the poorest.

The Experience of Poverty

2

The Law and the Poor: Institutional Support and Economic Need in Italy[1]

YURI KAZEPOV

SUMMARY

THIS CHAPTER, DRAWING on the author's recent research findings aims to clarify some key aspects of the relations between "law" and "poverty", in relation to the forms of institutional support existing in Italy to deal with economic need between 1977 and 2000.

The chapter is divided into three parts. The first describes the overall fragmented picture of Italian policies against poverty developed during this period, focusing in particular on the heterogeneity of social assistance schemes and considering the different territorial authorities (the municipality, the region, the state) responsible for their definition and implementation.

The second part examines in greater depth how the legal frameworks deal with the conditions of economic need in a number of Italian cities. In particular, it shows how the law structures the areas of protection and vulnerability at the regional and municipal levels in a very differentiated way. Formal criteria and practices are analysed in relation to their institutional design and implementation process.

The third part shows some of the implications of the legal framework described by pointing out some crucial problems which informed the debate on Italian welfare state reform before the approval of the new framework law on

[1] This contribution is based on pilot research on *The Local Policies Against Social Exclusion in Italy*, which the author co-ordinated for the Poverty Commission established by the Presidency of the Council of Ministers. The research focused on four policies: 1) minimum economic benefits (*minimo vitale*); 2) supporting measures for the homeless; 3) fosterage policies; and 4) home care for the elderly; implemented in 14 cities: a) Turin, Milan, Piacenza and Bologna for northern Italy; b) Florence, Pesaro, Ancona and Rome for the centre; and c) Naples, Cosenza, Bari, Messina and Catania for the south of Italy. These cities represent about 15% of the national population and are located in 11 regions: a) Piedmont, Lombardy, Trentino-Alto-Adige and Emilia Romagna in the north; b) Tuscany, Marche and Lazio in the centre; and c) Campania, Apulia, Calabria and Sicily in the south. My best thanks go to Chiara Saraceno, who followed the research and actively supported it for the Commission. The results of the research have been published by the Istituto Poligrafico di Stato in Rome (Kazepov, 1996a). A first analysis of the results also appears in Kazepov (1996b) and (1998). This chapter, based on that documentation, also includes analysis of the economic support measures existing in Bergamo, Brescia, Bolzano, Urbino and Reggio Calabria, realised in a second phase, with different funding, but following the same methodology.

an integrated system of social services and provisions. In particular these relate to the need to ensure equal rights, equal access to benefits and less discretion. The persisting exclusion of specific groups from even the possibility of claiming for some benefits, and the institutional north–south divide, require a complex reorganisation of the protection mechanisms.

THE FRAGMENTATION OF RIGHTS IN ITALY

In 1977, by Decree No. 616, the Italian legislature shifted responsibility for "public charity" and social assistance from the national to the regional and local authorities. This decision represents the loss of one of the main opportunities within Italian social policy to combat poverty.

The regions and the municipalities inherited the assets and functions of a series of charitable bodies (some of which still exist and are funded) which intervened for specified categories (e.g. single mothers, orphans and prisoners) instead of focusing on the situations of need *per se*. However, until October 2000 the state gave no clear guidelines or tools for establishing standard access criteria and building up a coherent system of social security able to guarantee a safety net for people in a condition of economic need. This lack of a framework law had its roots in political reluctance and has left regions and municipalities in a *vacatio juris* for nearly 25 years whose negative consequences have not yet been resolved.[2]

In order to apply the 1977 decree, many regions have approved a regional law on social assistance. This has brought some problems. First, not every region had a regional framework law; secondly, in approving these laws, the regions did not co-ordinate their efforts, so that we had, and still have as the implementation of the new law will last several years, different criteria for access to benefits and services in different regions. There are of course similarities but, as we will show, more at the level of stated principles than of actual measures. This situation is highlighted by the differences in the implementation guidelines, which were intended to make the principles concrete, but which have helped to increase the variation between access criteria, benefits and services. Within this framework a further problem emerged from the municipalities. In some cases they designed specific rules for specific categories, often disregarding the regional basic laws. In other cases they interpreted the outline laws in a very loose way, maintaining a high degree of discretion within the decision-making process which underlies the distribution of benefits.[3]

[2] This issue has been analysed by many authors. The most significant contributions are by: Antoni (1990); Motta and Mondino (1994); Rei (1994); Negri and Saraceno (1996). For a critical analysis of the proposals for a framework law until the 1990s see: Giumelli (1991); Rinaldi (1998).

[3] Not until 1990 did national Law Nr. 142 on decentralisation and re-organisation of all regulatory criteria at the local level set a process of change in motion. However, only some municipalities have unified proceedings and criteria for access to social services for all groups; the process is still underway and has not yet solved the problem of inter-municipal differences, not to speak of the fact that it touches only the formal aspects, and not the practices which in many cases still categorise claimants and recipients.

A range of approaches is a common feature for a large number of Italian policies against social exclusion. This heterogeneity is a result of the effect of existing formal and informal differences. The intervention varies apparently without reference to any coherent and uniform criteria. There are different policies and there are different ways of implementing these policies. In other words, in contexts which are similar in socio-economic terms, we may have different policies dealing with similar problems, while in social and economically different contexts we may have different applications of similar policies.

One important consequence of this complex situation was the consolidation of different systems of social rights. Within these systems, *citizens* are entitled to different sets of rights, related less to their condition of need than to the specific features of the entitlements and the specific way in which social services are organised in the place where they live (see: Kazepov, 1998). Local differences in social policies do not in themselves necessarily represent a problem. On the contrary, there is a tendency to consider differences positively, because through them it should be possible to give more specific individual responses to the increasingly distinct contexts. The problem lies in the fact that distinction must not entail a difference in rights. A social entitlement can require different strategies to be effectively implemented, but, faced with the same situation of need, it must grant equal access to adequate provision, in terms of both the law and practice. The question is complex, because it refers to two different levels of analysis. At the more abstract level, for example, there can be the aim to grant minimum economic support to everybody in a situation of need, i.e. to ensure socially defined and accepted "decent living conditions". At a more concrete level, the implementation of this right requires from social workers in different situations, to organise interventions differently. Paradoxically, this means that a truly homogeneous enforcement of social entitlements (a standard provision for everybody, independently of the actual individual situation) would reproduce the unequal condition of the claimants as they were before they approached social services. Financial protection schemes, then, have to plan for different strategies of implementation, to enable everybody to attain minimum "decent living conditions".[4]

Given the fact that difference is not negative *per se*, the aim of this chapter is to give details of the matters discussed, showing the situation at the local level in Italy. The subsequent analysis is based on the measures aimed at providing economic support to individuals and families in a situation of need, before the approval of the new framework law on integrated social services and provisions in October 2000 (Ln 328/00). In particular it shows the possible consequences for social citizenship rights arising from the highly fragmented nature of Italian social policies and the difficulties of guaranteeing minimum "decent living conditions" at the national level.[5]

[4] The international debate on social policies is now going in this direction. For Germany see Hanesch (1995); for France see Paugam (1993); for Italy see Negri and Saraceno (1996).

[5] As far as this point is concerned it would be appropriate to open a theoretical debate on the meaning of federalism in relation to social assistance policies, but the complexity of the issue would

LEGAL FRAMEWORKS AND CONDITIONS OF NEED: THE WHO, HOW AND HOW MUCH OF SOCIAL ASSISTANCE

More or less all Italian municipalities granted between 1977 and 2000 some kind of financial support to satisfy the basic subsistence needs of both individuals and households. This statement may sound encouraging; however, the benefits differed in many ways, for instance in relation to how the benefit was and still is calculated, who is entitled to it and for how long he/she can claim it.[6]

There are two main explanations for these differences: first the abovementioned lack of standard criteria established in national law for more than 20 years, and secondly the fact that the regional reorganisation of social services laws (where they exist[7]) often shifted the definition of the support criteria to the municipalities. At this lower level it is not unusual to find classification of claimants into categories of people (minors, the elderly, single mothers, etc.). This may seem curious, given that most of the regional framework laws identify the potential claimants in all residents with no distinction (nationality, for instance, should not play a role). There are of course inclusive and exclusive interpretations, but all residents should be entitled by the fact they are in a condition of need. This is the *sine qua non* for the right to social security benefits. However, few regions define what is meant by *condition of need*. Among those included in our survey, only Lombardy, the Autonomous Province of Trent[8] and partially the Autonomous Province of Bolzano provided such a definition.

drive us far beyond the aims of this chapter. Nevertheless it is worth mentioning that, for instance, Germany, despite its federal administrative organisation based on a high level of decentralisation, also in fiscal terms, has regulated social assistance according to the *Bundesozialhilfegesetz* (BSHG, the federal law on social assistance) since 1962. This law states the rights and duties of people in economic need for the whole Federal Republic, even if implementation is the responsibility of the municipalities (partially supported by the *Länder*). The levels of variability and discretion within the municipalities are very low, even if the institutional mechanism allows some flexibility in the individualisation of the benefit. The core question is, therefore, how to define the different political and spending responsibilities at the different territorial levels (local–national) for granting equal rights to "decent living conditions" throughout the whole nation. Social assistance is in this sense the "last safety net" for people in a condition of economic need and also has a redistributive function at a minimal level for widely different socio-economic contexts. For an overview of the German system and its effects on the impoverishment processes see Leisering and Leibfried (1999), Hanesch et al. (2000).

[6] Benefits based on the *minimo vitale* are not seen explicitly in all municipalities considered in this chapter. In many cases the reference is implicit in the statement about the guarantees of "minimal decent living conditions" included in most of the framework laws. We consider here all economic support benefits which integrate the claimants" income up to a specific threshold and are supposed to last as long as the condition of need persists.

[7] Among the 11 regions considered in this contribution: Lazio, Campania and Apulia did not approve a regional Framework Law aimed at reorganising social services until December 31st 1995. Lazio approved such a law only in September 1996. Campania approved its LR Nr. 47 in 1985, aimed at creating a unified fund for social assistance, but without reorganising the social services and redefining any access criteria. In Apulia each municipality regulates autonomously the organisation of social services.

[8] Article 4.2 of LP 14/91 of the Autonomous Province of Trent states that: "The condition of need depends on at least one of the following elements: a) the insufficiency of the family income in

In these definitions, the "condition of need" does not refer exclusively to an inadequate income, but also to a range of circumstances which affect individuals and households, and which can combine with one another in very different ways, or can arise separately (i.e. the presence of dependent persons needing specific assistance or care, such as elderly people, the disabled, minors at risk, etc.).

This expansion of the "condition of need" to include issues other than those related only to income reveals the ambitious intention of the regional legislators to overcome a strict administrative definition of need. However, this intention led them to confuse two fundamentally distinct elements: on one hand, the recognition and evaluation of the condition of need; on the other, the administrative aspect of granting a minimum protection to persons in such a condition.

The process of identifying and evaluating an existing condition of need cannot depend on discretion, whose variability can threaten the certainty of the individual right to a "minimum decent condition of life". On the contrary, it should foresee the possibility of intervention also in borderline situations, thus underlining the preventive nature which financial support should have, particularly when combined with other social measures.

In those regions in which the definition of the "condition of need" is not tackled directly, the "persistence of the condition of need" is used to define the period during which the individual can be economically supported by the social services. In any case, income represents the main indicator to define the appropriate amount of financial support and therefore, at least implicitly, to recognise a state of need.

Given these limitations, the regional laws granted, in principle, universal "minimum decent living conditions", as happens in the majority of the European welfare states, with a relatively sophisticated institutional set-up. No economic need below a certain threshold is ignored. The regions considered in this contribution respect, at least formally, the EU recommendations on social policies, which foresee a minimum standard of living for everybody.[9] The regional laws for the re-organisation of the social services represent a positive policy innovation, especially in comparison to the complex mix between the Crispi Law (No. 6972 of 17 July 1890) and the categorisation which occurred during the Fascist era, which characterised the system of social assistance before the 1977 Decree.

relation to the basic needs of all household members, when there are no other people who should provide or that *de facto* provide to integrate the income; b) the total or partial incapacity of a person to provide for his/her own needs or when the family is not able to ensure adequate assistance; c) circumstances not included in a) and b), in which individuals or families are in a condition of particular need (also from the affective/educational point of view) or risk social exclusion; d) judicial measures towards the individual, that impose or make social services' intervention necessary". Similar articles are to be found in LR 1/86 of Lombardy (art. 12.3) and in LP 69/73 of the Province of Bolzano (arts 8 and 8bis).

[9] The reference here is to art. 3 of the EU Directive No. 1408/71 on equal social security treatment for people resident in EU countries. More recently (1992) the Council adopted a Recommendation on the convergence of social security policies and social policies in general (92/442/EEC L245). For more details about the Commission's perspective see: European Commission (1994).

Some basic problems, typical of the whole Italian system, still remained up to the approval of the new framework law. The rights of people in a condition of need were stated formally in one place and were formally limited in another. This process of limitation of rights took place through:

a) the guidelines for the implementation of the regional laws (where these existed); and
b) the regulation and practice at the municipal level.

The guidelines for implementation of the regional laws

The guidelines for the implementation of social assistance laws, at both the regional and the municipal level, highlight the problems of institutional fragmentation in defining how to apply the stated principles. Analysis of the guidelines shows that:

- although there is no explicit categorisation of claimants in need, very often there is the recommendation of categorising the interventions (e.g. in respect of single mothers, minors, and the elderly);
- even if the threshold is not always explicitly mentioned (as in Lombardy and Sicily) the common implicit reference is to the minimum INPS pension, to which the amount of housing costs is usually added. The final sum should then be compared with the real (or estimated, as for Trent and Bolzano) income of the individual/household applying for the benefit;
- benefits are usually divided into: a) continuous economic support provided while the condition of need persists; and b) benefits provided to satisfy specific necessities;
- very often, social services are subject to budget constraints: they provide economic support only if financial resources from regions and city councils are available, independently (although not totally) from people's conditions of need (i.e. in Lombardy, Calabria and Lazio).

These features (among others) are more or less common to all implementation guidelines. Their main effect is to introduce specific limits to the rights which people with economic needs should have in economically advanced societies. The greatest formal limit which challenges the principles stated at the regional level is that of budgetary constraints.[10] In contrast to most EU member states, economic benefits in Italy are dependent on the financial resources of the municipality. In this way, the right to economic support is subordinated not so much to the condition of need *per se*, but to the wealth of the municipality concerned. The guidelines recommend prudence in granting economic benefits, and this

[10] Some of the analysed framework laws do not explicitly limit the financial benefits in general, but only the extraordinary payments (e.g. Trent and Bolzano) but each situation is evaluated singly in relation to its seriousness.

becomes a tool of discretion in the definition of both the advisability of paying the benefit and its amount and duration. In other words, discretionary power is supposed to prevent public services from a potential economic collapse, rather than to enable them to answer specific conditions of need more adequately. The lack of certainty to which this situation gave rise in terms of criteria for access and possible distortions for clients is problematic. To rely on the certainty of guaranteed "minimum decent living conditions", defined in advance, does not necessarily imply that interventions have to rely on bureaucracy. A well designed measure of economic support can easily be tailored to the individual and integrated with other non-economic accompanying measures, as stated by the implementation guidelines themselves. This complex intervention, which was available for certain categories, such as minors or elderly people, more than for others, such as able-bodied adults, shows that the historical tendency to categorise persisted for quite a long time beyond fascism.

The local policies: rules and practices of economic support

A further element of variation comes from the different ways in which the municipalities apply the regional guidelines. This situation made it even more difficult to build up a homogeneous system of rights for the whole country without a national framework law, and increased the uncertainty of the law by impeding the full implementation of the principles stated at the regional level. To complete this picture, we must add those cities within regions which have a basic law and which were following those criteria even before 1977 or which are following their own distinct criteria.

The relationship between the supporting interventions at the local level resulted in a scarcely coherent range of measures and access criteria.[11] This has occurred in spite of the fact that the majority of the cities implicitly refer to the *minimo vitale* to plan their policies. The other cities, as we will see, use different thresholds.

The minimo vitale *support*

Despite the persisting local differences, economic support measures in the cities considered do have some common features.

[11] In the municipalities analysed the implementation of the regional framework laws has not been an easy process. Between approval and implementation there is often a long delay, and the law is not always applied. We can identify four typical situations:

a) municipalities which anticipated the regional law (e.g. Turin, Ancona, Piacenza, Firenze and Catania);

b) municipalities which are applying the regional or provincial law (e.g. Trent, Bolzano, Milan, Bergamo, Pesaro and Reggio Calabria);

c) municipalities that do not apply the regional law (e.g. Cosenza and Messina);

d) municipalities located within regions without a regional law (e.g. Rome until September 1996, Naples and Bari).

- The support usually refers to an income threshold corresponding to the minimum INPS pension (685,000 lire per month in 1997) which is updated annually. Those who have an income below this threshold are considered to be in a condition of need.
- The economic support should theoretically be calculated as the difference between that threshold and the real income of the individual/household. In practice, however, not everybody in a condition of need is equally entitled to benefit. Claimants come under the auspices of different offices and each of the latter deals with a specific category and provides the support with varying degrees of discretion. Among these groups is, for instance, the elderly, which includes women aged over 60 and men aged over 65, who normally benefit from income support up to the level of the threshold automatically and on a regular basis, while the condition of need persists. Similar provisions are granted to disabled people (but the degree of invalidity needed to access the benefits varies from city to city).
- Those assessing groups of people with less formal protection, such as able-bodied adults, have a high degree of institutional discretion to determine both the existence of the condition of need and the amount of the benefit.
- Budgetary constraints can affect the payments, for instance by reducing them; several cities have also established a maximum level of spending on economic benefits.
- According to article 433 of the Italian Civil Code the law *obliges* relatives to support those in need. However, since legal claims to enforce this principle have to be made by the individual in need, municipal support is often provided in any case; nevertheless, the relatives under this obligation are taken into account in calculating the household's available income.

Beside these common features which reinforce the limitations present in the implementation guidelines, the measures are described differently in every city and have their own characteristics (see Table 2.1). These latter derive from the local implementation guidelines which often establish their own criteria and limits, so changing the sense of the intervention and increasing the uncertainty of the right to support. This situation has helped to establish very unclear and variable borders of inclusion/exclusion, and to make the comparison difficult, even between cities within the same region. In the local context, the organisation of claimants by categories persists: in fact, categories still determine the distribution of resources. Many elements[12] depend on this rather than on the existence of a condition of need *per se*. As a consequence, at the local level, although the regional law states that all resident citizens in a condition of need are entitled to public support as soon as their income falls below a certain threshold, in reality only elderly people, the disabled, low-income households

[12] For instance the regularity of the payments, the criteria for determining the threshold and the benefit, etc. In some contexts the continuity of the support is related not only to the availability of resources, but also to a more or less formalised bargaining between social worker and claimant.

Table 2.1: Regional framework laws and foreseen economic benefits (social assistance)

Municipality Regional laws	*minimo vitale* (MV) Continuing and temporary (year of implementation)	Different from the *minimo vitale* (year of implementation)	Extraordinary benefits (year of implementation)
TURIN LR 20/82 LR 62/95	• *Minimo vitale* (1978) • Reduced *minimo vitale* (also on a temporary basis) • As a loan	• Subsistence allowance (1984, 1993)	• Integrating measures of the *minimo vitale* (1978) • Services (1984) • Special benefit (2MV)
MILAN LR 1/86	• *Minimo vitale* (1988)	• Allowances for adults (1990) • Allowances for minors	• Extraordinary one-off benefits (1990)
BERGAMO LR 1/86	• *Minimo vitale* (1988)		• Extraordinary one-off benefits (1988)
BOLZANO LP 69/73 LP 13/91	• *Minimo vitale* (1973, 1991)	• *Taschengeld* (pocket money) • Special family allowances	• Extraordinary one-off benefits (1991)
TRENT LP 14/91	• Continuous financial assistance (also on a temporary basis) (1980, 1991) (1994: 402,000 lira)		• One-off benefits (1991)
PIACENZA LR 2/85	• Financial support added up to the *minimo vitale* threshold (1980) • *Minimo vitale* paid by the local health unit (USL)		• Extraordinary municipal allowances (1980) • Extraordinary allowances USL • Heating allowances (municipality)
BOLOGNA LR 2/85	• *Minimo vitale* (1971, 1986)	• Continuous financial support from the municipality (1993) • Continuous support by the USL (1991) • Continuous support instead of services	• One-off benefits (1971, 1986) • Extraordinary allowances (USL)

Table 2.1: *cont.*

Municipality Regional laws	*minimo vitale* (MV) Continuing and temporary (year of implementation)	Different from the *minimo vitale* (year of implementation)	Extraordinary benefits (year of implementation)
ANCONA LR 43/88	• Regular allowance for basic needs (1981) • Temporary allowance		• One-off allowances (1981)
PESARO LR 43/88	• Continuous financial assistance (also on a temporary basis) (1982)		• Extraordinary financial benefits (1982) • Financial support for health expenditure (MV+20% for the elderly)
REGGIO CALABRIA LR 5/87	• *Minimo vitale* (1986, 1992)		• Extraordinary municipal allowances
FLORENCE LR 42/92	• Continuous financial assistance for basic needs (n.a.) • Temporary financial assistance		• Extraordinary municipal allowances
CATANIA LR 22/86	• *Minimo vitale* (1983)		
ROME	• None until September 1996 when LR 38/96 was approved	• Regular allowances (1982) 800,000 lira (elderly) 700,000–1,000,000 lira for families	• Special allowances (1976, 1984)
NAPLES LR 47/85	None available up to 1998	• ex ECA subsidy for the unemployed; • ex ENAOLI subsidies; • Subsidies for ex-prisoners and their families: all suspended since 1993 because of financial constraints	• Extraordinary allowances at the discretion of the mayor (1958): suspended since 1993

Municipality Regional laws	*minimo vitale* (MV) Continuing and temporary (year of implementation)	Different from the *minimo vitale* (year of implementation)	Extraordinary benefits (year of implementation)
COSENZA LR 5/87	None available		• Pre-1977 assistance (1977, 1983)
BARI (no)	None available	• Basic financial assistance (1987, never implemented)	• Extraordinary municipal allowances (1987)
MESSINA LR 22/86	None available	• Services for single mothers services (1991) • Ex enaoli subsidy (1986) • Ex anmil subsidy (1986)	• Financial solidarity support (suspended since 1990)

with dependent children and children with relatives in prison have access to more regular economic support. These categories were already legally protected by means of wider and specific measures[13] and there is less discretion about who has access and for how long. On the other hand, in order to receive economic benefits adults outside those groups must satisfy several conditions of need[14] and prove that they have a need. The assessment of both these factors involves a high degree of discretion.

Given the substantial convergence in considering the minimal INPS pension, the income threshold and the basic amount for the economic support (except for Trento and Bolzano), there is a point where the criteria diverge: the equivalence scales used to determine the support in relation to the dimensions of the household. These scales, defined by the regional laws (e.g. of Lombardy, Sicily and Calabria) or at the local level, again show a very high degree of variation without any obvious reason (see Table 2.2).

[13] The heritage of the cultural climate which characterised the development of social policies and of measures protecting those who are not guilty of determining their condition of need (minors and the elderly) is evident. For this same reason able-bodied adults (mainly males) were excluded. Contributory policies have reproduced this pattern, making benefits depend on one's position in the labour market.

[14] The accumulation of conditions of need implies the co-presence of one or more conditions of deprivation which in sum create the economic disadvantage, so reducing the actual and potential autonomy of the household.

Table 2.2: Equivalence scales used to define the *minimo Vitale* threshold taking the size of the household's into account

	TO	TN	BZ	BG	MI	BO (1)	PC	FI	AN	PS	CT	RC	CIPE (2)
1 person	100	100	100	100	100	100	100	100	100	100	75	100	100
2 persons	70	75	70	65	65	89	70	59	50	50	25	66	66
3 persons	40	50	40	35	47	82	50	46	33	33	35	47	56
4 persons	40	50	40	35	42	82	50	37	24	24	15	42	50
5 persons or more	40	20	30	35	39	82	50	37	24	24		41	46
Single person		120	120										

Source: The author's calculations on deliberations of the analysed municipalities.

(1) For an elderly couple the municipality of Bologna pays the basic amount minus 11%. For larger households (three or more) the municipality adds 18% for each additional member.

(2) The equivalence scale of the Poverty Commission has been determined considering as a threshold (=100) the average per-capita consumption of a two-member household; in order to compare with the other equivalence scales the proportions have been recalculated putting =100 the *minimo vitale* threshold for 1 person.

The differences shown in Table 2.2 have many implications. For example, given the same condition of need and the same available income, the entitlement of a family to a minimum benefit will depend also on these scales. Theoretically, a family in Bologna with double the income of one in Catania will be entitled to the same benefit. In practice, however, things are even more complicated because in most cases, as we have seen above, the family will only be entitled to the benefits if there are other conditions of need which involve economic deprivation.

Other elements of variability stem from the fact that in order to define the income threshold below which the person or family is to be considered in a condition of need, housing costs (e.g. rent, heating) are usually added to the basic amount. In some cases the final amount of the support cannot be higher than a certain sum; in others a standardised amount is fixed for each room; in yet other cases the actual rent is taken into account.[15]

As a result of these differences[16] the amount of actual economic support may vary considerably from city to city, irrespective of the conditions of need *per se*.

[15] The highest payable rent fixed in 1995/1996 was 108,000 lira in Turin, 300,000 lira in Ancona and 400,000 lira in Reggio Calabria. In some municipalities the rent and heating costs are not added to the *minimo vitale* but subtracted from the claimant's income in the definition of the benefit (the result is almost the same). In Bologna the maximum possible deduction was for a single person's household of about 127,000 lira. The variability of these amounts does not reflect the different housing conditions of the different contexts, but only the heterogeneity of the existing criteria and the different degrees of public generosity.

[16] In defining the amount to be paid to the person in a condition of economic need, there are two further elements of variability: a) the possible contribution from the relatives of the person in need;

In addition to this, in practice it is not unusual for the entitlement to be paid only in part or for a limited period of time (and not as long as the need persists), thus contributing to the uncertainty of the right to minimum decent living conditions.

Other measures of economic support

In those cities where financial support is not provided on the basis of the *minimo vitale*, the situation is even more variable. The criteria vary from municipality to municipality, and in some cases from district to district within the same municipality.

- In Rome, economic support is granted primarily to elderly people. Minors and younger adults also have the right to claim support, but for them the intervention is limited by more selective procedures, involving more discretion. The duration of the support depends also on the continuation of the condition of need, but the threshold of this need is higher than in the other cities, at least for the elderly (800,000 lira). For families it varies from 700,000 to 1,000,000 lira, irrespective of the household's size. Despite these thresholds the amount provided varies considerably, because each district may adopt different criteria and each has a different budget at its disposal. In any case, the social services never pay more than 200,000 lira per month. Finally, the people who benefit from this support cannot claim for other services provided by the municipality. This rule clearly restricts multi-dimensional intervention, which goes beyond mere economic support.
- In Naples all basic economic support has been suspended since 1993, when the city's financial bankruptcy was declared.[17] From 1958 to 1993 the mayor had the power to decide the supply of special support benefits on an irregular basis, usually varying from 200,000 to 500,000 lira. From 1993 up until 1998, when a minimo vitale was established, the only benefits actually covered by specific national transfers (such as those for minors) have been paid. Since 1999 Naples has participated in the RMI testing phase
- In Bari the municipality passed a new regulation in 1987 which includes basic economic support measures, although the *minimo vitale* is not explicitly referred to. However, the measures have never been implemented because the authority decided its funds were too limited for this. For this reason, the

and b) the methods to calculate the amount. Both can bring about very different thresholds. As for the obligation of relatives to intervene in case of need (art. 433 of the Italian Civil Code), only some municipalities consider this possibility. Turin, Ancona and Pesaro, for instance, have very precise regulations determining the exact amount of the contribution in relation of the respective income. Other cities (e.g. Florence) reduce the benefit by 20%. Able-bodied claimants are supposed to earn a certain amount, even if they are unemployed (e.g. 311,000 lira in Trent, 300,000 lira in Bolzano and 200,000 lira in Piacenza).

[17] In Naples, "financial embarassment" has been declared according to art. 25 of the LN 144/89. Until the late nineties the financial situation of the municipality has been managed according to Decree DL 77/95. The main consequences of this declaration for the people in a condition of economic need were retrenchments and more severe control procedures.

income thresholds—which were already lower than the minimum INPS pension—have never been updated. In practice, the nine municipal districts pay a sum ranging from 200,000 to 300,000 lira as a special support measure, trying to manage the limited funds available. This limit on resources seriously affects the adequacy of intervention.

- In Messina, basic economic benefits are provided only to those categories of people who were awarded benefits before the 1977 decree, e.g. single mothers and orphans (previously in charge of the ENAOLI) and the relatives of war victims. Here again, the income thresholds are very different for each group, as well as the amount and the length of time for which the benefit can be claimed.

WHAT VARIATIONS IMPLY: POLICY MAKING AND ENTITLEMENTS

The diversity of ways in which economic support is granted has many consequences. In particular the synergetic effect of these diversities makes understanding local policy mechanisms very difficult. All these variations in fact cause several problems.

The first and crucial problem caused by the range of measures, guidelines and practices described is the management of information. Welfare systems have to produce information about their working, to enable better planning of social policies. From this point of view, the central state has been unable to manage and control a phenomenon like that of dependency, while this is growing. The same can be said for the regional level where, with few exceptions, the quality and quantity of information available is relatively poor. Different policies result in the production of different data, and these can be compared only when aggregated at a higher level, often only in terms of expenditure without taking into account the basic socio-demographic characteristics of recipients. Even in the municipalities the situation is not really any better. Few of the cities analysed have an adequate monitoring system (e.g. Bologna, Turin, Trento) and the range of institutions also use different ways of collecting data: the kind of data that is considered to be relevant differs as well as the degree to which this information is available.

All these features make it hard to compare different contexts and to give a detailed interpretation of the social dimension of this phenomenon. Data does not necessarily show more or less vulnerable situations, but it does reveal the lack of clear and reliable criteria for accessing benefits. They are an indicator of the different ways in which institutions *prestructure* the profiles of recipients, rather than an indicator of the real weight of the problem (Kazepov, 1999). A higher number of recipients can indicate either a socially deprived area or an area with good access to benefits. Similarly, a low number of recipients can indicate that claims are ignored, or alternatively that there are few specific problems in that area. The question is particularly relevant, because data should be used to understand the local situations and to plan more effective policies at each territorial level: local, regional and national.

A second crucial problem arises from the fact that institutional and social disadvantages it Italy are concentrated in the southern regions. There the amounts are lower, support and benefits are provided for shorter periods, some categories (such as adults) are completely excluded from any benefit, the social services have no proper staff, access criteria are stricter, and at the same time the degree of discretion is much higher. In many cases the laws which regulate social assistance are not implemented and monitoring systems do not exist. In the northern and central regions the situation is far better, but still not as good as might be expected.

These situations have put Italy—together with Greece, and to some extent Spain—at a disadvantage, compared with other EU countries, from the point of view of citizenship rights. What made Italy different from the other south European countries was the co-existence of some very advanced policies (mainly concentrated in the north and centre) with more traditional and stigmatising ones (mainly concentrated in the south). The new national framework law approved in October 2000, laid down common standards could promote equal access criteria and equal support to the conditions of need throughout Italy.

A third crucial problem is linked to the fact that, despite the many and persisting differences, there has been a slow but steady trend towards the formal adoption of some of the regulatory features of the *minimo vitale* threshold by all municipalities. This occurred in both northern and southern Italian municipalities, but there are considerable doubts as to the adequacy and advantages of this trend. In fact, municipalities were converging to maintain, at least in the implementation of the guidelines, an approach which defined categories of people and provided different degrees of protection for people with the same condition of need. Able-bodied adults (mainly males) were specifically excluded from this last safety net, partially in the north and totally in the south, while mothers and/or families with dependent children are relatively well protected. In addition, the degree of discretion was high for decisions about everyone, throughout Italy, even if in the northern cities the discretion was in some cases used to widen the range of the intervention opportunities and not just to restrict them. Finally, elderly people enjoy better rights than others because the social pension was one of the financial supports automatically provided in case of need. This is also available in cases of invalidity, although the amount in no way guarantees decent living conditions, particularly when the individual is affected by a serious disease.

CONCLUSIONS

From a political point of view, this situation offered a great potential for confusion especially when we consider the ongoing retrenchments in the social security systems made in view of the European Monetary Union. These tendencies also weakened those groups which were well protected through their position in the labour market.[18] Italian social policies of the 1950s and '60s, when there was relatively full employment (particularly in the north) were aimed at securing the job of the male *breadwinner,* and so maintaining the household's income. These policies, which did not foresee the problem of adequate income support for non-workers, appear now to be inadequate. This is true despite the fact that in Italy, especially in its northern regions, the unemployment rates for adult males are still among the lowest of the European Union.[19] In fact this should not prevent us from recognising that chronic structural long-term unemployment (mainly in the south) and the decrease in work opportunities and the growth of unemployment (mainly in the north) on one hand, and the retrenchment policies, on the other, will increase the numbers of people who will soon be outside any protection scheme other than social assistance. The joint effect of these tendencies creates the *institutional preconditions* for a process of downward mobility, i.e. from a contributory and insurance-based system of social protection to means-tested social assistance.

When unemployment becomes long-term and the right to claim contributory benefits disappears, then social assistance should be the last safety net. However, as we have seen, the Italian system of social assistance has not been able to ensure adequate protection to people in economic need, who have no other support, such as other family members. The high degree of discretion intrinsic in most aspects of the access procedures up to the new law made the groups at risk even more vulnerable. This does not mean that there was and is an automatic and direct relationship between discretion and vulnerability. However, it is not difficult to imagine that it increased the variation of the policies, so consolidating the inequality of rights which existed in the different local contexts. In fact the system has not been able to face the conditions of need equally, that is to say it has not been able to implement similar measures to answer similar needs. The importance of this aspect, however, represented a challenge, arising from the variability of the risks of falling into poverty, which the fragmented and unequal Italian welfare system tried to overcome with the new framework law on an integrated system of social services and provisions.

[18] The causes of this situation are to be found in the way in which the Italian welfare state developed, and in the particularistic mechanisms that it created to achieve consensus. Social groups could obtain specific benefits only if they were able to exercise some pressure on the political body, which helped to create a system of social security characterised by a juxtaposition of different measures which tend to categorise welfare claimants. For an overview of the Italian welfare model and its development see: Ferrera (1984, 1993, 1998), Ascoli (1984), Paci (1990) and Fargion (1997).

[19] Italy has one of the lowest male unemployment rates in the European Union. This is particularly true of some northern regions where the unemployment rate is nearly fractional: e.g. Lombardy (4.1% in 1995) and Trentino-Alto-Adige (2.7% in 1995) (Eurostat, 1996). Young people are in a very different situation. The high levels of protection granted to the male (or female) adults employed within large and medium-sized factories has created a deficit of labour mobility and a kind of *frozen employment*, which slows down the generational turnover. With Spain Italy has the highest youth unemployment rate in Europe: in Campania (1995) it reached 68.7%.

This law (Ln 328/00) sets up the frame for an integration of the existing services and provisions in view of homogenising criteria and avoid institutionalised inequalities. It establishes also the *Reddito Minimo d'Inserimento* (Rmi), a French style last safety net. In doing so, the law took seriously the suggestions given by the Poverty Commission in 1995 (CIPE, 1995) and re-elaborated by the Onofri Commission in 1997, to develop a national measure of economic support (similar to the minimo vitale) as a fundamental individual right of people in need. In the view of the legislator, the Rmi should become a support to be given automatically to any individual whose income is lower than the threshold. The new access criteria reduce the degree of discretion and are complemented by other supporting measures to help people out of their condition of economic need more actively and effectively. The criteria regulating the *Reddito Minimo di Inserimento* support will be defined more concretely in 2001, after the end of the testing phase of the Rmi, which lasted from January 1999 to December 2000. It should, in any case, be characterised by being independent of the budgetary constraints of municipalities and should force public bodies to develop innovative and efficient individually designed projects in order to avoid a growing deficit. In such a way, economic support is only one element of a global strategy for reducing the likelihood of dependency and increasing chances for individual autonomy. With such a policy Italy would come closer to the other mainland EU countries, whose social protection schemes are explicitly moving in this direction, for instance the *Revenue Minimum d'Insertion* in France, *Sozialhilfe* in Germany and the *Maatwerk pilot project* in the Netherlands. Here, institutions were obliged to develop empowering strategies because of the legal right of the individual to have his/her claims recognised as soon as he/she fulfils specific criteria. Spain and Portugal are also moving in this direction, having introduced similar programmes of *Renta minima* (see: Guibentif and Bouget, 1996).

The question is now whether the Italian political actors will be able to implement the recently approved welfare reforms allowing Italy to enter Europe, in terms of concrete social rights.

REFERENCES

Artoni, Roberto (1990), *Welfare State e politiche sociali*, Milan: Franco Angeli

Ascoli, Ugo, ed., (1984), *Il Welfare state all'italiana*, Bari: Laterza

Cattaui de Menasce, G. (1963), *L'assistenza ieri e oggi*, Rome: Editrice studium

CIPE (Commissione d'Indagine sulla Povertà e l'Emarginazione) (1995), *Verso una politica di lotta alla povertà: l'assegno per i figli e il minimo vitale*, Presidenza del consiglio dei Ministri, Dipartimento per l'Informazione e l'Editoria, Rome: Istituto Poligrafico dello Stato

European Commission (1994), *European Social Policy: A Way Forward for the Union. A White Paper*, DGV, COM(94)333, Brussels

EUROSTAT (1995), *Statistiche dell'Unione Europea*, 32nd ed., Brussels

Fargion, Valeria (1997), *Geografia della cittadinanza social in Italia*, Bologna: Il Mulino

Ferrario, Paolo (1988), *Politica dei servizi sociali*, Rome: Nuova Italia Scientifica
Ferrera, Maurizio (1984), *Il welfare state in Italia: Sviluppo e crisi in prospettiva comparata*, Bologna: Il Mulino
—— (1993), *Modelli di solidarietà*, Bologna: Il Mulino
—— (1998), *Le trappole del welfare*, Bologna: Il Mulino
Giumelli, Guglielmo (1991), "Assistenza: una legislazione incompiuta", Materiali per il dibattito, *Marginalità e Società*, 17: 73–105
—— (1994), *Anziani e assistenza: Dalla carità verso la sicurezza sociale*, Milan: Franco Angeli
Guibentif, Pierre and Denis Bouget (1997), *Minimum Income Policies in the European Union*, Lisbon: União das Mutualidades Portuguesas
Hanesch, Walter, ed., (1995), *Sozialpolitische Strategien gegen Armut*. Opladen: Westdeutscher Verlag
—— Krause, Peter and Bäcker, Gerhard (2000), *Armut und Ungleichheit in Deutschland*, Hamburg: Rowohlt Taschenbuch Verlag
Kazepov, Yuri (1996a), *Le politiche locali contro l'esclusione sociale*, Rome: Istituto Poligrafico dello Stato, Presidenza del Consiglio dei Ministri, Quaderni della Commissione Povertà
—— (1996b), "La legge non è uguale per tutti", *Assistenza Sociale*, 50: 115–34
—— (1998), "Urban Poverty and Local Policies against Social Exclusion in Italy: The North–South Divide", in *Empirical Poverty Research in a Comparative Perspective*, ed. by Hans Jürgen Andreß, Aldershot: Avebury Press, pp. 391–422
—— (1999), "At the edge of longitudinal analysis. Welfare institutions and social assistance dynamics" *Quality and Quantity* 33, 305–22
—— (2000), "Italia, Europa: il RMI tra sperimentazione e generalizzazione", Prospettive Social e Sanitarie XXX, n. 20/22, 44–7
Leisering, Lutz and Leibfried, Stephan (1999) *Time and Poverty in Western Welfare States: United Germany in Perspective*, Cambridge University Press
Mariani, Gaetana and Tognetti Bordogna, Mara, eds., (1995), *Politiche sociali tra mutamenti normativi e scenari futuri*, Milan: Franco Angeli
MISSOC (1995), *Social Protection in the Member States of the European Union: The Situation at July 1st 1994 and Evolution*, Brussels: European Commission
Motta, Maurizio and Mondino, Franco (1994), *Progettare l'assistenza: qualità e diritti nei servizi*, Rome: La Nuova Italia Scientifica
Negri, Nicola and Saraceno, Chiara (1996), *Le politiche contro la povertà in Italia*, Bologna: Il Mulino
Paci, Massimo (1989), *Pubblico e privato nei moderni sistemi di welfare*, Naples: Liguori
—— (1990), *La sfida della cittadinanza sociale*, Rome: Edizioni Lavoro
—— ed., (1993), *Le dimensioni della diseguaglianza*, Bologna: Il Mulino
Paugam, Serge (1993), *La Société Française et ses pauvre: L'expérience du revenue minimum d'insertion*, Paris: PUF
Ranci Ortigosa, Emanuele (1990a), *Welfare state e politiche sociali in Italia*, Milan: Franco Angeli
—— (1990b), "La politica assistenziale", in *Le politiche pubbliche in Italia* ed. B. Dente, Bologna: Il Mulino
Rei, Danilo (1994), *Servizi sociali e politiche pubbliche: modelli, percorsi, casi*, Rome: La Nuova Italia Scientifica
Saraceno, Chiara (1996), *Reti familiari e politiche sociali*, Milan: CGIL-SPI

3

Strategies for Police Accountability and Community Empowerment

ROSS HASTINGS and R.P. SAUNDERS

SUMMARY

THIS CHAPTER ADDRESSES the extent to which the accountability of public police to local governments and their communities has resulted in a meaningful shift of power to those groups traditionally most disadvantaged in local political processes. Using the example of the legal regime governing civilian oversight of police forces in the province of Ontario (Canada), the paper argues for the need to examine accountability from a wider perspective, which adopts a more integrated approach to the control of public police and which attempts to tie these efforts to a broader range of policing reforms at the structural, educational, professional and police-work levels in order to increase not only accountability, but more importantly the empowerment of those communities which are currently most disadvantaged.

INTRODUCTION

A recurring theme in the literature on law and poverty is the limited ability of formal legal regimes and their institutions to improve the lives of the poor. This chapter examines traditional approaches to police accountability and argues that these have not been sufficiently effective in establishing control over the public police by local governments and the communities they serve. The connections between poverty, community mobilisation and the control of crime highlight the need for better ways to make the police accountable to the communities most affected by their actions. We argue that an effective police accountability mechanism is a key element in the empowerment of disadvantaged communities.

Traditionally, crime and its management have tended to be peripheral concerns for law and poverty scholars. This is in spite of the fact that the impact of crime on the poor, whether financial, physical or emotional, has been well established. Moreover, the causal impact of poverty on crime—through factors such as cyclic abuse and violence, lack of education and opportunity, and unstable family and community lives—is well documented in the criminological literature. Also, an effective and transparent accountability mechanism is a necessary element in any attempt to reduce the traditional animosity between many disadvantaged communities and their police agencies. We examine ways in which community control over the public police might be better established and maintained, and identify specific and constructive mechanisms of control and accountability.

The primary focus of the paper is the potential of police accountability mechanisms to assist members of these communities (especially the poor or disempowered) to mobilise for political action and to exercise greater control over their destiny. The institution of the public police is central to the everyday life of the poor and their communities. There are a number of reasons for this, all of which centre around the impact of crime and disorder on the lives of the poor. The poor are more likely to be involved in crime and disorder, either as victims or as the objects of police activity. In addition, the impact of recent fiscal and economic policies on the availability of social services has left the police in the position of being the only all-purpose twenty-four-hour-a-day crisis management and problem-solving service available to many people. Finally, the police are playing an increasingly important role in community development activities, largely because they have human, financial and organisational resources which are well beyond those available to most community-based groups.

Whether responding to demands for service which originate from the public or attempting to develop proactive responses to the problems of dealing with crime and disorder, the police are central to the creation and maintenance of the minimum level of social order necessary to permit the mobilisation of community-based political activities. In this context, the accountability of the police to the communities they serve is an issue of growing importance. It is imperative that the poor and other disadvantaged groups have access to structures and processes which allow them to influence police decision-making in a meaningful manner, and to hold the police accountable for their performance. In addition, they must have access to the resources necessary to participate actively and effectively within these same structures and processes.

It is our position that current approaches to police accountability largely ignore the wider relationships between inequality, power, crime, and social control. Instead, there is a tendency to focus on the identification and sanctioning of individual "rule violators" in an atomised and isolated manner. The result is a police complaints industry which is effective as an ideological mask for the realities of economic and political inequality, but which is often irrelevant to the needs and desires of disadvantaged communities.

We will argue for a broader conception of the notion of accountability, one which better reflects the range of issues and concerns which characterise the communities the police must serve. The chapter is divided into three principal sections. The first briefly describes the professional model of policing which has dominated discourse in policing since the 1950s and the formal-legal approach to accountability which it has privileged. The second section involves a case study of the experience with civilian review of the police in the province of Ontario (Canada), particularly since the introduction of the *Police Services Act (1990)* which mandated a shift towards emphasising community policing. The third section describes the key rhetorics and strategies behind the current attempts to reform police organizations or the legal regimes which govern them. The emphasis is on community approaches to policing. We argue that the apparent consensus around the notions of community and partnerships masks major divisions and disagreements over the definition of the notion of "community policing" and over the question of the strategies and techniques to be used to implement organisational reform. We identify three different approaches to policing reform, each of which implies a different orientation to police accountability and a different approach to the design and implementation of accountability mechanisms.

THE PROFESSIONAL MODEL AND POLICE ACCOUNTABILITY: AN OVERVIEW

The professional model of policing

The professional or law enforcement model has dominated the conception of the police function and the approach to organising police services and bureaucracies since the 1950s (see Leighton, 1991; Reiner, 1992; and Goldstein, 1990 for excellent detailed discussions of both the professional model and the later community models of policing). The professional model argues that the key roles of the public police are law enforcement (crime fighting), order, maintenance and emergency response. The police have two basic strategic approaches to their mission. One is based on a commitment to prevention, usually through reliance on some version of the tactic of random patrol. The premise in this case is that the public's awareness of the existence of patrols will raise the objective risks of arrest and sanction, and will thus deter individual offenders. The other strategy is based on a faith in the deterrent effect of punishment. In this case, the police focus on their ability to clear cases: to identify offenders and deliver them for processing by the courts. Unfortunately, recent research has produced strong evidence that there are important limits to the ability of realistic changes in police tactics to have a significant impact on crime rates or on individual or community safety and security (see Reiner, 1992 for an overview of this research).

The key to the professional model, for the purposes of this chapter, is that the police remain largely autonomous from outside control in the performance of their duties. They are obviously dependent on their political masters for issues related to resource allocation, but their basic responsibility is to the law. In this context, the police have argued for a model of "self-policing" which is characteristic of other professions (such as lawyers or doctors), and which thus leaves them with considerable autonomy in the control of their affairs. In practice, approaches to public accountability for their performance have tended to focus on rule-breaking by individual officers, and have tended to exclude areas relating to police policies and practices.

Police accountability: the North American experience

In North America the history of the debates surrounding the accountability of the public police is relatively short. The debates have been most keen—and then only intermittently—since the 1960s. Interestingly, and certainly in Canada, the issue has not generated much public interest, particularly outside larger urban areas. Where debates about and around accountability have occurred, this has usually been within the broader framework of the control of crime, law and order, and the unique needs of the police to do their job. When such debates did focus specifically on the issue of accountability, they almost always arose (especially in the 1960s and 1970s) in the context of a confrontation between the police and minority groups over their treatment at the hands of front-line police officers in a particular community. These debates were usually framed around the civil rights of minorities and, importantly, around individualised notions of officer misconduct; they were *not* structured in the context of larger organisational concerns or systemic misconduct. It is not that this larger context was not known or not spoken to, but simply that the principal thrust of the discourse around accountability quickly developed into one of the accountability of an officer for his or her misconduct. The quest then became one of finding an appropriate legal regime for ensuring that clear rules and regulations specified appropriate lines of conduct/misconduct in order that individual officers were brought to "justice". It was hoped that this would restore the mythic legalistic "balance" in the community. In practical terms, the debate centred attempts to wrest some of the traditional (legalistic) accountability mechanisms in the hands of the police administration (and chief) from the police department and vest them to some degree in the community or its representatives.

The debates, as they developed, were almost invariably framed in *negative* terms. The spotlight was on the alleged misconduct or wrongdoing of individual officers. This raised then a criminal justice model of accusation and defence, giving rise to claims by aggrieved citizens for redress and counterclaims by the officers, stressing their legal rights and the unique requirements of the job. Where civilian review was instituted there followed a juridification of the process of complaints by citizens. The civilian review accountability models followed a route much more in harmony with the civil or criminal courts' focus on individual rights and wrongs, rather than a less limiting path which might have allowed for more proactive and interventionist approaches. In fact, it was much the same route as had been followed by internal complaints systems within police departments, though arguably with even less effect.

More importantly, the focus on this type of review served to divert attention from other meanings and practices of accountability. Given the "misconduct" orientation and adversarial character of the processes set up and their confining and legalistic nature which focused on the individual's misdeeds, a rights discourse tended to overwhelm the debates and practices around accountability, and transform the concept into an ineffective shell of what it could have been. The problem for the poor is how to transcend such a system, even one which is relatively "progressive" and citizen-oriented, and claim greater accountability to and for their community. The rhetoric around policing and the reform of police organizations in recent years suggests that the answer is to be found in some variant of community policing. The final section of this chapter discusses the promise of this approach and its relationship to police accountability. To provide the context for this discussion, we consider next civilian review in the province of Ontario (Canada), which illustrates an attempt to develop a progressive and relatively strong system of civilian review.

THE TRADITIONAL FACE OF ACCOUNTABILITY: A CASE STUDY

Overview

The organization and delivery of policing services in Canada reflects the federal character of the country. There are several layers of policing authorities corresponding to the federal, provincial and municipal jurisdictions and spheres of control. While the formulation of criminal law is within the federal jurisdiction, the responsibility for policing rests primarily with the provinces, which in some cases delegate their authority to the municipalities (which are provincial creations). This scenario is further complicated by the contractual arrangements between the federal government and all the provinces except Ontario and Quebec. In the other eight provinces, the effective provincial forces and many of the municipal forces are members of the federal Royal Canadian Mounted Police who provide policing services under contractual agreements with either the province or the municipality. Ontario and Quebec have their own provincial forces—the Ontario Provincial Police and the Sureté du Québec—as well as a large number of municipal forces which operate under provincial legislation. The result is a large number of laws, regulations and policies which separately and collectively govern the approximately 55,000 fully sworn police officers operating in Canada (Leighton and Normandeau, 1990: 5).

In the past the province of Ontario has been in the forefront of attempts to breathe life into the concept of accountability and the practice of civilian review of the police in Canada. That experience, as in the rest of North America, has a relatively short history. In Ontario the movement for civilian review took root, not surprisingly, in Toronto where there had been a series of high-profile incidents (beginning in the early 1970s) involving officers of the Toronto police and members of visible minority communities, notably the black community. As a result of complaints from members of these communities and the impact of the surrounding publicity on the attributions of legitimacy in general, there was a series of investigations and reports on the conduct of the Toronto police and on their handling of complaints against them (Lewis, 1991: 154–5). Each of the reports came to the same conclusion: the existing internal complaints system of the police department was found wanting, and the creation of some form of external civilian oversight to restore confidence in the system, notably the confidence of the visible minority communities in the city, was recommended (Lewis, 1991: 154–5).

The case of Ontario

The Toronto Initiative

In 1981 an initiative was launched in Toronto as a pilot venture under the authority of the Ontario legislature's Metropolitan Police Force Complaints Project Act (1981). According to Lewis (1991:153), it was the "first successful Canadian effort at 'civilianization' of police complaints procedures". With a few modifications, it became a permanent feature of the Toronto system in 1984, and later of the entire province. It should be noted that when the Toronto scheme was introduced, it met with vociferous opposition by the police officers themselves. This mirrors the experience of attempts to institute civilian review accountability procedures in most North American cities (see, for example, Terrill, 1991: 300–3, and Skolnick and Fyfe, 1993: 220–3). However, unlike many similar experiences in the United States, the Toronto scheme survived, in part due to the failure of the police to generate much public support for their cause. There has been, at best, an attitude of grudging acceptance of the system now in place throughout Ontario, a system which, in spite of the changes recently enacted and discussed below, continues to reflect the basic principles and direction of the original pilot project legislation.

The pre-1997 legislative regime

In 1990 the Police Services Act essentially enshrined the Toronto scheme and applied it across the province. That same Act also introduced a new set of guiding principles for the police services in the province, focusing in particular on the need for community policing and partnerships. At its core was the review agency—the Office of the Police Complaints Commissioner—which was fundamentally an agency intended to *monitor* the processing by individual police agencies of complaints in the province. The province's individual police agencies had been mandated under the Act to establish complaint bureaus, and these bureaus were given the primary task of investigating complaints in the first instance. Of the review agency itself, Lewis, referring to the original Act setting up the Toronto scheme, states:

> "The basic scheme of the Act provided that the Office would:
> 1. monitor the handling of complaints by the police;
> 2. perform initial investigation in unusual circumstances;
> 3. reinvestigate and review findings when the complainant was dissatisfied with action taken by the police;
> 4. when the public interest required a hearing, refer cases to a civilian adjudicative tribunal with direct disciplinary power; and,
> 5. perform a preventive function, making recommendations to the chief of police, the board of commissioners of police, the Attorney-General, and the Solicitor-General, with respect to policing issues arising out of complaints." (Lewis, 1991: 157)

Like other agencies of its genre, it was not intended to replace the traditional method of discipline for officers who commit misdeeds or otherwise break departmental codes or policies. That power was meant to rest principally, though not exclusively, with the managerial sector of police bureaucracies (in spite of their very poor record in the area of disciplining officers accused of misconduct against citizens). Moreover, strong protections were built into the Ontario system for ensuring due process and other constitutional guarantees for individual officers, as well as the right to appeal any discipline decisions to the courts (Lewis, 1991: 161–3). In virtually all of these types of agencies, the "most pressing issue . . . remains the question of independence" (Terrill, 1991: 315). How "civilianized" and independent the agency is, and what powers of investigation and sanctioning it has, are the issues most often at the heart of the debates over the relative merits of oversight agencies. By most accounts, the Ontario scheme provided for the functional independence of the oversight agency, and provided the agency with the tools necessary to enforce its decisions, at least in regard to the individual officer. In particular, the powers of independent investigation and direct discipline (including dismissal) were noted by supporters as evidence of the existence of an effective body against police misconduct and as an indication of its standing as a relatively potent agency for its type, especially when compared to many similar American agencies.

Furthermore, in regard to the practices and procedures of the police department as a whole, the Police Complaints Commissioner was authorised to make recommendations and forward them to the Attorney-General, the Solicitor-General, the chief of police, the local police association and the police services board where such existed. This provision addressed, at least in a small way, the argument by Goldsmith and other writers that review agencies can and should serve a broader policy function, using complaints as "sources of knowledge and opportunities for self-correction" (Goldsmith, 1991: 15). The chief, the association and the board could comment on these non-binding recommendations, but it was generally the chief who decided whether or not to implement any proposed changes.

The enforcement record

In practice, the work of the Office of the Police Complaints Commissioner did not result in many changes in the disposition of complaints nor, many would argue, should it have been expected that many changes would result. As Skolnick and Fyfe state, "[n]o matter how effective civilian review is, most of the time cops will be exonerated, and probably should be" (Skolnick and Fyfe, 1993: 229). Such sentiments are based on the fact that there are many spurious claims against the police due to unrealistic expectations and demands on the part of aggrieved citizens and the simple fact that many disputes cannot be resolved due to lack of corroborating evidence (the Rodney King case in Los Angeles being a notable exception).

Under the scheme which existed until 1997, as was the case elsewhere under similar systems, the dismissal rate remained very high (Goldsmith, 1987: 621). As a result, some critics of the system saw it as a farce, serving more as a public relations vehicle than as an effective brake on police misconduct (see for example, early criticisms of the Toronto pilot project in McMahon and Ericson, 1987: 47). It can be argued that the state recognised that something had to be done to deal with the increasing public concerns about the police agency's ability to police itself, and the answer lay in the creation of an outwardly external, independent and civilian review process. However, the result might have been called a triumph of form over substance, along the line of Sykes' criticism when discussing the reform of policing in more general terms: "Such reforms may provide an image of change without the substance. . . . [T]he reform movements may have succeeded in creating the appearance without the substance of fundamental reform" (Sykes, 1989: 296–7).

The pre-1997 Ontario system was praised in the civilian review literature as being among the more "progressive" systems of oversight, though it received little attention in the popular press and therefore in the wider public mind in Ontario since its inception. The concerns expressed by representatives of various community and visible minority groups were not picked up by the larger public. The public appeared less concerned about police accountability, at least in regard to their alleged misdeeds, and more concerned with crime in the streets, personal and property safety, and fiscal responsibility. The larger public's sense of accountability continues to reflect not such much concern with the individual misconduct of the officer on the beat or with the larger issue of dealing with the structural anomalies which lie behind and even encourage such behaviour. The focus is on the need for budgetary accountability, a traditional concern with politicians and the public writ large. This concern in part motivated and is reflected in the most recent amendments.

The 1997 amendments

The changes were adopted in mid-1997 in Bill 105, An Act to Renew the Partnership between the Province, the Municipalities and the Police and to

Enhance Community Safety. By all appearances, they represent, a step backwards. Under the revisions, the Office of the Commissioner was abolished in the name of cost-cutting and efficiency, and the oversight responsibilities (as modified in the legislation) have passed to the appointed local police services boards which have traditionally been very close to the local police, and ultimately, by way of review, to the Ontario Civilian Commission on Police Services, a pre-existing body whose duties previously related only to the overall provision of police services in the province and the review of internal disciplinary dispositions. While it is still very early to assess, the changes appear to be a move to treat public complaints in the manner of internal discipline infractions, with the locus of initial investigation moving from an internal bureau of complaints (which would no longer be mandated) to the local chief of police. Boards of inquiry, which were rarely empanelled under the old scheme, were also abolished by the legislation.

The new measures reduce the independence of the oversight process by shifting greater control to the local chief of police. In this regard, it is noteworthy that while the Office of the Police Complaints Commissioner was under the authority of the Attorney General, the Civilian Commission is under the authority of the Solicitor General, the same ministry which is in charge of the police in the province. The new review provisions are weaker than the former provisions (for example, no independent investigation resources are provided for the Commission) and stress even more than before the adversarial, individualistic nature of the complaint process. Significantly, section 57 of the legislation restricts eligible complainants to those who have been "directly affected by the policy, service, or conduct that is the subject of the complaint". Broader notions of organisational accountability to the community will be more difficult to raise in the future; complaints regarding the general policies and practices of the local force are allowed for, but such complaints are to be made to the local chief and are also require the complainant to have been directly affected.

Those changes came in response to a number of criticisms from the police and some members of the public about the delays and alleged duplication in the system of police governance: the changes were an attempt by the right-wing government both to satisfy those concerns and to save money. The ultimate effects of the amendments are yet to be seen. However, given our conclusions on the very limited success of civilian review as a vehicle for achieving police accountability and on the potential for community policing in this area, any effect may be unimportant or irrelevant in the long term.

THE REFORM PROCESS IN PUBLIC POLICING

There can be little doubt that the notion of community policing has been the organising framework for the reform of most policing organizations in recent years. We next describe briefly a model of the reform of policing in an attempt to identify some of the key issues and concerns in policing and police accountability which emerge at different stages of the reform process. The focus is on the notions of partnerships and the co-production of social order which are central to the concept of community policing, and on the implications of different approaches to the implementation of community policing for the empowerment of disadvantaged groups and the effective accountability of the public police to the communities which they are supposed to serve.

Community policing: the reform process

In spite of the tremendous popular appeal of the rhetoric of community policing, there is still no consensus on the precise definition of the nature of this concept and strategy, nor is there much agreement on how exactly to transform a police organization so as to equip it to take on the challenge of incorporating community policing into its overall activities as efficiently and effectively as possible.

In our view, part of the problem is the difficulty in finding a common ground on which to situate some of the debates. One possible solution is to identify and describe the stages of the police reform process, and to discuss the key questions and issues which emerge at each stage. For our purposes, we have identified four stages:

1. the recognition of the impact of social change on the function of policing, and on the resources available to accomplish the tasks assigned;
2. the shift to a broader mandate for public policing, involving greater responsibilities for the public police and greater expectations on the part of the public (in terms of performance and scrutiny);
3. the identification of new strategic approaches for addressing the new mandate; and
4. the reform of police organizations on the basis of a commitment to one (or a combination) of the possible strategic approaches.

Each of these stages is worthy of some discussion.

Social change and policing

Few police organizations are unaware that the world is changing faster than ever, and that many changes have significant consequences for public policing. One result is that both governments and the police now expend considerable time and effort in attempting to anticipate the demands and priorities they will have to face, and to identify the types of resources they are likely to have at their disposal to accomplish their assignments. The basic methodology used in this work is a variation of what is usually called environmental scanning: essentially, this involves projections on the basis of available demographic, social or economic data in an attempt to describe the future.

In the context of policing, the projections suggest that it will be increasingly difficult to create and sustain an adequate level of social and communal order in the future (see Hastings, 1994: 50–3). A large part of the problem is that the institutions traditionally responsible for the production of order are becoming progressively less able to accomplish their role. For example, families now face greater challenges to their ability to socialize children and to prepare them for participation in a complex and demanding world. As a result of social and geographical mobility, family breakdown, an unstable economy, inequality, and other factors, the modern family is smaller, and has access to a more limited range of social or community resources and support. This is compounded by the growing limits placed on our educational systems, which are now being asked to achieve more (especially in the face of the retreat of the family and the increase in social heterogeneity) with less resources (in the face of constant budgetary cutbacks). Politically, we are becoming a more fragmented society, in which it is ever more difficult to create a common set of rules or conflict-resolution mechanisms which all groups can accept as fair and legitimate. Finally, recent economic developments have tended to increase the gap between social classes, and to trap some groups in our society (especially underprivileged youth) in positions of hopelessness and fatalism about their potential to occupy a valued place in society.

The result is a system which is generating ever more pressure towards crime and disorder. This is obviously not without significance either for the police or for the underprivileged communities which tend to bear the greatest weight of this type of development. The problem is exacerbated by the fact that both the welfare system and the less formal network of community supports and institutions are less and less able to cope with these developments. The pattern in recent years is for more of the "work" previously performed by community-based institutions or by the welfare system to be diverted into the purview of the justice system.

This development has significant implications for the relations between the police and the poor. To begin, the increase in crime rates and the emergence of new types of criminal activity are likely to have a greater impact on the poor, both as victims of crime and as residents of communities where high levels of fear and distrust make communal mobilisation for political action much more difficult. Moreover, the poor (especially the youth in this category) are over-represented as the objects of police activity. Current developments are likely to increase the sense of injustice already felt by many members of this class, and to make the task of gaining legitimacy for their interventions ever more challenging for the police. On the other hand, the cutbacks in social and community services have made the police ever more important as the only twenty-four-hour-a-day response service available to the poor and the underprivileged. In this context, the police have the potential to play a crucial role as partners in community problem-solving or social development activities (if only because the police have human and financial resources which are beyond the imagination of almost any local community-based group).

The role of the public police

The result of the trends described in the previous section is that the police are faced with the dual challenge of doing more of the "old" work of control and law enforcement (largely due to increases in problems related to crime and disorder) and at the same time taking on "new" work (largely because of their expanding role as partners in community problem-solving or social development activities). The problem is that there is little indication, at least in the recent Canadian experience, that the police will be provided with any significant new resources to accomplish these tasks; on the contrary, indications are that resources will at best be stable, and more likely there will be some cuts in police budgets in the years to come. The result is that the police are being asked to achieve more, in terms of both amount and type of work, with fewer resources.

The shift to a broader conception of police roles and responsibilities means that the police will have a new and broader role to play in the community. The heart of this new role is to be found in the notion of the police as a partner in the co-production of order. This has implications for our discussion of the relationship between the police to the poor, and for the issue of police accountability. The broader role or function of the public police means that their performance will increasingly be judged by new types of output criteria. There will be increasing pressure to shift from the former reliance on output criteria such as clearance rates or response time towards impact criteria which measure the actual results or consequences of police activity on crime rates or community problems, or which assess the satisfaction of community clients with the performance of the police.

The result of this development is that a new and much more politicised conception of police accountability is being added to the existing reliance on formal legal accountability mechanisms. The partnership role of the police with the community, however it is conceived, links the police to local politics in a manner which was inconceivable in the professional law enforcement model of policing. This problematizes the position of the police *vis-à-vis* other community actors, especially in situations characterized by high levels of heterogeneity and conflict. In this context, mechanisms of police accountability become crucial components of a community's ability to control its destiny, and of the ability of a police service to earn and sustain a level of legitimacy which allows it to perform its function. We argue that the conception and operationalization of accountability will depend to a great extent on the type of community approach to policing which is given priority by a police organization or by the communities it must serve.

Police and community: new strategies for policing

Community approaches to policing

The crux of the argument in the discussion of the previous stage is that the concern to reform police organisations cannot and must not be reduced to a simple question of improving the economic efficiency of these organisations. The challenge faced by modern policing is not simply to do more with less (although that is a considerable part of the problem) it is also to do new and different kinds of work while retaining the traditional responsibility for crime control and law enforcement. There is an apparent consensus within policing and public policy circles that the solution to this problem is to be found in some variant of the community approaches to policing. As we shall see, each of these variants has considerable consequences for the problem of designing and implementing an effective legal and political accountability mechanism. First, however, a brief description of the community approaches to policing is necessary.

The baseline for this discussion is the idea that most police organisations, at least in North America, have spent the better part of the last generation attempting to move as far as possible toward a professional model of policing. In brief, this model emphasises the role of the police as autonomous law enforcers. In this context, accountability mechanisms are primarily designed to assure that the police practice their trade within the limits set by the law and by local departmental policies. The key point is the tendency to defined accountability almost exclusively of individual performance, rather than in terms of the responsibility of the police to account to the community for the nature (to say nothing of the success) of their performance.

Community models of policing and crime prevention take a different approach. There are three common themes: commitment to proactive strategies, inclusion of the community as a partner and reliance on inter-agency partnership in the delivery of programmes and initiatives (see Hastings, 1993b: 10–32). All versions of community policing insist on the necessity of balancing reactive approaches to crime and disorder (associated with the professional models of law enforcement) with more proactive or preventive strategies. The focus is increasingly on the need for preventive strategies which address factors associated with crime and disorder before problems emerge or worsen. The second theme is the insistence on including the community as a partner in the co-production of solutions to the problems of crime and disorder. However, there are two very different views of how this should be done. One focuses on the *responsibility* of the community to participate in the work of policing: this usually involves attempts to include members of the community as volunteer workers in the delivery of police services (in programmes such as Crime-Stoppers or Neighbourhood Watch). The other shifts the focus to the *right* of the community to influence decisions about the definition of policing problems and priorities, and about the implementation and evaluation of police strategies.

The third theme is the necessity for co-operation among the various government sectors and community agencies which are active in the realm of social control. The argument is that the efficient use of the limited available resources requires greatly increased levels of interagency co-operation.

The three notions of prevention, community and co-operation seem at first glance to signal the emergence of a consensus around which to organise the reform of justice systems. The problem is that this consensus is illusory (Hastings, 1993a; 1993b: 26–33): in our rush to rally around the flags of prevention and community, we have failed to debate and resolve key theoretical and policy issues. For example, the near universal agreement on the need to address the factors associated with crime proactively does little or nothing to settle the issues of what these causes are, and what the most effective and efficient solution might be. The result is that we are still a long way from a basis for concerted action. Similarly, the agreement on the need to include the community has not yet resulted in much agreement on how exactly we identify communities and their legitimate representatives (especially in cases of inter- or intra-community conflict). Moreover, there has been little or no progress towards designing mechanisms through which the police can share power and control with their community partners in a real and meaningful way. Finally, the commitment to interagency co-operation ignores the real cost in terms of human and financial resources to community agencies who wish to get involved in partnership exercises. All too often the consequence is a cutback of other activities, usually at the expense of client populations. Nor have there been many constructive proposals about how agencies (who tend to be concerned with preserving their control over their resources and their client bases) will share power and control in partnership initiatives. In the end, one is forced to conclude that the apparent consensus may still be at a stage where it promises more than it can deliver.

This might explain why the apparent consensus over the need for "community policing" has resulted in very different approaches to the operationalisation of this strategy. Three models or ideal types can be identified: community-based policing, problem-oriented policing, and community policing (Hastings 1993b: 33–55). Each model emphasises a different aspect of the apparent consensus, and each has implications for how the concept of accountability should be defined and operationalised.

Community models of policing

The first model is *community-based policing*. The emphasis here is on the responsibility of the community to participate in the delivery of policing services and programmes. Typically, this reflects the growing realisation that the police cannot "do it all" by themselves, and that the community must help out by being their "eyes and ears". It also reflects the growing recognition by the police that their success depends to a large extent on their access to information from members of the community (especially victims and witnesses of crime or disorder).

What needs to be emphasised here is that this represents primarily a change in the delivery of policing services by the inclusion of volunteers—there is little indication of any attempt to challenge the notion that arrests and convictions will have a deterrent effect on rates of crime or disorder. The practical consequence, for the purposes of this paper, is a tendency to emphasise programmes aimed at improving the quantity and quality of contacts between police and public (for example, by establishing police mini-stations or instituting foot patrols). There is a correlative tendency in this approach to equate the popularity of the police *with* the public and the accountability of the police *to* the public.

The second model is *problem-oriented policing*. The emphasis here is on the need for a proactive response to the factors associated with crime and disorder. The basic premise is simple: crime and victimisation are not random phenomena. A significant proportion of police work is repetitive, in the sense that the police tend to deal recurrently with certain offenders, victims or situations which generate a high level of demand for services. That being the case, appropriately targeted proactive measures hold considerable promise both for reducing the demand for police services, and for increasing the safety, security and satisfaction of members of the community. The practical consequence of this model is a tendency to equate accountability with the appropriate forms of community consultation during the stages of identifying problems and designing, implementing and evaluating solutions. This is, at least potentially, a much more political approach to accountability than is easily imaginable in the professional law enforcement model.

The final model is *community policing* in its real sense: the politicisation and democratisation of issues related to the broad concerns with public safety and social control, and the more specific issue of the role of the public in this sphere. The emphasis here is on the right of the community to participate in and influence decisions related to police policies and practices. The goal is to include the community as fully and as actively as possible as a partner in the co-production of order and control. Obviously, this involves a dramatic change in the nature of the political relations between the police and the communities they serve. Equally obviously, the old formal legal models of individual accountability which characterise the professional approaches to policing (and the juridico-legal approaches to accountability) will not be sufficient to support the implementation of community policing. The juridic approach addresses only the legal responsibility of individual officers to perform their duties within the limits defined by the law and by the policies of individual departments. However, this highly individualised approach goes only part of the way towards creating the kinds of transparency and accessibility necessary as a basis for active partnerships between the police and the community. Individualised approaches to accountability contribute little to the successful empowerment of underprivileged groups who might wish to mobilise in order to influence the design, delivery or evaluation of policy strategies in their communities.

Organisational renewal and the police

The question of how the public police can best reform the organisation of their structures and work processes is beyond the scope of this paper. However, it is worth briefly mentioning the motives of police organisations which take up the challenge of reform. In simple terms, there are two basic reasons why organisations take up (or are pushed into) the challenge of reform: economic necessity, and the desire to adapt the organisation to the types of strategies necessary to meet the challenge of the broader role of modern policing. Arguably, few organisations are motivated by only one of these; in the real world, reform usually reflects a combination of these two factors.

However, we argue that the need for cost efficiency tends to be the primary drive behind many of the decisions made by police organisations. For example, few cases of organisational renewal in policing fail to investigate the possibilities of "delayering" the organisational structure and decentralising the decision-making process. The logic of delayering is to streamline the organisational structure so as to bring the top levels of command closer to the operational frontline. One need not be too cynical to realise that "delayering" also offers the promise of cutting costs with relatively few consequences for the quality of service offered to clients. The holy grail of cost efficiency sometimes obscures the fact that "delayering" also has two very negative consequences: it engenders enormous resistance within the rank and file who are expected to carry out organisational reform (it is, after all, their potential for promotion which is being eliminated) and the thinness of the command structure is independent of the transparency of the organisation to outside observers and the access of the community to the policy-making process. In other words, decentralisation may actually generate so much resistance that the success of reform attempts is threatened. The rhetorical commitment to community approaches may also serve as an ideological gloss for the fact that little or no progress is actually being made in the empowerment of communities, or in the accountability of the police to those communities.

Police, communities and accountability

The arguments set out above reveal the complexity of the notion of accountability, and show how the concept can be defined and implemented in different ways, depending on the operational strategy pursued by a particular police organisation. This discussion is summarised in Figure 3.1: our point is that different strategies of police practice are guided by different goals and concerns, and are based on different conceptions of the nature of the partnership which ought to exist between public police organisations and the communities they serve. Our concern for the moment is not so much to argue for the advantages of any particular approach as to describe the gap between the organisational possibilities of accountability and the actual practices which govern most police organisations in Canada. As we argued above, accountability tends to be limited to the attempt to hold individual police officers accountable for certain types of violations either of the criminal law or of the rules established by governing or supervisory bodies to limit the behaviour of officers in the exercise of their function. As yet there is little indication of mechanisms which establish organisational accountability, or which effectively assist in the empowerment of communities wishing to mobilise for action.

Figure 3.1: Policing strategies and accountability

MODEL	STRATEGIES	ACCOUNTABILITY
PROFESSIONAL	Apply law in an effort to punish, deter and rehabilitate offenders, and maintain social control	Organisational autonomy and individual accountability
COMMUNITY-BASED POLICING	Improve police—community relations → better enforcement (through information and co-operation)	Limited community participation: focus on quality of relations
PROBLEM-ORIENTED POLICING	Proactive response to factors associated with crime and disorder	Limited community participation: focus on impact of service on clients
COMMUNITY POLICING	Democratize and politicize key aspects of policy and practice	Participation and empowerment: mobilized communities exercise degree of influence and control (in part through political processes)

An important dimension of the problem is the lack of any real guidelines or direction in the governing legislation, the Police Services Act (1990). The Act stipulates in section 1 the "need for co-operation between the providers of police services and the communities they serve" and mandates in section 3 the development and promotion of "community-oriented police services", but nothing else in the act sets out the type and degree of co-operation or the exact nature of community policing to be provided. This gap in the legal regime has left the door open to interpretations which deny more effective partnerships in the co-production of order and stability. Given the realities of power and resource inequities faced by members of disadvantaged or poor communities, there is little hope that such a vague and ambiguous legal provision will create an effective terrain for political mobilisation or community development. If there is to be effective use of the practices and strategies required in the more democratic and participatory forms of community policing, social and economic realities and history suggest that these forms must be specified explicitly and in detail in the governing legal regime. The internal rules and regulations of the various forces will not accommodate the more community-oriented variations of community policing, variations which offer much more hope of generating effective systems and practices of accountability to the public being served.

CONCLUSION

The message which emerges from the experience of civilian review of police misconduct in Ontario is similar to findings from most other North American jurisdictions: there is little in either current legislation or practices which broadens the notion of police accountability beyond the assessment of the performance of individual officers and its conformity with either the criminal law or other policy and procedural regulations.

There is little indication that the popular notion of police service and accountability to client communities has been translated into operational structures and processes which give those communities a partnership role in decisions relating to the definition of problems and priorities within a community, nor in the design, implementation or evaluation of the programmes or initiatives which constitute the service to these clients. This point becomes even more salient when one considers that many of the communities in which the police operate are characterised by high levels of disorder, tension and conflict. The performance of the police in such a context can have a significant impact on the way in which a community evolves and develops.

At its heart, the problem begins at the conceptual level with the failure to distinguish adequately between the different operational meanings of the general notion of involving the community (as either client or partner) in policing, and of the more specific concern with the relationship of police accountability mechanisms to this process. Accountability should be viewed as a continuum involving a number of different options and approaches. The continuum runs the gamut of possibilities between the two extremes of complete police autonomy and complete community control. Obviously, neither of these extremes is desirable or realistic; they serve as end points for debates about where exactly to locate a workable approach to accountability.

The first possibility is to involve the public as *complainants* in accountability processes. This has been the most popular position to date. It reflects the consensus that individual officers must work within the confines and constraints of the criminal law and other relevant regulations. In operational terms, the result is a tendency to involve the public as victims or witnesses of police abuse who may bring complaints to the attention of the relevant police authority (usually, at least initially, the police service in which the officer is employed). The key point here is that neither the complainant nor the general public exercise any control over the process beyond the complaint, and many of these processes also fail the test of transparency. Even if it were possible to develop a perfect system for identifying and sanctioning individual officers, this approach does little or nothing to address problems at the corporate level of a police service. In addition, it neglects the broader structural factors which are responsible for current trends in crime and disorder, and the maintenance of the legitimacy of the police among client groups and communities.

The second possibility is to include the public either as an *advisor* to the police or as a *participant* in the delivery of policing services. The benefit of this approach is that it helps to open up a police service to public input. Moreover, public participation seems to have a beneficial impact on the quality of the contacts and relationships between the police and the public. The problem is that the relatively autonomous police professionals retain control over what to do with the public's input, and over the nature of the activities in which the public is allowed to participate. This is merely a new approach to the *delivery* of traditional types of police services, with little or no real increase in community power or control.

The third possibility is to involve the community as a *partner* in the design and delivery of policing services. The focus of accountability here shifts from the individual officer to the police service. The aim is to develop structures and processes for addressing and redefining the problem of the redistribution of power and control in what are supposed to be partnerships between the police and the community in the co-production of social order. In this approach accountability provides mobilised community groups and their representatives with a real and significant role within these partnerships. A crucial element in such accountability is the construction of a legal regime which guarantees meaningful participation by all sectors of the community, particularly the least powerful. This also places a responsibility on either the police or another government agency to assist disadvantaged groups to mobilise.

Current accountability mechanisms fail to do this. They not only are unable to address the larger notions of police accountability and responsiveness but, more importantly, in appropriating the discourses of accountability they mask the real challenge which remains to be faced in the next few years. It is only by establishing transparent and effective accountability mechanisms that the poor and the disadvantaged can hope to democratise criminal justice within their communities. Until this happens, their chances of success remain severely limited. While the accountability of the public police to their communities represents only one element in the reproduction and transformation of social relationships, it is critical to the larger social project of constructing community well-being. The law and its formal regimes serve important but often unexamined functions within this project.

REFERENCES

Blumberg, Mark (1989) "Controlling Police Use of Deadly Force: Assessing Two Decades of Progress", in R.G. Dunham and G.P. Alpert, eds., *Critical Issues in Policing: Contemporary Readings*, Prospect Heights, Illinois: Waveland Press

Goldsmith, Andrew J. (1987) "Complaints Against the Police in Canada: A New Approach", *Criminal Law Reports* [1987]: 615

—— (1991) "External Review and Self-Regulation: Police Accountability and the Dialectic of Complaints Procedures", in Andrew J. Goldsmith, ed., *Complaints Against the Police: The Trend to External Review*, New York: Oxford University Press

Goldstein, Herman (1990) *Problem-Oriented Policing*, Toronto: McGraw-Hill

Goode, Matthew (1991) "Complaints Against the Police in Australia: Where We are Now, and What We Might Learn about the Process of Law Reform, with Some Comments about the Process of Legal Change", in Andrew J. Goldsmith, ed., *Complaints Against the Police: The Trend to External Review*, New York: Oxford University Press

Hastings, Ross (1993a) "La Prévention du Crime: L'Illusion d'un Consensus", *Problèmes Actuels de Science Criminelle* VI:49–69

—— (1993b) *Leadership in Community Policing in Canada: A Report Submitted to the Canadian Police College*, July 1993 (unpublished)

—— (1994) "Address to Atlantic Crime Prevention Workshop", *Building Safer Communities: Final Report of the Atlantic Community Safety and Crime Prevention Workshop*, June 1994, Charlottetown, PEI: Community Legal Information Association of PEI Inc

Kerstetter, Wayne A. (1985) "Who Disciplines the Police? Who Should?", in William A. Geller, ed., *Police Leadership in America: Crisis and Opportunity*, New York: Praeger

Leighton, Barry N. (1991) "Visions of Community Policing: Rhetoric and Reality", *Canadian Journal of Criminology* 33: 485–522

—— and André Normandeau (1990) *A Vision of the Future of Policing in Canada*, Ottawa: Minister of Supply and Services

Lewis, Clare E. (1991) "Police Complaints in Metropolitan Toronto: Perspectives of the Public Complaints Commissioner", in Andrew J. Goldsmith, ed., *Complaints Against the Police: The Trend to External Review*, New York: Oxford University Press

Lindsay, John A. (1991) "Managing Police Liability: A Strategic Perspective", in Dan Ogle, ed., *Strategic Planning for Police*, Ottawa: Canadian Police College

McMahon, Maeve W. and Richard V. Ericson (1987) "Reforming the Police and Policing Reform", in R.S. Ratner and John L. McMullan, eds., *State Control: Criminal Justice Politics in Canada*, Vancouver: University of British Columbia Press

Petterson, Werner E. (1991) "Police Accountability and Civilian Oversight of Policing: An American Perspective", in Andrew J. Goldsmith, ed., *Complaints Against the Police: The Trend to External Review*, New York: Oxford University Press

Reiner, Robert (1992) *The Politics of the Police* (2nd ed.), Toronto: University of Toronto Press

Skolnick, Jerome and D.H. Bayley (1986) *The New Blue Line*, New York: Free Press

—— and James J. Fyfe (1993) *Above the Law: Police and the Excessive Use of Force*, New York: Free Press

Sparrow, Malcolm K.; Mark H. Moore and David M. Kennedy (1990) *Beyond 911: A New Era for Policing*, New York: Basic Books

Sykes, Gary W. (1989) "The Functional Nature of Police Reform: The Myth of Controlling the Police", in R.G. Dunham and G.P. Alpert, eds., *Critical Issues in Policing: Contemporary Readings*, Prospect Heights, Illinois: Waveland Press

Terrill, Richard J. (1991) "Civilian Oversight of the Police Complaints Process in the United States: Concerns, Developments, and More Concerns", in Andrew J. Goldsmith, ed., *Complaints Against the Police: The Trend to External Review*, New York: Oxford University Press

Wagner, Allen and Scott Decker (1989) "Evaluating Citizen Complaints Against the Police", in R.G. Dunham and G.P. Alpert, eds., *Critical Issues in Policing: Contemporary Readings*, Prospect Heights, Illinois: Waveland Press

Strategies to Confront Poverty

4

Poverty, Social Exclusion and the Impact of Selected Legal Measures against Caste Discrimination in South Asia

KALINGA TUDOR SILVA and AJITH HETTIHEWAGE

SUMMARY

AMONG THE MANY factors responsible for widespread poverty in South Asia, caste has attracted relatively little attention.

While caste was understood by some social scientists as a model of social solidarity ensuring social security for the downtrodden, others view it as an oppressive social system resulting in social exclusion of and discrimination against groups such as Untouchables in Hindu society. Legal measures for dealing with caste in India include constitutional safeguards against caste discrimination, on one hand, and positive discrimination for the disadvantaged in the system, on the other. While the position of social outcasts has improved considerably over time, the extent to which this may be attributed to the relevant legislation is unclear. Despite this improvement, the continuing nexus between poverty and untouchability suggests the need for a more comprehensive programme of social justice and positive economic measures.

BACKGROUND

Nearly half of the global poor population live in South Asia, which accounts for less than 5 per cent of the total land area on earth (Silva and Athukorala 1996). According to the estimates of the Independent Commission of Poverty in South Asia, 30–40 per cent of the population in South Asia live in conditions of poverty (SAARC 1992). Entrenched poverty in South Asia is characterised by acute physical deprivation as well as multiple discriminations, disabilities and disempowerment resulting from oppressive structures of class, caste, gender and spatial inequalities. This chapter focuses on social exclusion resulting from caste, its relation to poverty in South Asia and the impact of selected legislation on the reduction of caste inequality, the removal of hereditary disadvantage and poverty alleviation in general.

Much of the discussion on poverty in South Asia deals with either macro-economic issues relating to underdevelopment and stagnation or household-level characteristics such as landlessness, lack of capital or lack of marketable skills, without paying sufficient attention to the mediating structures of class, caste and gender. Even the recent literature on social mobilisation and participatory approaches to poverty alleviation pays inadequate attention to issues of discrimination and social exclusion as factors inhibiting broad-based participation of the poor in government-sponsored or even in "community-based" programmes of various kinds (Berraman 1967, Wignaraja 1990). While poverty and social exclusion need not always go hand in hand, the relative ineffectiveness of most of the poverty alleviation programmes calls into question the underlying assumptions of these programmes. In this context anti-discriminatory legislation, such as that applicable to caste discrimination, should be more carefully considered in the light of its effect on removing the disadvantages of being poor, socially excluded and underprivileged.

This chapter presents a brief introduction about caste, mainly for the benefit of those unfamiliar with this unique South Asian social institution. Two contrasting views of how caste may be related to poverty are then discussed. There follows a review of some legal measures designed to overcome disadvantage resulting from caste and their impact. Finally the implications of anti-discriminatory legislation intended to promote social justice and poverty alleviation in South Asia are examined.

CASTE

Castes are arranged into a hierarchical social order, members of each caste having a more or less fixed position predetermined by custom, social interaction and notions of purity and pollution which are particularly strong in Hindu society. In the first place a caste system is a scheme for allocating social status, i.e. the level of dignity or social honour to which each person is entitled, within a fixed and neatly defined social hierarchy. Patterns of distribution of wealth and power may or may not conform to this social hierarchy since *artha* (lit. the search for material prosperity and power) is considered subordinate to *dharma* (lit. good deeds) in Hindu orthodoxy (Dumont 1980).

Each caste has a hereditary caste occupation or a calling, giving rise to a static division of labour in society and related exchange of goods and services across caste boundaries. Certain types of social relations are only permitted within each caste, due to considerations of purity and pollution. For instance marriage (but not necessarily sexual relations) can only take place between men and women of the same caste. Similarly, the sharing of food, drinking water sources or common seating arrangements is considered appropriate only among persons of identical caste status. On the other hand relations between persons of different castes are limited to economic and social obligations which reinforce status differences and patterns of interaction which are necessarily hierarchical.

Even though the caste system imposes one restriction or another on all the castes, the Untouchables or outcasts in the Hindu caste system encounter severe social exclusion by virtue of the high levels of pollution attributed to them by custom. The disabilities imposed upon them include minimal social contact with those above them in the caste hierarchy, denial of access to places of worship and drinking water sources used by the upper castes, as well as other inhibitions restricting their spatial and social mobility (Jayaraman 1974, Hollup 1994). In some areas they have been forbidden to wear trousers or a wrist watch or even to use an umbrella. These extreme forms of social discrimination have been maintained through a combination of ideology, social pressure and physical violence against Untouchables who have defied the system. Sexual violence against untouchable women has also been an important form of caste oppression in parts of India. The Untouchables, who now identify themselves as Dalits (lit. oppressed people) constitute about one-sixth of the total population in India. Organised collective efforts to overcome oppression against Dalits have led to violent confrontations with their oppressors in recent years (Mitra 1994).

THE INFLUENCE OF CASTE ON POVERTY IN SOUTH ASIA

While the above analysis implies that caste and related social discrimination are likely to have contributed to high levels of poverty in South Asia, the relationship between caste and poverty is far from straightforward. Poverty is by no means restricted to those at the bottom of the caste hierarchy. Nor are the "outcasts" uniformly poor. Among social scientists there are two contrasting views regarding the relationship between caste and poverty. One view holds that the caste system, at least in its traditional form, provided some protection against poverty and victimisation for those at the bottom of the caste hierarchy. Others, however, either explicitly or implicitly suggest that there is a nexus between poverty and caste-based social discrimination in South Asia.

Leach (1960) in his functionalist explanation of caste essentially argued that it provided some protection to those at the bottom of the social hierarchy.

> "In a class system social status and economic security go together—the higher the greater; in contrast, in a caste society, status and security are polarised. . . . In a class society the 'people at the bottom' are those who have been forced there by the ruthless processes of economic competition; their counterparts in a caste society are members of some closely organised kinship group who regard it as their privileged right to carry out a task from which all the other members of the total society are rigorously excluded" (Leach 1960: 6).

However, Leach was fully aware that in contemporary South Asia low castes were often economically underprivileged. He interprets this as a manifestation of the disintegration of the caste system.

> "The low castes suffer economically not because they are low castes but because present conditions have turned them into an unemployed working-class. What has put them in this position is not their caste but the recent rapid increase in population, coupled with the fact that caste rules which formerly compelled the high-status landlords to support their low-status servitors have been progressively destroyed by arbitrary acts of 'liberal' legislation extending over the past 150 years" (Leach 1960: 6, emphasis in the original text).

While signifying a conventional anthropological bias against modern legislation in line with a predominantly functionalist interpretation of the role of indigenous social institutions, the last statement highlights the need to examine the impact of modern legislation on social inequality in South Asia more closely.

On the basis of the caste ideology, even those at the bottom of the social hierarchy could think of themselves as having "certain inalienable rights" and "privileges" as claimed by Leach. However, those rights were by no means legally binding on their social superiors. They were more like voluntary social obligations on the part of the upper-caste establishment towards those conforming to customary modes of conduct, deference and demeanour. For instance, the Rodiyas, the lowest of the Sinhalese castes in Sri Lanka, had the "right to solicit alms" from those above them, but the only sanction they had against those refusing to oblige was to curse or cast a spell on them. It was in the nature of the caste system that the lower the status, the higher the likelihood that a person"s life chances depended on the goodwill and support of others. Any notion of fundamental human rights applicable equally to all human beings was alien to the social values underlying the caste system.

Other researchers argue that there was traditionally a broad correspondence between caste status and economic position in much of South Asia. For instance Berreman (1967: 402) concluded that "Generally, caste status and economic advantage go together in India". Similarly, based on his intensive fieldwork in a village in South India, Beteille (1971) argued that wealth and power in rural society was traditionally concentrated in the hands of a land-owning upper-caste elite which had a vested interest in maintaining the subservient position of the Adi Dravidas (farming and labouring castes). As low castes set their sights on the good things in life (like education, government jobs, representation in decision-making bodies) with social change still restricted to the social elite, the fund of goodwill between the lower and upper castes is progressively diminished and conflicts of interests come to the surface. This analysis implies that the low castes encounter new opportunities as well as new challenges in the emerging social set-up, having lost whatever protection and minimal guarantees they had in the traditional system.

The rigid caste hierarchy prevalent in parts of South Asia has contributed to entrenched poverty in a number of ways, including the institutionalisation of social inequality, social exclusion, prejudice and discrimination, creating barriers to social mobility, promoting passive acceptance of the status quo and making it difficult for the poor to organise themselves across caste lines (Beteille 1991, Silva *et al.* 1996). To the extent the caste system provided any social security for the downtrodden, such social security quickly disappeared in the modern era, leaving them vulnerable to both social deprivation and economic insecurities.

LEGAL MEASURES TO ELIMINATE CASTE INEQUALITY

Legislation against caste seeks to guarantee individual rights where the caste system has subordinated individual freedom to a collective will sanctioned by tradition and cultural ideology. Such legislation is based on principles of individual freedom and egalitarianism, whereas caste is based on the recognition of hierarchy, i.e. fundamental inequality between human beings and the need for co-operation among them in spite of unequal status (Dumont 1980). Even though Leach referred to "arbitrary acts of liberal legislation" impacting on caste, they are not arbitrary in so far as they are guided by a fundamentally different ideology.

However, there is considerable ambiguity in the applicability of legal measures against caste. While the Indian government has consistently resorted to legislation to create a "level playing field" among people of different castes, the Sri Lankan government has for the most part maintained a "hands-off" attitude towards caste, assuming that it will die a natural death due to the impact of modernisation and market forces. While the difference in the responses of the two governments may be partly attributed to the difference in the severity and socio-political impact of caste in the two countries and the absence of a notion of untouchability among the Sinhalese (the majority ethnic group in Sri Lanka), it also indicates a sharp difference in the public response to caste. While caste is an important public and policy issue in India, in Sri Lanka it is one of those social realities it is more or less taboo to discuss in public.

In contrast to the Sri Lankan constitution, which is more or less silent on caste, the Indian constitution has adopted two contrasting measures to deal with caste inequality and related social issues. On the one hand the constitution outlaws discrimination on the basis of caste, gender, race or place of origin. On the other hand it provides for positive discrimination in favour of the "backward castes and backward classes" as a means to reduce existing social inequalities. This dual approach, trying to tear down the caste system while at the same time using it as a framework for facilitating its own destruction, brings into sharp focus some contradictions involved in the current policies and programmes.

This issue is discussed below. We will next examine how the Indian constitution deals with caste discrimination.

PROHIBITIONS AGAINST CASTE DISCRIMINATION

Article 15 of the Indian Constitution highlights its general egalitarian ethos. Article 15(1) specifies that the state shall not discriminate against any citizen on the grounds of religion, race, caste, sex or place of birth. According to the constitution, the enforcement of any disability on the basis of "untouchability" is an offence punishable by fine or imprisonment. According to Article 17, untouchability is abolished and its practice in any form is forbidden. This provision was further strengthened under the Untouchability (Offenses) Act (UOA) of 1955. The power of the civil courts to recognise any custom, usage or right which would result in the enforcement of any disability is withdrawn by this Act. The more recent Civil Rights Act is even more far-reaching in its prohibition of untouchability.

The definition of the term "untouchability" varies depending on the legislation. While the notion of untouchability is closely associated with that of ritual pollution, Article 17 and the UOA do not apply the term "untouchability" to every instance where a person is treated as ritually impure or unclean. Certain temporary states of uncleanliness, such as those attributed to women during menstruation or childbirth or those associated with the death of a family member, are not included in the legal concept of untouchability. According to one author the legal definition "is confined to that untouchability ascribed by birth rather than attained in life" (Galanter 1968: 313). The first court to administer this legislation identified as Untouchables "those regarded as 'Untouchables' in the course of historic development" or those relegated "beyond the pale of the caste system on grounds of birth in a particular caste" (AIR 1960). Any disability imposed by one caste on another falls outside the prohibition of Article 17 in so far as the victims are not the customary outcasts.

There has been considerable confusion in legal circles as to whether the prohibitions apply to disabilities imposed on the Shudras who constitute the fourth *varna* and are therefore very much within the pale of the caste system, even though they are not included among the twice-born. These people—Brahmins, Ksastriyas and Vaisyas comprising priests, rulers and traders respectively—have special status within Hindu society. In much of South India only those below the status of Shudras, namely Dalits, have obtained the protection granted by the legislation.

The categories of people covered by the prohibition of untouchability are not readily identifiable given the ambiguities about what constitute forbidden forms of untouchability. The relevant legislation only applies to social situations where a person of designated untouchable status is barred from places "open to other persons professing the same religion or belonging to the same religious denomination or section thereof". In so far as the social discrimination may be attributed to a religious or denominational difference, rather than to a caste difference, the rights of the Untouchables are weakened. For instance in the case of *State of Kerala v. Venkiteswara Prabhu*, the court decided that the prohibition against Untouchables entering the inner chamber of a Brahmin temple was not an offence as it was a religious prerogative of the relevant group of Brahmins to restrict entry to this temple to those belonging to their own denomination. Since these laws do not extend protection to non-Untouchables, proof of untouchable status was left to the victims of discrimination. Several states in India enacted supplementary legislation to overcome the limitations and inconsistencies of the Constitution of India and the UOA.

Legislation in both India and Sri Lanka seeks to facilitate access to places of worship for the social underclass. This conflicts with Hindu notions of ritual cleanliness and the desire of the ritually pure *varnas* or castes to prevent those of ritually inferior castes from entering their places of worship. The Prevention of Social Disabilities Act of 1957 in Sri Lanka, for instance, was intended to help depressed castes in Jaffna to gain admission to certain Hindu temples, entry to which was traditionally forbidden to them (Jayawickrama 1976, Pfaffenberger 1990). However, this legislation was not enforced, principally because the law enforcement machinery was staffed mainly by the Vellalars, the dominant caste in the Jaffna peninsula.

The exact relationship between untouchability and high levels of poverty in rural India is not known. While poverty is by no means restricted to specific castes in Indian society, a disproportionate level of poverty, malnutrition and economic insecurity has been reported in untouchable communities (Moffatt 1979). Often the social exclusion of Untouchables goes hand-in-hand with extremely limited assets and related economic deprivation. As Pfaffenberger (1990) has described in relation to Jaffna society, the social exclusion of the Untouchables was one way of ensuring a cheap supply of labour for upper-caste landlords. Most of the economic activities of Untouchables, including leather work, street sweeping, garbage disposal and the handling of dead bodies, are of an unstable nature even though the notion of pollution keeps those of a higher status away from such activities. However, the prohibition against untouchability seeks to remove social and cultural barriers against them rather than to help overcome any economic disadvantages they suffer. This becomes clearer when we examine legislation on access to public places of a secular nature.

Legal measures to ensure access to secular public facilities

Article 15(2) of the Indian Constitution specifies that no citizen shall on grounds of religion, race, caste, sex or place of birth, be subject to any disability, liability, restriction or condition with regard to a) access to shops, public restaurants, hotels and places of public entertainment; or b) the use of wells, tanks, bathing ghats, roads and places of public resort maintained wholly or partly out of state funds or dedicated to the use of the general public. A series of related Articles forbid discrimination in educational institutions maintained by public or private funds (Articles 28(3) and 29(2)). These provisions address any disabilities imposed by the caste system in regard to the use of public facilities for satisfying the necessities of life, including food, water, communication, education and entertainment. The constitution seeks to ensure individual freedoms while the caste system emphasises social obligations and restrictions applicable to different categories of people.

Legal measures to facilitate public access to secular facilities were available even during the British period. The courts declared that no right could be maintained to exclude other castes or sects from the use of streets and roads. The provisions regarding the use of water sources were even more elaborate. As far back as 1926 a Lahore court held that other users had no right to prevent Charmers (an untouchable group) from drawing water from a public well (AIR 1926). However, some courts held that a right to exclusive use might be upheld where a custom of exclusive use could be proved. Proof of exclusive use of water sources was not easy to establish even in this early period. In *Marriappa v. Vaithilinga,* while the right of exclusive use of a well was granted, Shanars obtained a court order allowing them to use a large tank also used by higher castes. In contrast to a well, fewer precautions against pollution were needed in the case of a tank given the larger volume of water.

However, the impact of this legislation in terms of improving social justice for the underclass in South Asian society cannot be overstated. A prominent low-caste politician stated in Lok Sabha in 1983 that "throughout India the fourth caste-Sudra had been denied education, social status and opportunity to taste anything good in life for more than twenty centuries, because of Hinduism" (Rao & Ahluwalia: 1990). This background provided the justification for a policy of positive discrimination in favour of the social underclasses.

Legal measures for positive discrimination

The Indian Constitution provides for positive discrimination favouring the social underclasses in the fields of legislative assemblies, public service, education and social welfare. The idea is that the reduction of existing inequalities requires not just equal rights for those on the lower rungs of the caste hierarchy but the widening of opportunities and allocation of greater resources by the state on their behalf. The state is authorised to move away from the indifference to caste required by the constitution in following terms "Nothing in this article . . . shall prevent the State from making any special provision for the advancement of any socially and educationally backward classes of citizens or for Schedule Castes and Scheduled Tribes".

Under Article 16(4) of the constitution, 15 and 7.5 per cent of jobs in central government and public sector undertakings have been reserved for members of the Scheduled Castes and the Scheduled Tribes respectively. Groups identified and listed in a schedule of disadvantaged communities prepared by constitutional experts in consultation with various lobbies are referred to as scheduled castes and scheduled tribes. A proposal by the V.P. Singh government to reserve an additional 27 per cent of jobs for a further category of Socially and Educationally Backward Classes (SEBC) in 1990, in accordance with recommendations of the Mandal Commission, was abandoned due to vehement opposition from anti-reservation lobbies comprising youth drawn mainly from the so-called forward castes (Rao and Ahluwalia 1990, Karlekar 1992).

By contrast with the prohibition against caste discrimination, in the selection of groups for positive discrimination it has been mandatory to supplement notions of the ritual standing of groups with appropriate social and economic criteria (sometimes referred to as a "means test"). Although the constitution also refers to backward *classes*, the units selected as backward have typically been caste groups of low ritual standing. However, the courts have been increasingly reluctant to accept as backward groups those determined by ritual criteria alone (Galanter 1968). As a result, the Mandal Commission formulated a set of eleven social, economic and educational criteria for designating SEBCs, who would benefit from the proposed reservation policy. These criteria ranged from castes or classes where the number of children aged between five and fifteen who never attended school was at least 25 per cent higher than the state average to castes or classes where the average value of family assets was at least 25 per cent below the state average (Karlekar 1992).

With caste being a qualification for preferential treatment by the state, many legal disputes have arisen about which castes are to be included among the beneficiaries, and about the caste identities of individuals. In *Chatturbhuj Vithaldas Jesani v. Moreshwar Pareshram* the Supreme Court decided that a Mahar (a member of a scheduled caste) who joined a Hindu sect which repudiated caste remained a Mahar and was thus eligible to contest a reserved seat in the legislature as he continued to identify himself as a Mahar and was accepted as such by the Mahar community (AIR 1960).

In trying to determine the "backwardness" of castes and other social groups for the purposes of positive discrimination issues of poverty have come up in various ways. While the discourse about caste has continued, given the communal character of political competition and the readiness of politicians to mobilise communal identities for the purpose of attracting votes, the problems addressed are of a socio-economic nature and relate to high levels of poverty and related social conflicts. Of the eleven socio-economic criteria of backwardness identified by the Mandal Commission, ten have a direct or indirect relationship to poverty. This reveals the critical importance of poverty in defining backwardness, which in turn was seen as the basis for positive discrimination.

The effects of the legal measures of positive discrimination have been hotly debated and keenly contested. These measures have led to considerable political agitation by those social groups which saw such measures as interfering with their fair share of social and economic benefits. Adherents of the anti-reservation movement typically frame their arguments in the language of merit and equality. Both of these are said to be violated by special provisions for the benefit of the "backward classes". It is claimed that reservation policies allow mediocre and incompetent people to rise to positions of authority which in turn may adversely affect the capacity of the society as a whole to achieve rapid social and economic development. They also argue that the decadent institution of caste, which is likely to die a natural death if left alone, has acquired a new lease of life due to reservation policies. According to those critics, these policies have favoured a nucleus of upwardly mobile and forward-looking people in each designated backward caste without helping the socially and economically disadvantaged, who are typically in the majority, to join the mainstream process of economic and social development (Rao & Ahluwallia 1990, Karlekar 1992).

Advocates of reservation policies, however, are convinced that they promote social justice and open up opportunities for the socially and economically disadvantaged. For instance, Mitra (1994) claims that the double instruments of legal equality and positive discrimination have had the effect of severing the nexus between *jati* (subcaste) and occupation. The rise to high positions by persons of untouchable origin and their successful performance of duties assigned to them, it is argued, undermine the ideological basis of the *varna* scheme. Parekh and Mitra) make the following observation about reservation policy:

> "While legitimising caste at one level, it subtly undermined it at another level. Dissociated at its material roots, the consciousness of caste becomes purely formal, a badge of politically convenient self-classification to be manipulated and waved when necessary. A Charmer does not automatically and instinctively think of himself as a Charmer: rather now he presents himself as one to secure certain advantages . . . Caste consciousness is a ladder he uses to climb out of a social cul-de-sac, and having got to the top he kicks it away. The dialectic of reservation is far more subtle than is generally appreciated" (1990: 108).

In Sri Lanka caste has not been used as a basis for positive discrimination, at least within the legislative framework. Until 1977 the state was committed to a comprehensive programme of social welfare covering education, health services, transport services, food supply and all citizens irrespective of social class, caste, creed, ethnicity or gender. However, some of the politically motivated welfare programmes like the Gamudawa (Village Reawakening) Movement in the 1980s were targeted mainly at depressed low-caste communities with the implicit assumption that special intervention was needed to improve their well-being and social status. Similarly the Paddy Lands Act of 1958 was intended to help the share-tenants, many of whom were from disadvantaged caste backgrounds, by making it illegal to evict such tenants and regulating the rent paid to landlords. Yet the grievances of the low castes have in recent years also surfaced in Sri Lanka. Youth from depressed caste backgrounds have played a significant role in both the JVP uprising in the South and the ongoing Tamil liberation movement in the North-East.

CONCLUSION

Social exclusion associated with caste has taken many forms in India and parts of Sri Lanka. In Hindu society, characterised by the most rigid caste system, it has had the effect of producing a category of social outcasts who are kept out of mainstream society through the notion of untouchability. Even though the caste system primarily encompasses a value system applicable to ritual domain and social relations, it also determines the relative worth and level of dignity of human beings, affecting their overall position including their livelihood security, freedom and adaptation to a modern market economy.

The legal response to caste has taken two primary forms: laws for eliminating disabilities imposed by reason of caste and laws for facilitating positive discrimination in favour of the outcasts. There is an apparent contradiction between these two types of legal measures in that one seeks to outlaw caste discrimination and the other seeks to open up opportunities for those identified as disadvantaged by reference to their caste. There is insufficient data to determine fully the impact of these two types of legal measures, but it is evident that caste identities have been reinforced, at least among the scheduled castes, as a result of the legal recognition of caste for the purposes of affirmative action. However, this does not indicate that caste-based social exclusion and discrimination have remained intact.

On the contrary, there is some evidence that the social exclusion of Untouchables and discrimination against them in fields such as education, employment and politics have gradually decreased over time. It is, though, difficult to determine how far the observed changes can be attributed to legislation rather than to other fundamental changes in society, such as improved communication, market mechanisms and urbanisation. It would be useful to compare the experiences of India and Sri Lanka in this regard. However, since legal measures have not been utilised to any significant extent in Sri Lanka, such a comparison is not possible due to the altogether more relaxed nature of the caste system in Sri Lanka in general.

The legal measures for preventing caste-based social exclusion can be expected to have both negative and positive consequences on poverty. In so far as such measures have the unintended consequence of removing whatever protection and social security was provided by the caste system (converting co-operation into conflict and trust into mutual suspicion in the process) without creating alternative structures of social welfare, they may be expected to enhance poverty and vulnerability at least in the short term. On the other hand, to the extent such legal measures have the effect of bringing the socially excluded into mainstream society, and ensuring their fundamental human rights in the process, they are likely to help overcome poverty and deprivation among the disadvantaged in society. Further research is necessary to determine the contrasting effects of the legislation in question.

Anti-discriminatory legislation has an important role to play in promoting equity and social justice in South Asia. However, to be fully effective such legislation needs to be part of a comprehensive programme of social justice and economic improvement targeted at disadvantaged groups in society in general. The nexus between poverty and social exclusion can only be broken if there are parallel and equally vigorous efforts to address the problems on both fronts.

REFERENCES

Berreman, G.D. (1967), "Caste and Community Development", in *Peasant Society: A Reader*, J.M. Potter, M.N. Diaz and G.M. Foster, eds., Boston : Little, Brown and Co. 398–406

Beteille, A. (1971), *Caste, Class and Power*, Berkeley: University of California Press

—— (1991), *Society and Politics in India: Essays in a Comparative Persepctive*, Oxford: Oxford University Press

Dumont, L. (1980), *Homo Hierarchicus*, Chicago: Chicago University Press

Galanter, M. (1968), "Changing Legal Conceptions of Caste", in *Structure and Change in Indian Society*, M. Singer and B.S. Cohn, eds., Chicago: Aldine Publishing Company, 299–336

Hollup, O. (1994), *Bonded Labour: Caste and Cultural Identity among Plantation Workers in Sri Lanka*, New Delhi: Sterling

Jayaraman, R. (1975), *Caste Continuities in Ceylon*, Bombay: Popular Prakshan

Jayawickrama, N. (1976), *Human Rights in Sri Lanka*, Colombo: Ministry of Justice

Karlekar, H. (1992), *In the Mirror of Mandal*, Delhi: Ajanta

Leach, E.R. (1960), "What Should We Mean by Caste", in *Aspects of Caste in South India, Ceylon and Northwest Pakistan*, Cambridge: Cambridge University Press, 1–10

Mitra, S.K. (1994), "Caste, Democracy and the Politics of Community Formation in India", in *Contexualizing Caste*, M.S. Chatterjee and U. Sharma, eds., London: Blackwell, 49–71

Moffatt, M. (1979), *An Untouchable Community in South India*, Princeton: Princeton University Press

Parekh, B. and Mitra, S.K. (1990), "The Logic of Anti-reservation Discourse in India", in *Politics of Positive Discrimination*, S.K. Mitra, ed., Bombay: Popular

Pfaffenberger, B. (1990), "The Political Construction of Defensive Nationalism: The 1968 Temple Entry Crisis in Nothern Sri Lanka", *Journal of Asian Studies* 49 (1): 78–96

Rao, K.N. and Ahluwalia, S.S. (1990), *Mandal Report X-rayed*, New Delhi: Eastern Books

SAARC (1992), *Meeting the Challenge: Report of the Independent South Asian Commission on Poverty Alleviation*, Kathmandu: SAARC Secretariat

Silva, K.T. and Atukorala, K. (1996), "Poverty in South Asia: an Overview", in *Poverty: A Global Review: Handbook on International Poverty Research*, E. Øyen, S.M. Miller and S.A. Samud, eds., Oslo and Paris: Scandinavian University Press and UNESCO, 65–85

—— *et al.* (1996), *Approaches to Poverty Alleviation in Sri Lanka*, A Report submitted to GTZ Working Group on Self-Help Promotion and Organizational Development in Sri Lanka and Interdisciplinary Working Group on Poverty Alleviation, Eschborn, Germany

Wignaraja, P. (1990), *Women, Poverty and Resources*, New Delhi: Sage

5

Disability and Poverty in the United Kingdom

PETER ROBSON and NICOLA LOUGHRAN

SUMMARY

WE EXAMINE HISTORICAL and contemporary reasons behind state intervention through law and the welfare state in areas relating to disability in Britain. The link between poverty and disability has long been recognised in the UK, inspiring a succession of legal and social policy measures which address the additional problems faced by disabled people. However, since the 1980s anti-welfare ideologies have been canvassed anew, heralding a retrenchment exercise which has sought to restrict the scope and extent of state welfare provision. Nevertheless, although the general atmosphere in Britain throughout the 'eighties was one of retrenchment, legal rights and benefits for people with disabilities remain relatively intact. This chapter discusses that paradox. A consideration of key legislative innovations concerning people with disabilities in Britain suggests that historically the state intervened because of the obvious link between poverty and disability. On closer inspection, however, it is apparent that wider economic reasons, not entirely altruistic, also formed a major spur. People with disabilities have also always been regarded as part of the "deserving" poor—a view still popular today. In fact, it is possible that the current "underclass" debate, which has fuelled penalisation of those sections of the community considered "non-deserving", may have (perhaps unintentionally) strengthened the legal and political position of those deemed "deserving". This has insulated people with disabilities from the brunt of recent legislative assault.

The second section asks whether legal rights and remedies available for people with disabilities have actually increased, and if so why empirical research shows that this has not resulted in their improved social and economic standing in the UK. This second familiar "paper rights" paradox we label "legislative entrenchment with financial retrenchment". We suggest that gains may have occurred in the realm of legal rights. On the other hand, levels of financing and resources available to people with disabilities in the UK have diminished. As most of this community relies upon a spectrum of services provided by local authorities, the effects of central government funding cuts over the past decade appear to a great extent to have negated positive developments in the legal field.

The paper closes with some familiar themes. Legislative and legal entrenchment are clearly valuable strategies for populations in poverty. Advances in the legal and political arenas, however, rarely transform into substantive social and economic gains without financial backing. The economic underpinning which historically has played such a constant factor in influencing state intervention to the present day, simultaneously poses problems for short-term government aims as well as providing an incentive for states to approach social, economic and legal change with long-term objectives.

HISTORICAL REASONS FOR STATE RECOGNITION OF "DISABILITY"

Introduction

The most obvious reason for state recognition of "disability" is the link between disability and poverty which has always existed, although in Britain it was for some years hidden.[1] The early use of institutions for education, working and living separated disabled people from society which disguised the impact of the market on their incomes. However, when state provision for the disabled was introduced, it seems to have been motivated from the very start by a decidedly economic rationale, designed not solely with the welfare of citizens with disabilities in mind. In fact, a consideration of key legislative developments for people with disabilities suggests that wider economic concerns may have been the driving force behind most instances of state intervention.

Legislative provision in the UK for people with disabilities

Special education

The first statutory recognition of disability as a category of need in itself requiring special provision came in 1893 when the government established special education for blind and deaf children, on the ground that such children, given special training, were perfectly able to become useful citizens and workers, but left neglected would become dependent paupers.[2]

Protected work

The hidden link between poverty and disability was exacerbated by the solution chosen to promote the economic viability of disabled war veterans following the

[1] In 1914, for example, 12,015 blind persons were counted as receiving Poor Law relief.

[2] Topliss, 1979: 10–11.

Great War: protected work environments. Sheltered employment was designed for people with disablement capable of employment but not of coping with normal working conditions. Government re-employ factories utilised pay scales for workers reflecting their speed of work. Consequently they were never expected to be profit-making, but were intended to cover costs. Sheltered employment remained popular until the end of the 'seventies.[3] The provision of workshops and retraining centres, coupled with statutory assistance in finding employment, suggests again, however, that the primary aim of successive governments was to make self-supporting and productive those who would otherwise be an economic burden.

Integrated work

It was not until the reconstruction legislation following World War II that integration into the mainstream workforce was seen as a more appropriate strategy for the disabled workforce. Again, however, a range of perspectives operating culminated in a ground-breaking piece of legislation. In the aftermath of the War, it seems that the government's prime concern was with a particular section of the population with disabilities.

In the passage of the Disabled Persons (Employment) Bill in 1944, emphasis was for the first time placed on inclusivity and universality. All disease was included, whether caused congenitally, through illness, accident, industrial injury or war. Until then, special reverence had been accorded to ex-servicemen.[4] However, the symbolic need to continue this tradition was strong enough for the government of the day[5] to give assurances that if the "needs of all [were] not adequately met" there would be no hesitation in ensuring that the needs of the war disabled and ex-servicemen would be met first. This principle was even enshrined in clause 16 of the Bill, although in practice it was never called upon. It resulted, however, in the official creation of two distinct categories of disabled persons: the "deserving" and the "more deserving".

Thus, it appears that in the immediate post-War period in Britain the spur to legislate was born principally from political imperatives with traditional undertones. There was an over-riding desire to cater for the war disabled, while those with disabilities from birth remained a secondary priority. Nonetheless the 1944 Act was welcomed as an exceptional step in bringing together in practice the needs of the war disabled, the congenitally disabled and the industrially injured,

[3] The total sheltered labour force approximated 13,700 in 1978. Although the demand was greater than could be accommodated, one investigation of a group of people wanting sheltered employment revealed that 40% were too severely disabled to be acceptable even for work in sheltered conditions.

[4] The real motivation behind the failed attempt to distinguish the war disabled from the rest, according to Bolderson, was class driven: "The desire to carve out a special case for the ex-servicemen constituted, on the part of the ruling classes, an attempt to divide the working classes (trade unions against ex-servicemen) and maintain their own privilege" (1991: 115).

[5] Bevan and Tomlinson.

thus "cutting right across the views held before the war that collective liability existed only for war pensioners".[6]

Affirmative action

The 1944 Disabled Persons (Employment) Act[7] was also groundbreaking in the UK for another reason: it constituted one of the earliest versions of affirmative action. Employers were required to meet a 3 per cent target of people with disabilities in the workforce.[8] Exemptions, conditions and disqualification regarding entry to the register of those available for work were controlled by the Minister for Labour. One basic condition of entry was that individuals were capable and desirous of obtaining and keeping employment. Disqualified were individuals unable to undertake work on their own, such as patients in hospital,[9] and those who were, in the opinion of the Minister, of habitual bad character.

Local District Advisory Committees representing employers, workers and others appointed by the Minister dealt with questions concerning eligibility for and dismissal from the register and exemptions for employers regarding a reduction of their standard quota. After referring to the advisory committees the Minister could also dismiss from the register "malingerers": disabled people unwilling to attend a vocational training or industrial rehabilitation course or suitable employment without reasonable cause. Final decisions lay with the Minister, who was also advised by a National Advisory Committee on the Employment of the Disabled. There was no appeal tribunal for people with disabilities. There were, however, provisions for prosecution and penalties in the case of an employer ignoring the quotas.

That balance of disqualifications of the disabled worker on one hand, and penalisation of the employer on the other, has been interpreted as revealing a desire on the part of the government of the day to avoid bringing the scheme into discredit with both workers and employers.[10] Indeed a general seal of approval upon the operation of both the quota system and the rehabilitation services was given by the 1956 Piercy Report. However, the system could not be enforced because insufficient numbers of disabled persons registered to enable all employers to fill their quota.[11] Despite the obvious disenchantment of people with disabilities, and later recommendations from the Department of Employment (1972–4) for the abolition of the quota system, the employment

[6] Bolderson: 117.

[7] Which received the Royal Assent on 1 Mar. 1944, but was not fully implemented until 1946.

[8] Regulations regarding the quota came into effect from March 1946. The target was fixed at 2% (raised to 3% the following year) in order not to oblige employers constantly to apply for exemption permits.

[9] The disqualification from entry into the register of mentally ill patients was revoked in 1959 by the passing of the Disabled Persons (Registration)(Amendment) Regulations 1959, SI No. 1510.

[10] Bolderson: 117.

[11] Some individuals even requested that their names be removed from the register (Topliss: 50).

register and the practice of designating certain occupations (such as car-park and lift attendants) as "reserved for registered disabled only",[12] these policies continued into the 1990s.

Co-ordination of services

The importance of a co-ordinated approach to services to people with disabilities was officially recognised in Britain from the mid-'fifties. The Piercy Report in 1956 re-emphasised the role of rehabilitation and resettlement services, but expressed concern about the lack of co-ordination both within the National Health Service (NHS), and between the NHS and the employment services. A later report in 1972[13] also recommended closer integration of services, this time between hospitals and vocational assessment units. Since medical, personal, psychological and social factors are inextricably bound up in an individual's chances of rehabilitation, hospital assessment clinics were urged to include consultants, patients' GPs and local authority social services personnel.[14]

This gradual move in the UK on the part of the state towards encouraging an integrative and comprehensive approach to services for people with disabilities was clearly another positive development. However, bearing in mind the wider political and economic consequences, this strategy might even be seen as evidence of an over-riding preoccupation on the part of the state with supporting those who could potentially return to the workforce, with its stress on maximising the economic contributions from as many citizens as possible.[15]

DISABILITY AND THE WELFARE STATE

Introduction

Like the early legislative developments, the financial benefits provided in Britain initially had a limited range of coverage, addressing only the issue of long-term sickness. Again developments in welfare were conceived amidst economic considerations which were wider than a simple desire to improve the position of individuals with disabilities.

[12] Topliss: 51.

[13] Rehabilitation, Report of a Sub-Committee of the Standing Medical Advisory Committee of the Department of Health and Social Security, HMSO, 1972.

[14] Topliss: 52.

[15] Topliss: 57. In a similar vein, the Department of Employment consultative document on sheltered employment (1973) stressed that disabled workers should be encouraged to move out into open employment if able, although this led to the loss from workshops of the most productive employees and left those least able to reach high productive levels.

Work-based contributions

Like the 1940s Beveridge reforms, which developed the early Liberal benefits dating from 1908 and 1911 into a systematic approach to welfare provision, these benefits were work-based. Sickness benefit, for example, was extended to those who were chronically sick but it remained contingent on work capacity and was subject to withdrawal on resumption of work. The British approach was therefore from its earliest days always tied to workers' contributions, and premised upon the norm of able-bodied (male) self-sufficiency.[16]

The disincentive thesis

The issue of disability also complicated the debate over whether or not provision of benefits provided a disincentive to work. Helen Bolderson notes that between the wars sickness and disablement benefit were so low that the resumption of work could rarely have resulted in financial loss.[17] As the number of sickness and disablement claims rose, however, due to lulls in employment opportunities, the fear that benefits intended to replace earnings would create a disincentive to work and prolong dependency grew. This belief in turn led to the adoption of stricter control and further justification for low benefits.[18] It was not until after World War II that higher sickness benefit made it possible that a disabled person's return to work or permanent part-time employment could cost the worker money.[19] However, the "disincentive" thesis came to be viewed as inappropriate for people with disabilities. Proposals to downgrade benefit for disablement were later resisted, because it was felt that this would further depress the position of those to whom incentives could not apply.[20] Instead, 1934–46 saw the provision of training allowances. Levels of benefit, then, were influenced not only by the ebb and flow of adherence to the "disincentive" view and popular sympathy for the (war) disabled, but also by fluctuations in the employment market and the overall state of the fiscal purse.

Rehabilitation

A less obvious connection between the provision of benefit and rehabilitation suggests that state support of rehabilitation after World War II was also not motivated entirely by simple therapeutic aims. Beveridge's failed attempt to use rehabilitation services as a direct means of controlling sickness benefit claims

[16] MacGregor: ch 1.
[17] Bolderson: 165.
[18] Ibid.
[19] Ibid.
[20] Ibid.: 166.

suggests, once more, a fiscal motivation. The rejection of Beveridge's plan because it might import into industry unwilling or inefficient workers indicates which group interests were again given paramount consideration by the government of the day and which were not.

Thus after 1946 the volatile inter-relationship between benefit, rehabilitation and employment on one hand and between people with disabilities, the state and employers on the other invariably pulled all three groups in conflicting directions. More importantly, we can see that the mesh of legislation, policies and social welfare affecting people with disabilities which evolved in Britain had clearly "sprung from a host of other considerations",[21] primarily economic, and often viewed from the perspective of those already in positions of political and financial power.

Poverty findings

Unsurprisingly, the unequivocal conclusions of successive research projects from the 1960s onwards confirmed the existence of poverty among people with disabilities. The government's own survey of the disabled in 1968–9, documented by Harris,[22] found that disabled people tended to be worse off financially than the rest of the population.[23] Peter Townsend's 1979 study *Poverty in Britain*[24] echoed the Office of Population Censuses and Surveys' work in underlining the problem of exceptionally high levels of poverty amongst people with disabilities.

Disability and citizenship

Aligned with findings of widespread poverty was the growing recognition of the wider social invisibility and exclusion from society of people with disabilities. Several pieces of legislation in the 1970s attempted to address these issues.

The Chronically Sick and Disabled Persons Act 1970

This Act made it obligatory for local authorities to provide people with services which they had power to provide under the National Assistance Act 1948. Local authorities had to identify all disabled people within their jurisdictions and

[21] Ibid.

[22] Harris, A.I, *Handicapped and Impaired in GB, Part I*, Office of Population Consensus and Surveys, HMSO, 1971.

[23] A large number of those in the Harris sample were elderly, a group of the population known to have low incomes. Of those of working age and not full-time housewives, 55% were then in employment.

[24] Chs. 21 and 22.

inform them of all services relevant to their needs. Local authority housing departments had to have regard to the special needs of disabled people when planning future housing developments.[25] The Act sought to extend access to public buildings by requiring all new public building to make provision for the needs of disabled people, subject to the "reasonable and practicable" qualification.[26] The Act also attempted to ensure that disabled individuals themselves participated as members of councils or committees dealing with matters affecting them.[27] The National Health Service and local authorities were required to provide statistics on the number of chronically sick and disabled people under the age of sixty-five who were accommodated in units housing the elderly.[28]

Despite the wide-ranging provisions, it is important to recognise that the Chronically Sick and Disabled Persons Act dealt with a limited range of the problems facing disabled people. It was essentially a long-term measure, and its impact is visible a quarter of a century later in the greater accessibility of public buildings and extended facilities for the disabled population. Its impact on poverty was tangential. At best, it made employment for disabled people more feasible by encouraging accessibility throughout new buildings.

The limited achievements of the 1970 legislation

Reasons for the failure of this piece of legislation to live up to expectations are documented in various sources. The Silver Jubilee Committee found that the access provisions in the 1970 Act were not widely known among property developers, and even when acknowledged, the waiver clause permitted them to be ignored, often on the grounds of "economy and safety".[29] For some critics, the inclusion of the "waiver" clause in effect meant that "the needs of disabled people continued to be disregarded almost as widely as before the Act in the building of new or substantially reconstructed premises".[30] A later report pinpointed the Act's lack of "teeth" to bring about any reallocation of funds to promote the services highlighted.[31]

Another reason for the legislation's lack of impact came to light later through the actions of the UK government in 1978. In an attempt to prevent one arm of local government passing the financial responsibility onto another, the Government drafted a circular reminding housing departments of their duties under the 1970 Act.[32] The fact that the Act imposed statutory responsibilities on

[25] S. 3.

[26] S. 4. This included toilet facilities (ss. 5–6).

[27] Ss. 9–15.

[28] Ss. 17–18.

[29] Topliss, 1981: 128–9. The Committee urged that consideration be given to the way in which fire and safety regulations acted as a barrier to other attempts to improve access to buildings.

[30] Topliss, 1979: 128.

[31] *The Implementation of the Chronically Sick and Disabled Act*, Social Policy Research, National Fund for Research into Crippling Diseases, Sussex, 1973.

[32] Department of Environment Circular 59/78 considerably modified s. 2 of the 1970 Act.

social services departments was not to be made an excuse for the failure of housing departments to use their own powers to carry out modifications on properties of disabled people.[33] Structural adaptations of private properties (such as the provision of ramps and handrails or the installation of an entry-phone system) were made the responsibility of the housing department, which could claim back a subsidy for such work undertaken to make a dwelling suitable for a disabled person. From a critical perspective, however, the buck appears merely to have been passed in a different direction: away from central government at Westminster.

By the late 'seventies, it was clear that the passing of legislation onto the statute book was only the first of many steps needed to bring about reform in favour of a disadvantaged group. Just as motivations prompting the conception of legislation and social security were inextricably linked to the wider financial objectives of central government, explanations for the inadequacy of legislation could also be traced to fiscal considerations. As with the pioneering 1970 Act, lack of financial backing—either directly from central government or indirectly via pressure on local government—proved crucial. As successive pieces of legislation were enacted in Britain, this pattern was set to be repeated.

BENEFIT REFORM AND SEVERE DISABILITY

Introduction

In order to assess more fully the wider implications of benefit reform in the UK, we will turn briefly to the development of state responses to those with more severe disability. Two major issues were initially identified concerning people with chronic disabilities: care at home by relatives and the cost of mobility.

Constant care

The first target of welfare reform were people whose disabilities necessitated constant care. In 1971 the Government introduced a non-contributory payment, the Attendance Allowance. The level of dependence and care was assessed by doctors. Claims were made through local Social Security offices, of which approximately 60 per cent were granted. A review system to a specialised appeal body separate from those dealing with other sickness and social security benefits operated. One-third of rejected claims were submitted for review and of these 60 per cent were successful.[34] The Attendance Allowance was paid as a

[33] Topliss, 1981: 126.

[34] However, Carson stressed that many of the very severely incapacitated who are eligible for Constant Attendance Allowance are likely to be elderly, and unable to make the effort to insist on a review (D. Carson, "National Insurance Attendance Allowance: Appeals", *New Law Journal*, 2 Nov. 1972, 973–4.

simple addition to any other income of the claimant. The principle of contributions had proved to be inappropriate in this field since likely recipients might well never have entered the waged workforce. Until this benefit was introduced the invisibility of disability under the Beveridge Report had resulted in disabled people figuring heavily amongst those in poverty (National Superannuation and Social Insurance (1969), Cmnd. 3883; Report on Social Security Provision for Chronically Sick and Disabled People, 1973–74, HC 276). The benefit was also non-taxable. Nor was it taken into account in assessing the income of the recipient for eligibility for any means-tested benefits. The benefit was payable for those requiring attendance and supervision night and day.

It soon became apparent that the terms of qualification for the allowance had been drawn too narrowly to cover many with serious medical problems (Ogus and Barnedt, 1982: 171) A two-level benefit was quickly introduced. Since 1973 then a lower level of allowance has been payable in respect of those at home who need the attention of another person either by day or night.[35] However, the level of payment was regarded as inadequate to pay for the amount of personal care which a disabled person must require in order to qualify for the allowance.[36]

Mobility

A welfare benefit to enhance mobility was engineered in 1976. The Mobility Allowance[37] was payable to disabled people unable or virtually unable to walk, but not confined to bed. This sum, again, was payable free of tax on top of other benefits and ignored for the purposes of means-tested benefit eligibility. However, the allowance alone, was not sufficient to enable an individual, who could not otherwise afford a car, to buy and run one.[38] Before 1976, a person eligible for a vehicle had one provided and maintained free of charge.[39] Further assistance, however, materialised in 1978: recipients of Mobility Allowance were exempted from Vehicle Excise Duty, and the government supported the voluntary organisation, Motability, which assisted recipients to lease a car in exchange for their Mobility Allowance.

[35] Topliss: 107. The introduction of the lower rate was phased, going first to those of working age who were eligible and then, from October 1973, to the children, and finally, from December 1973, to those elderly who qualified. By 1974 the full attendance allowance was being paid to 110,000 persons, and the lower rate to 55,000.

[36] £15.60 per week full rate and £10.40 partial rate in 1979 (Topliss: 108).

[37] The Sharp Report published in 1974 had recommended that the invalid tricycle be replaced by suitably converted standard small cars with the help of a modest annual grant. The government did not adopt these recommendations and opted instead for the Mobility Allowance.

[38] Valued at £10 per week in 1979 re. Topliss: 108.

[39] Albeit a three-wheeler.

Carers

In 1975 a benefit was introduced to encourage carers by providing a benefit for those caring for recipients of Attendance Allowance in the form of the Invalid Care Allowance. However, not all carers were eligible. This exposed in the clearest light the gendered ideology underpinning the British welfare system. If the person giving the care was a married woman she was ineligible to receive the care allowance. As Topliss noted:

> "This effectively excluded the vast majority of those caring for a severely disabled relative—wives of disabled men, mothers of handicapped children, and married daughters caring for elderly parents."[40]

Viewed fiscally, of course, the payment of state support to married women would have translated into a colossal bill.

ASSESSING THE 1970S BENEFIT REFORMS

Objectives of the welfare state

It is clear from this brief examination of state benefits introduced before the 1980s that there was an element of schizophrenia in the approach to financial support for the long-term sick and disabled. On one hand there was a recognition of a group of people who did not fit into the contribution-based benefits system which had been developed following Beveridge. For them a separate set of benefits was constructed with no need for contributions. In addition, these benefits were payable irrespective of the income or capital of the applicants. Disability was recognised as a costly calamity for which the community should shoulder significant financial responsibility. On the other hand, another group of people in a related position of long-term sickness were unable to satisfy the contributions' conditions and were made subject to stigmatised means-tested benefits. The system of benefits provided for them, however, was constructed specifically to maintain the insurance or contribution principle. For one group of citizens the principle is crucial; for another, not dissimilar group it could simply be abandoned.

This suggests a system whose rationale was never crystal clear and which external events have rendered even more cloudy and confused. On the other hand, recurring themes have emerged from the above brief examination of key legislative and benefit reforms. The first is a deepening resolve on the part of the state to intercede on behalf of its citizens with disabilities, urged by their exceptionally high levels of poverty and social exclusion, as documented by successive

[40] Topliss: 108.

pieces of research. The other theme which we have noted is the wider economic considerations which have constantly played a major role in shaping both the type and scope of government action to date.

The issues of poverty and state spending are of equal concern to both government and citizens today. However, the lack of historical clear-cut objectives behind the evolving welfare system in Britain may be particularly critical at the end of the millennium when the concept of universal welfare is under increased pressure from those keen to retrench and restrict welfare provision. The following section of this chapter considers recent developments in law and social policy more generally in areas where the retrenchment exercise of the 1980s has succeeded. The second half of the chapter considers whether, and to what extent, retrenchment has occurred specifically in the area of disability, and gives possible explanations.

WELFARE RETRENCHMENT?

Introduction

In global terms spending on social security has risen from £15 billion to £90 billion between 1978 and 1996 (Social Trends). The view had been expressed that once the state was involved in an area it could not be easily rolled back (Gilbert, 1970). This argument has been extended to welfare (Piven and Cloward, 1972). On the other hand, some areas, it is argued, are more susceptible to radical change than others (Pierson, 1994; Banting, 1979).

Opinions on whether retrenchment as an exercise has "worked" in Britain vary. At one end, Pierson (1994) suggests that retrenchment efforts in both Britain and America have been spectacularly unsuccessful. The best that Mrs Thatcher could achieve, he suggests, was the initiation of reforms which were "superficially striking but largely devoid of any content".[41] Pierson does recognise that the long-term implications of policy change must be considered "because retrenchment advocates often pursue strategies that hide the magnitude of cuts by minimising the short-term negative consequences".[42] Even applying a long-term lens to the UK, however, he notes that "spending levels have not diminished" and that "privatisation initiatives have been limited, and programme structures have shown more signs of continuity than of change".[43] In contrast to this view, we will briefly consider some areas of social policy in the UK which have clearly encountered a measure of retrenchment, and why this may have occurred.

[41] Ibid., chs 5 and 6.
[42] Ibid., 143.
[43] Ibid., 146.

Areas of retrenchment

Sections of society which have been targeted for retrenchment are those which have attracted the label "undeserving of state aid". A variety of different approaches has taken over the years by those whose goal is to lessen the role of welfare. These include overt ideological appeals to the undesirable effects of welfare provision, centring on the deleterious moral impact of reliance on benefits both on the working population and on those in retirement. There has been concern about parenting[44] and the decline of the two-parent family.[45] Some states in the United States, such as New Jersey and Michigan, have introduced benefit capping as their solution to this perceived welfare dependence.

There have also been "technical" critiques of the levels of welfare provision in terms of the burden of welfare in the future based on demographic projections. These essentially suggested that the burden of welfare for an ageing population could not be sustained by a shrinking labour force. For a number of years welfare cutters have been able to rely on such assessments as evidence of the inevitability of restrictions in welfare provision.

There are also a number of areas in which discreet forms of retrenchment have been essayed. Regulation of market exploitation has been replaced by means-tested benefits in the rental housing market, for instance. In some cases a benefit has been removed or replaced; in others either the level of benefit or the way in which it is calculated has changed.[46] Other attacks have been less subtle. Pierson notes, for example, that for Child Benefit and Unemployment Benefit "retrenchment took the form of 'death by a thousand cuts' ".[47]

DISABILITY AND RETRENCHMENT

Introduction

Against this background of general benefit contraction and the crumbling of the central philosophy of the Beveridge welfare state, the treatment by the benefits system of disabled people appears at first glance to be in marked contrast. A whole series of social policy changes in the 1980s, reflecting ideological developments, resulted in positive outcomes for disabled people.

[44] Ruth Lister, *As Man and Wife?* Poverty Research Series 2, Child Poverty Action Group, 1973, describes how social security payments to unmarried mothers were effectively determined by subjective moral evaluation of their sexual behaviour. In particular social security officers decided whether a mother was being supported by a man, which was very often inferred simply from a suspected or reported sexual relationship.

[45] Murray, 1988.

[46] E.g. the impact of legislation in 1988 limiting the overall eligibility for the following : Single Payments from the Social Fund, Job Seeker's Allowance, Incapacity Benefit, Pensions, and Child Benefit.

[47] Pierson, 101.

Social security

The main proposals which followed the OPCS disability surveys in 1988 and 1989,[48] coupled with the 1988 report from the Social Security Advisory Committee[49] resulted in a positive package, consisting of:

- an extension of Severe Disablement Allowance to benefit those disabled at birth or at an early age;
- the Disability Living Allowance extending Mobility and Attendance Allowances;[50]
- a new Disablement Employment Credit, similar to Family Credit, paying a supplement to disabled people earning low wages; and
- the abolition of the earnings-related component of Invalidity Benefit.

Similarly, the amended Attendance Allowance in the 1990s, albeit renamed and made more complex, does extend coverage to those with more limited disabilities. It remains tax-free, non-contributory and non-means-tested.

In 1988 there were actually slight increases in benefits, including two reforms which pointed to a will to strengthen the incentive for disabled people to work. Provision was made for benefits to be retained while people attended employment rehabilitation courses (in place of the rehabilitation allowance) and the therapeutic earnings limit was dramatically increased. The intention to make it easier for those in receipt of Invalidity Benefit and Severe Disablement Allowance to undertake some work appeared to signify an attempt to alleviate some of the conflict between benefit and rehabilitation policies.

A slight shift could also be detected in respect of the Severe Disablement Allowance and the Disability Allowances. These amalgamated and extended existing benefits, based on an assessment of work incapacity, but placing greater emphasis on the principle of loss of function.[51] Again positively, the rules which link periods of interruption of employment were changed to make it easier for people to requalify for Invalidity Benefit or Severe Disablement Allowance if they took up work for a while but then suffered a relapse.[52]

Public discourse on disability

Such gains in policy and legislation could not have occurred had developments not taken place in the discourses employed in the social and political arena on

[48] OPCS Surveys of Disability in GB (HMSO) 1988 and 1989.

[49] Social Security Advisory Committee, Benefit for Disabled People: *A Strategy for Change* (HMSO, London 1988), para. 2.4.

[50] There are new lower rates for those slightly less severely disabled. Mobility Allowance was also extended to people who were deaf and blind.

[51] The 1990 White Paper "*What is Disability*" nevertheless retains the loss of faculty principle as one route to eligibility for Severe Disablement Allowance, now the Disability Living Allowance for most new claimants after Nov. 1990.

[52] Bolderson: 171.

disability. British government pronouncements gradually adopted a broader concept not only of disability, but of disablement, referring to the overall effect of disabilities and focusing on the power to enjoy a normal life, drawing on the World Health Organisation Classification.[53] These developments have in turn been inspired by influential writings and action from the disabled movement itself. Most importantly, perhaps, has been the widespread acceptance of a "social" or even "political" model of disability as opposed to the old "medical" model premised on stereotypically negative imagery. As Barton explains:

> *"Terms like 'cripple' or 'spastic' reinforce an individualised definition in which the functional limitations predominate. Thus, disability is viewed in terms of an individual's personal inability to function. . . . This type of perspective legitimated an individualised, homogenised and static view of disability. It assumes an idealised notion of 'normality' against which disabled people are being constantly compared. 'Able-bodiedness' is seen as the acceptable criterion of 'normality'."*[54]

By contrast, a "social" or "political" model suggests (for most people) a completely different way of viewing people with physical or mental "handicaps", which reminds us that people with disabilities also have talents and capabilities.

Consequently, a number of pioneering developments reflecting this growing shift in perceptions around the issue of disability have raised the potential of disabled people to participate in society. These include the raised profile of independent living,[55] the operation of the Independent Living Fund,[56] major changes in health, social services and the benefits system, specifically the closure of long-stay institutions, the implementation of new community care legislation, and the transfer of social security money to local authorities.

[53] WHO, International Classification of Impairments, Disabilities and Handicaps (Geneva 1980).

[54] Barton: 237.

[55] The meaning of Independent Living, examined by Jenny Morris (1993a), refers to people's ability to achieve their own goals and control their own lives with whatever assistance is needed to do so. It thus entails a rejection of the traditional "medical", "personal tragedy", "come to terms with", way of thinking. Similarly, the focus is on the limitation of opportunities owing to social, physical and attitudinal barriers, i.e. a "social model" of disability is used, firmly in the context of human and civil rights. Additionally, the idea of integrated living in the community is highlighted, referring to much more than just personal assistance. Seven basic needs have been identified as essential to achieving independent living: appropriate housing, personal assistance, transport, access to the environment, advocacy and training, information and counselling and equipment or technical assistance. It is hoped that these will open the door to additional mainstream opportunities such as non-segregated employment.

[56] The Independent Living Fund was a charity financed by a government fund, to make payments to severely disabled people for the cost of domestic help or personal care, in an attempt to quell complaints that the most severely disabled people were the heaviest losers under the new scheme: Ann Kestenbaum: 1.

RESILIENCE TO RETRENCHMENT

Introduction

In order to try to unravel some of the reasons why the retrenchment exercise of the 1980s looks, on this evidence, to have by-passed the community of people with disabilities, we turn next to areas which have proved most susceptible to retrenchment and consider why this has been so.

Public support

Retrenchment tends to occur where supporting interest groups are weak or where the government has found ways to prevent the mobilisation of supporters.[57] Conversely, where dense networks of personnel are employed, it is very difficult to dismantle jobs that have been safely established over time.[58] Both of these reasons would partly explain why any effort to retrench existing "rights" for the disabled would falter. Perhaps most important of all, however, is the element of public support surrounding an issue:

> "Few groups are more likely to be considered more deserving of public support than the sick and the disabled, and thus it might be expected that efforts to achieve retrenchment in this area would be difficult."[59]

So as long as people with disabilities continue to be viewed as "deserving" of public (and consequently state financial) support, the future from this assessment looks bright. That a sudden swing of popular feeling *against* people with disabilities will ever arise seems unlikely. From this standpoint, retrenchment in the area of "disability" looks like, in Lukes' words (1972), an "area of non-debate".

"The deserving poor"

A related explanation for this paradox of expansion during a climate of retrenchment appears to be rooted in the persisting idea that people with disabilities are part of the "deserving poor". Like Pierson's "public support" thesis, this explanation centres on the traditional division between the deserving and the non-deserving. The same kind of split can also be seen in the case of benefits

[57] Ibid.: 6.

[58] See Cohen 1996: ch. 36, for a not dissimilar thesis on why methods of social control spread and become entrenched partly due to the professional and expert structures of employment which rely on "the system" for their livelihood.

[59] Pierson: 139.

for children. Child Benefit has been stoutly defended as a concept over the years by politicians of all shades as performing an important ideological function of demonstrating the centrality of the family in society. However, it can be separated into discrete segments: child benefit *good*; single parent benefit *not good*. This view proved extremely popular in the late eighties and nineties fuelled by the media and polemics against "the underclass", blaming single mothers for the reported crisis of undisciplined youth and juvenile delinquency.[60] By the same token, people with disabilities are "deserving" and therefore entitled to society's support. The same cannot be said about those who are merely sick: they may be malingerers.

In spite of these recent gains in both law and welfare which point to an absence of retrenchment (even to further entrenchment of rights and benefits) thanks to ideological hegemony and long-term economic expediency, a growing body of evidence appears to suggest that over the last decade people with disabilities are feeling "worse off". Quality of life for many has decreased, according to available social research. In fact, despite gains on some fronts, on others there have been signs of regression, if not retrenchment. The following section re-examines the "lack of retrenchment" conclusion, and asks: if social research contradicts this finding, could it be that retrenchment *has* occurred, perhaps subtly, in other areas related to disability? First, we discuss some of the theory which has prompted us to re-assess the retrenchment question, then review in detail findings across a range of empirical research on people with disabilities to re-examine this issue.

"SUBTLE" RETRENCHMENT?

Introduction

Retrenchment is easy to identify when it takes the form of a deliberate strategy or overt policy change. However, negative results similar to those of "deliberate" retrenchment could theoretically also occur as a consequence of simple political inactivity. Similarly, developments in other fields, say on the economic or cultural level, could also result in unplanned yet nevertheless negative consequences. According to Bachrach and Baratz (1970) the results of "*non*-decision-making" can be as invidious as planned decisions.[61]

One reason for the existence of non-decision-making is that political systems and sub-systems almost inevitably contain a "mobilisation of bias" or hegemonic view: a set of predominant values, beliefs, rituals and institutional procedures, or "rules of the game", which operate systematically and consistently to the benefit of some persons and groups at the expense of others.[62] This,

[60] See Murray (1988).
[61] Bachrach and Baratz: 44–51.
[62] Ibid.: 44.

arguably, sums up the difficulties faced by people with disabilities in society: politically, socially and economically the status quo does not favour them. Whether this is intentional or not is another question. The primary method of sustaining mobilisation of bias or hegemony is less through planned policies, which could attract attention and resistance, but through non-decision-making.[63]

This "subtle retrenchment" thesis is, we suggest, relevant to recent developments in law and social policy relating to disability. On this view, certain weaker groups in society are kept at a disadvantage simply by keeping things the way they are. Non-decision-making can result in broad acquiescence in the status quo.[64] It could also suggest that whatever entrenchment has occurred so far has not gone far enough. Whatever gains have been made are paltry in comparison with the accelerated position of other groups in society. At its most cynical, a subtle retrenchment thesis warns of the danger of believing that changes are being made and opposition is being heard: it gives "the illusion of a voice".[65] Demands can be distorted or transformed into something more innocuous. Again, all these claims have been made most loudly by those within the more radical wing of the disabled movement who stress the politics of disability.[66]

Looking for the tell-tale signs of obvious retrenchment in policy regarding people with disabilities, then, is too simplistic. An analysis which includes notions of non-decision-making, or even decision-making in other fields, in fact reveals traces of regression or even semi-retrenchment. To return to the question posed at the beginning of the paper—what would explain the paradox of an apparently strong legislative and social policy position erected over the course of the last century in relation to people with disabilities in the UK, on one hand, and social and economic indicators which appear far from progressive, on the other. We next attempt to answer these questions by reviewing key findings across a spectrum of empirical research on the social and economic position of individuals with disabilities in the UK, in order to re-assess the matter of retrenchment.

[63] Meaning "a decision that results in suppression or thwarting of a latent or manifest challenge to the values or interests of the decision-maker—a means by which demands for change in the existing allocation of benefits and privileges in the community can be suffocated before they are even voiced; or kept covert; or killed before they gain access to the relevant decision-making arena; or maimed or destroyed in the decision-implementing stage of the policy process" (ibid.: 44).

[64] Ibid.: 49.

[65] Coleman: 1957: 17.

[66] Campbell & Oliver (1996).

"SEMI-ENTRENCHMENT" OR LEGISLATIVE ENTRENCHMENT WITH FINANCIAL RETRENCHMENT?

Introduction

The conclusion which appears to be consistent throughout contemporary social research literature on people with disabilitics in the UK is that this community is in fact experiencing an overall decline in their quality of life. Economically, people with disabilities say they were feeling "worse off" in the last decade than previously. In particular, the quantity and quality of services available to them seems to have decreased.

Some current disability issues have been the site of conflict, on the ground of cost. This position we term "semi-entrenchment". Here we have a paradox where the political right has been keen to extend social welfare benefits to disabled people but unwilling to extend civil rights on the ground of the impact on business and profits. The debates around rejection of the Civil Rights (Disabled Persons) Bill and the introduction of the Disability Discrimination Act 1995 demonstrate these arguments (Hansard, 1995).

The potential impact of recent legislative reforms upon people with disabilities appears,on one hand, to be hindered by a current dearth of funding, but on the other, offset by policy change in other spheres. We next review key findings across a spectrum of current empirical research which stress that the social and economic position of people with disabilities in the UK has worsened over the last decade. The most important changes as far as people with disabilities are concerned have occurred in areas which most directly affect daily living, for instance in the number and quality of services available, work and training opportunities, rates of pay, standard of housing and changes related to social security benefits. The overall picture which emerges is that, either for reasons of cost-cutting or as the adverse effects of reform elsewhere, a situation of retrenchment related to disability does appear to have occurred—certainly in terms of funding.

Local authority services

Arguably, the biggest impact upon people with disabilities over the last decade has stemmed from the financial restraints which most local authorities faced in the 1990s. As local authorities are the biggest service provider for the vast majority of disabled people, budget cuts have resulted in leaner service provision from the late 1980s onwards. This situation is predicted to worsen in the 1990s unless Government funding is increased.

Local authorities have never had so much responsibility to provide care; unfortunately, they also face financial and organisational crisis. The new UK community care legislation imposes the very comprehensive and integrative model urged by the Piercy Report way back in 1956. Yet because of local government restructuring some social services departments are about to fragment. Furthermore, there has been an overall shift from state provision to the purchase of welfare services from the private sector, although not in a uniform way. In fact, variable and confusing local authority policy and practice and general lack of support for people unable to pay for services were the findings of the National Consumer Council in 1995.[67]

People with disabilities in Britain are now, it seems, increasingly having to pay for what were previously free local authority services.[68] Two reports in 1995 confirm that local authorities have begun to charge for their services: the Local Government Anti-Poverty Unit in their report *Charges for Social Care*[69] and the National Consumer Council's *Charging Consumers for Social Services*.[70]

The extra costs of disability

These added expenses stemming from cuts in local authority services appear to have exacerbated the financial position of people with disabilities, already compounded by disability-related expenditure. Average levels of disability-related costs for severely disabled people have been estimated at £20 per week,[71] £50 per week[72] and £100 per week.[73] The 1990 *Family Expenditure Survey* (FES) stressed, however, that it is not the extra burden on income which is the prime cause of poverty for people with disabilities, but their lower income caused by lack of employment opportunities.[74] Above all, the FES study stressed:

> "the influence of the extra costs of disability on the standard of living on disabled people is of much less importance than the income disparities between disabled and other households."[75]

[67] National Consumer Council (1995) *Charging Consumers for Social Services: Local Authority and Practice.*

[68] Kestenbaum: 42.

[69] Local Government Anti-Poverty Unit (1995) *Summary of Charges for Social Care 1993–95.*

[70] National Consumer Council (1995) *Charging Consumers for Social Services: Local Authority and Practice.*

[71] Martin and White: 1988.

[72] Berthoud *et al.*: 1993.

[73] Thompson *et al.*: 1990.

[74] *Disability, Household Income and Expenditure: Follow Up Survey of Disabled Adults in the Family Expenditure Survey*, DSS, Research Support No. 2, HMSO, 1990, ix and 31 (FES).

[75] Ibid., 31.

Extra strain on the poorest families

Spending

The effect of cuts in services appear to impact hardest upon the poorest. The FES found "clear evidence that extra costs exist" and that spending on disability is constrained by income—notably reduced spending on luxury items and transport. Conversely, where and when there is more money, more is likely to be spent on basic items such as food, fuel and help in the home.[76] The FES made the point that the overall picture, where households containing disabled people appear to spend more of their money on necessities and less on luxuries, suggests that they are more constrained than other households, and do indeed face extra costs as a result of their disability.[77]

Benefit reform

Current research confirms the finding that the poorest sections of the disabled community also appear to be bearing the brunt of some benefit reforms. The extent to which disabled people on low incomes rely on Disability Living Allowance (DLA) to "balance the books" was highlighted in 1996.[78] A large proportion of the benefit was found to be spent in meeting basic living expenses, rather than contributing towards the extra costs specific to disability. Moreover, significant numbers of people who were severely disabled and apparently eligible for the benefit were not receiving DLA. Additionally, despite the shift from reliance on medical examination to a self-assessed claiming procedure, they found that advocacy and advice remain crucial to a successful claim for this benefit. Most households in the study without disability benefits did not have sufficient resources to make ends meet. In the 1996 findings those with disability-related benefits were applying part of the "extra income" to meet their basic costs, such as food and clothing.

Key objectives in the 1992 reform of disability benefits were improvements and better targeting of funds to those most in need. Households in receipt of DLA appear to have had their overall income significantly enhanced by these additions. However, a significant proportion of the survey group was still not in receipt of DLA by mid-1994. In their sample, Disability Working Allowance was exceedingly rare. They concluded that although DWA appeared to have failed to meet its objectives, DLA has had some impact in enhancing the incomes of disabled people in low income households. However, the benefit is far from reaching the whole of its eligible population and DLA receipt largely allows households to make ends meet rather than compensating for the extra costs specific to disability. This research confirms earlier findings that the entire

[76] Ibid.
[77] Ibid.
[78] Smith *et al.*: 1996.

Disability Living Allowance is often used to repay debts and meet general household bills.[79]

Low-paid work and the benefit trap

Some legislative reforms appear to have particularly negative effects on the lower-paid disabled, creating inequities between those who reach work via the benefit system and those who simply work for low wages. How the system could trap disabled people who did small amounts of paid work, but whose benefits would be jeopardised if they took advantage of more work, was first documented by Zarb and Nadesh.[80] The current Disability Working Allowance was designed to address this problem and to help disabled people get jobs, but it appears to have worked for a very limited number of people.[81] Very few disabled people appear to have started work as a result of DWA. There are reasons for this: low levels of awareness of the benefit; the stringent means test; not receiving a qualifying benefit but otherwise eligible; inability to sustain the minimum sixteen hours of work per week.

Incapacity Benefit was introduced in April 1995, and requires disabled people to show that they are medically incapable of work, but it crucially fails to recognise that many impairments prevent full-time work but allow part-time work. Disabled people have campaigned for many years for a comprehensive disability income scheme, including a partial incapacity benefit, but without success.

Another recent double-edged initiative is the Employment Credit which commenced in April 1992.[82] It has been praised for avoiding some problems, but at the cost of making the benefit subject to means-testing and also excluding some of the poorest people who are disabled and working. For instance, the Credit[83] originally noted the gap in benefits for disabled people resulting in an inadequate basic income for disabled people who work but are not fully able to support themselves. In taking Family Credit as their model for drafting, the Social Security Advisory Committee, according to Helen Bolderson, appear to have intended not only help in the transition into work, but to head off poverty caused by low wages.[84] Yet the SSAC in its 1988 report rejected extending Family Credit to disabled people, proposing instead for disabled people earning

[79] Grant: 1995.

[80] Zarb and Nadash: 1994.

[81] Rowlingson and Berthoud: 1994; Kestenbaum (1996: 42) noted that although the government estimated that some 50,000 would eventually be claiming at any one time, only 5,000 currently qualified and 80% of these were already in work. The figures for July 1995 showed that 6,544 were in receipt of DWA, of which 63% qualified because they were in receipt of DLA (Parliament Update, Feb. 1996).

[82] Initially, individuals needed to satisfy a doctor that they were only partially capable of work. This was later replaced by a form of self-assessment. Eligibility for the Credit extends to single disabled people and disabled partners in couples with no dependent children.

[83] First recommended by the SSAC in Social Security Advisory Committee, *Benefit for Disabled People: A Strategy for Change* (HMSO, London 1988), para. 2.4.

[84] Bolderson: 173.

low wages a means-tested "top-up".[85] Consequently, the Credit is used for those in work only, and entitles disabled people earning low wages to have them topped up by a means-tested benefit. Not all low-wage earning disabled people, however, will be included and the benefit has been criticised for not providing no effective incentive to those who are presently working, not drawing any benefit and poor. This anomaly is explained, however, if the legislation is considered in light of the views held by the government at that time, namely that some people malinger because they are better off on benefit.[86]

In fact, many disabled people will indeed be better off on benefit than in work, according to Bolderson.[87] Pressure groups have also argued that financial penalties in the present "all or nothing" system creates barriers to re-employment. Moreover, given that the number of people receiving benefit has steadily risen, particularly since the mid-'80s, this has only added fuel once more to the malingerer thesis.[88]

It could therefore be argued that the crucial weakness of several major recent reforms is simply the failure to address the issue of poverty in the disabled community in general and amongst disabled wage earners in particular. The Credit, for instance, has been criticised as providing no more than an incentive payment for those people with disabilities who are currently not working but are thought to be partially able to do so.[89]

LONG-TERM IMPLICATIONS OF WELFARE REFORM

Introduction

Concern has also been raised over the long-term implications of a top-up based approach in terms of the adverse consequences on employment opportunities for people with disabilities. Financially, a top-up is of course welcome, but it may also be "coercive in imprisoning people in a part of the labour market which commands low wages and indeed contributes to the maintenance of a low-wage sector".[90] Alternative approaches ensuring adequate wages in exchange for work would have been to accelerate funding for the Sheltered Placement Scheme,[91] or to introduce a minimum wage. Furthermore, the

[85] See also Second Report of the Social Security Advisory Comm., 1982/83, HMSO, London 1983 ch. 5.

[86] Bolderson: 172.

[87] Ibid.: 173.

[88] Ibid.

[89] Ibid.: 174. "At its best, DEC may reduce possible disincentives to, or financial penalties connected with, entering work. But, it remains to be seen whether it will help those who wish to work or whether it will be a means of putting pressure on people to work regardless of whether this is truly helpful to them".

[90] Ibid.: 175.

[91] This was pioneered for the long-term mentally ill in Bristol in the 1960s and later developed by the Manpower Services Commission. Under the scheme a person registered as severely disabled can

recognition of individuals' abilities and their limitations in respect of work must be addressed. In particular, the needs to work more flexible hours, to be allowed more time to rest and to have a job close to home have all been found to constitute typical obstacles restricting access to employment for people with disabilities.[92]

The macro effect of such initiatives which "bridge the passage into low wage work" (the Credit being a prime example) has been assessed by Bolderson. In practice such benefits:

> "supplement low wages . . . further marginalise disabled workers in the labour market and allow them to be used as 'instruments of anti-inflationary economic policies'."[93]

The micro effect of such legislation upon individuals could be to strengthen the benefit trap.[94] Once eligibility for receipt of one benefit is triggered by the *a priori* holding of another,[95] as in qualification for the Credit, the incentive to break free from the benefit cycle is weaker. Consequently, such legislation may result in the penalisation of poor, disabled earners who have never been within the benefit system.[96]

Means-testing

Additional criticisms of recent reforms focus upon the return to means-testing and the possibility of benefit withdrawal, both of which encourage low take-up at the outset. Ideologically, of course, the reversion to means-testing has signalled an abandonment of the state's move away from means-tested policies since the late 1970s.[97] A major survey of disability commissioned by the government in 1984 and completed in 1989[98] recommended the introduction of premiums for disabled people as part of a general restructuring of the means-tested Supplementary Benefit scheme, which became Income Support in 1986.[99] These,

work in open instead of sheltered employment and receive the wage for the job. The employer pays on the basis of output and the difference between the amount and the wage is made up by the sponsoring organisation (local authority, voluntary body or Remploy) and either wholly or partly financed by central government.

92 Erens and Ghate: 127.

93 Bolderson: 176.

94 Ibid.: 174.

95 IVB, the Disability Allowance, Severe Disablement Allowance, Income Support or Housing Benefit Disability Premium.

96 Bolderson: 173 notes of the Employment Credit: "Some of the poorest disabled wage-earners may therefore not be included; for example, older workers with debilitating conditions which prevent them from continuing their work at full capacity, yet who do not qualify for, or have not just relinquished, disability related benefits.".

97 Ibid.: 174.

98 OPCS, Social Survey Division, OPCS Surveys of Disability in GB, Report 1–6. HMSO, London 1988 and 1989.

99 Social Severity Act 1986, ch. 50 and s. 22(3).

and community care grants under the Social Fund, replaced the special needs payments under the Supplementary Benefit scheme and resulted, according to Bolderson, in both gainers and losers.[100]

Employment and income

From the 'seventies, the link between poverty and employment has been stressed, with attention focusing particularly upon low income (Topliss, 1979). A Government White Paper in 1979, *Better Services for the Disabled*, suggested that as earning power is reduced by disability the solution lay with better employment opportunities. Sally Sainsbury had earlier found that disabled people at work earned on average only three-quarters of the current average earnings for the population as a whole, although the actual earning figures were likely to be even lower.[101] People with disabilities were over-represented in semi-skilled and unskilled manual categories.[102] The vast majority of disabled people who retrained on a government vocational training course retrained for manual work, and very few for clerical, administrative or professional work. The training courses offered hardly maximised the potential of disabled people: some were not trained, but offered manual work only.[103]

Later government figures show that disabled people are consistently three times more likely to be out of work, and unemployed for longer periods, than non-disabled people.[104] A man in the highest disability category[105] has 79 per cent less chance of having a job, and then a 29 per cent reduction in potential earnings.[106] Compared with non-disabled men of similar age and educational background, the loss of earnings can be as high as 85 per cent.[107] On average, disabled men in full-time work can expect to earn almost a quarter less per week than non-disabled men working the same hours. People caring for disabled partners may also have to give up work so couples can lose earnings twice over.[108]

When people with disabilities do find jobs, they are more likely to be poorly paid and low skilled. Only 12 per cent of the disabled workforce hold a professional or managerial position, compared with 21 per cent of non-disabled workers.[109] The overwhelming majority of disabled workers in government-sponsored workshops are also in low-paid, low-status occupations, while

[100] Bolderson: 171.

[101] Sainsbury, 1970. Since her research was based on those on local authority registers where the more severely handicapped are more likely to be registered.

[102] Buckle, 1971.

[103] *Registered as Disabled*, Occasional Papers on Social Administration, No. 35, 1970.

[104] Kestenbaum: 39.

[105] defined by the OCPS.

[106] Kestenbaum: 40.

[107] Ibid.

[108] Berthoud *et al.*, 1993.

[109] Kestenbaum: 39.

assessment, rehabilitation and training have been found rarely to lead to mainstream employment.[110]

In the light of these figures, the large increase in the numbers of Invalidity Benefit claims in the last decade[111] could be taken not so much as an indication of a common preference to rely on benefit, but rather of how difficult it remains for disabled people to find jobs.[112] The idea behind the Conservative Government's 1989 White Paper *The Way Ahead*, which proposed the tapered withdrawal of benefit as income rises, was sadly out of touch.[113]

The disincentive thesis

The 1993 Survey of Invalidity Benefit[114] compared levels of benefit received while on Invalidity Benefit (IVB) with respondents' earnings in their last job. Their findings did not square with the view that benefit is a disincentive to work. For half of the recipients, their benefits replaced only half of their previous earnings; for a quarter of disabled people, benefits replaced more than half of their earnings; for only 13 per cent did their benefits replace more than 80 per cent of their last earnings.[115] The report specifically stated that there was no evidence that levels of benefits had much influence on recipients' attitudes towards returning to work. "If anything the attached were more likely than the others to have high benefit/earnings ratios".[116]

Training

Like the government-run employment rehabilitation centres which preceded it, the modern system of agency contracts has been criticised for the frequent failure of short courses to provide intensive training.[117] Furthermore, as responsibility for state-supported training has shifted from government to employers such as the Employment Credit are more likely to be concentrated on those already employed and most easily employable.[118] Some schemes have been set

[110] Barnes, 1991b.

[111] Erens and Ghate, *Invalidity Benefit—Longitudinal Survey of New Recipients*, DSS Research Report No. 20, 1993, 7.

[112] Berthoud *et al.*, 1993.

[113] *Caring for People: Community Care in the Next Decade and Beyond*, HMSO, 1989.

[114] Erens and Ghate, 1993.

[115] Erens and Ghate: 125: women and younger recipients were likely to have a higher benefit/earnings ratio (80%) due to a combination of factors—more of them have dependent children and received lower levels of net weekly pay in their previous job (partly due to the large numbers of women who worked part-time before starting on IVB).

[116] Erens and Ghate: 127: although within the attached group, those who were successful in returning to work were marginally more likely than those not working to have lower ratios.

[117] Lakey and Simpkins, 1995.

[118] Bruce, 1991.

up to help people with learning difficulties to get ordinary jobs rather than be limited to sheltered schemes, by supporting them in the workplace with trainers.[119] However:

> "Overall, it has been predicted that employment and training for disabled people will decline further unless there is a specific policy that will protect and promote them."[120]

Housing

A startling figure attesting to an unprecedented rise in the number of homeless people with disabilities also gives the lie to the idea of general progress. Reports of an estimated rise of 92 per cent in homelessness among people with physical impairments between 1980 and 1988, compared with 57 per cent among all types of households, have been documented by Morris.[121] The crisis in public-sector housing has, it appears, hit the disabled community considerably hard.[122]

High rents are a particular problem. Local authorities used to subsidise a rent above the "reasonable market rent" if the claimant was in a protected community group. Although Griffiths (1995) acknowledged that the two-stage rent officer/benefit assessment process was widely regarded as unsatisfactory, from January 1996 this rights-based protection was abolished. Its replacement by a small, cash-limited, discretionary budget is predicted to reduce the housing security of vulnerable disabled individuals still further.[123]

A recent study of 1,500 disabled people revealed that only 29 per cent thought they had all the adaptations they required; tenants in private rented accommodation fared worst.[124] The standard of service seems to depend on where people live.[125]

The overlap in funding between housing and social services which involves statutory and discretionary Disabled Facility Grants (DFGs) as well as Home Improvement Grants, appears to cause uncertainties and delays. RADAR'S[126] study of how section 2 of the Chronically Sick and Disabled Persons Act 1970

[119] E.g. the Training in Systematic Instruction (TSI) supported by Joseph Rowntree: National Development Team, 1992.

[120] Kestenbaum: 40.

[121] Morris, 1990; cf. Laurie, 1991: 4.

[122] Simon Brisendon (founder of Southampton Centre for Independent Living) wrote *Disability, Handicap and Society:* "In 1986, the reality has worsened, compounded by the staggering increase in homelessness throughout the country. Government housing policy had favoured owner-occupation, but not everybody can afford to buy. And public sector housing provision has decreased sharply because of the acute housing shortage. The recession, rising unemployment, escalating rents and interest rates have also taken their toll. The results? Record number of homes being repossessed, thousands sleeping rough, thousands in temporary accommodation. The lack of decent affordable housing had caused a housing crisis and there is increasing evidence that the crisis has hit disabled people particularly hard." Vol. 1, no. 2, 173–8.

[123] Kestenbaum: 8–9.

[124] Lamb and Layzell, 1994.

[125] Heywood, 1994; Kestenbaum: 13.

[126] The Royal Association for Disability and Rehabilitation.

was being implemented by local authorities found that 57 per cent of complaints were from people in the process of applying for a DFG. Problems seem to stem from the process, the number of different agencies involved, the squeeze on available resources and the application of the means test.[127]

Personal assistance

Other signs of poverty within the non-able bodied community include the finding that only 10 per cent of those aged over 79 are in a position to purchase their own care out of disposable income (the choice preferred over having to rely on statutory services).[128] Despite the government's aims in the 1989 White Paper *Caring for People,*[129] Morris found that community care services can create barriers to independent living by their limitations and inflexibility.[130] Personal assistants are also reportedly having to undertake additional tasks, arguably outside their remit, because of unsuitable housing or lack of adaptations.[131]

Inadequate information

A basic problem among people of all types of disability[132] and service providers[133] is lack of awareness of benefits, services available and rights and duties under legislation. A specific problem, known as "gate-keeping", suggests that professional bodies control the information and disabled people only find out about services once they have been assessed as suitable for them.[134] One solution to this problem is to encourage self-organised groups of disabled people.[135] Problems of access to, and the complexity of, information are of course compounded for the poor[136] and for ethnic minorities who often face a language barrier.[137] There is strong evidence of particularly acute problems for disabled individuals from ethnic minorities who appear to suffer disproportionately not only from financial hardship, but also from racial harassment.[138]

127 Kestenbaum: 13.

128 Doyle, 1993; Lakey, 1994; Kestenbaum, 1992; Kestenbaum 1996: 17: over half aged 75 are not home owners.

129 HMSO, 1989.

130 Morris, 1993a and b.

131 Dawson, 1995.

132 Straughair, 1992; Kestenbaum: 12.

133 Barnes, 1995.

134 Greater Manchester Coalition of Disabled People, in Kestenbaum: 12.

135 King, 1994.

136 "Complexity is always regressive because the poorest people find it harder to deal with": David Donnison, Chair of the Supplementary Benefits Commission: in J. Simkins, and V. Tickner, 1978: 185.

137 Baylis *et al.*, 1994; Baxter *et al.*, 1990.

138 See e.g. Baylis *et al.*, 1994.

Assessing the evidence

The overwhelming weight of recent social research which provides insights into the actual standard of living of disabled people in the UK contradicts any positive message apparently suggested by an absence of legal retrenchment. A common conclusion is that all recent improvements in services for disabled people take place against a backdrop of resource cutbacks,[139] particularly those of local authorities. The financial resources relied upon by many people with disabilities (such as the Attendance Allowance and the Severe Disability Premium) are reported to be inadequate to cover personal assistance costs, which can amount to several hundred pounds per week.[140] Given the spectrum of critical conclusions upon the effects of recent reforms, it appears to be erroneous to assume that substantive social and economic improvement will necessarily follow from improved legislation and/or the absence of evidence of retrenchment. In spite of anti-discrimination legislation, the experience of women and ethnic minorities may provide a parallel with people with disabilities.

Just as economic expediency appears throughout to have played a prime role in the shaping of law and social policy,[141] the real motive behind the previous Conservative government's drive to reform disability legislation is questionable. For the sceptical observer of recent legislation affecting people with disabilities, there is hardly a debate:

> "the intention appears to be to deal in the main with those who are already on a benefit, by replacing their benefit with earnings and the DEC top-up, thus ensuring a net expenditure saving."[142]

Indeed, if plain evidence of a deliberate and premeditated government strategy to retrench financially in the 'nineties is required to confirm the suspicion of a cost-cutting exercise, an example can be found in a parliamentary answer given in the Commons in 1990, to the effect that in the Credit's first year of operation there might be a net saving in expenditure of £10 million".[143]

It appears to us that the cumulative direct and indirect consequences of various government reforms—many of which are not specifically related to disability legislation or social policy nor even directed at the disabled population—

[139] Silburn and Winfield, 1993.

[140] Kestenbaum: 20.

[141] See Evans, 1978, for reasons (primarily economic and imperialistic) why the state first formed a collectivist response to social problems around the turn of the century in Britain. Also, Topliss, 1979: 5–10 refers to the "principle of economic rationality" as a "central theme in the development of all social policies of the nineteenth century".

[142] Bolderson: 174 notes that it was estimated by the government that 50,000 people will receive the Credit, of whom 15,000 will currently be in work and 35,000 will be drawing incapacity-related benefits and not working.

[143] Hansard vol. 165, col. 910, 26 Jan. 1990. See also the BBC TV documentary on the explicit drive by Social Security Minister Peter Lilley to slash the burgeoning social security budget, "*The System*", 19 Sep. 1996.

appear in fact to have had deleterious consequences upon the social and economic position of disabled people. Retrenchment in funding has occurred. Before summing up, one prominent trend in law across various nations should be noted: the adoption of anti-discrimination and a rights-based approach. It is too early to assess accurately how successful this alternative may be in securing effective gains for people with disabilities.

CONCLUSION

The history behind the development of both legislative and welfare reform in Britain targeted on people with disabilities reveals that motivations for state intervention included not only an increasing desire to help one of the poorest sections of society but also wider concerns of economic expediency. Indeed, reasons of economic efficiency have inspired the most recent retrenchment exercise, evident in many areas of social policy, driven by right-wing politics on both sides of the Atlantic from the late 'eighties. However, this cost-cutting exercise does not appear to have impacted on the area of disability to quite the same extent, or rather, not in the same way. No legislative retrenchment has occurred. This appears to be largely explained by the commonly held notion that people with disabilities are "deserving" recipients of state aid, and should not therefore be targeted. Indeed, many of the more recent policy changes appear to be conceptually very progressive, holding out the promise of substantial improvement in the position of many people with disabilities in numerous ways, and some have produced definite gains.

On the other hand, government measures in the late 1980s and 1990s in the UK appear more frequently to have conferred at best mixed blessings on disabled people. In particular, numerous findings raise doubts as to the general ability of much legislation to produce concrete social and economic gains for individuals with disabilities, especially the poorest. A growing bank of empirical research stresses that the quality of life of many people with disabilities appears to have worsened, particularly as a result of the cut-backs in services provided by local authorities. "Financial" or "resource" retrenchment does appear to have occurred, albeit indirectly, primarily through extensive capping by central government of local government spending.

Just as state intervention in this area has historically been motivated and shaped by various considerations, primarily economic, we suggest, we see these tensions continue to shape recent developments. However, the past gradual building up of legislation and social policy in order to aid the disabled population and save state expenditure in the long term now appears almost to have been reversed. Recent developments similarly appear to be dictated by economic imperatives—saving government expenditure—but very much from a short-term perspective. But perhaps the crucial difference between earlier and contemporary developments is not so much the areas targeted for expansion and retrenchment, for these have always been dictated to an extent by ideology which appears to remain constant through time, and perhaps cross-culturally, in relation to the "deserving poor". The change is in the vehicle used to secure these savings. Historically, governments used legislation or policy change to secure cut-backs, and have done so today in areas which can be ideologically supported for retrenchment targeting. But for the same ideological reasons, the state has been reluctant to retrench in the area of disability in this way. We suggest that the UK's outgoing government of 1997 secured the same goals as its historic counterparts—to secure fiscal savings—but by retrenching in other ways, primarily through cutting back central funding to local government. The effects of capping local authority expenditure is the clearest example of this indirect retrenchment, and is paradigmatic of the subtle way in which central government can retrench in a substantive way yet, while appearing to uphold the rhetoric of civil rights and citizenship for its community of citizens with disabilities.

Evidence from other countries, notably Sweden and America, suggests that a mixture of legislative and rights-based reforms, but backed up with the necessary funding and resources, may be the best route to real advances for the disabled community. Ironically, if the state's motive to retrench is economic, long-term financial savings are more likely to occur from backing the positive initiatives proposed by various disabled interest groups.

Our final remarks on socio-legal reform may be as apposite to any country and any disadvantaged population as to Britain and its citizens with disabilities. How to square short-term political and long-term social and economic objectives is a problem which will continue to exercise governments, globally as historically. Entrenchment of rights and benefits and the promotion of opportunities for people with any disadvantage or obstacle to participation in society is not only beneficial to that community, but in the long term saves state spending because individuals become more independent. Ironically then, if the key reasons for retrenching are financial, though couched as ideological justifications, the ever-present economic rationale could provide the strongest incentive for governing bodies to entrench further, provided they can be persuaded to take a long-term view.

On the other hand, ability to withstand deliberate or formal legal retrenchment, though welcome, should not be accepted as an accurate indicator of general or overall progress. More telling indicators of quality of life—or as here, levels of poverty—can be found by looking at levels of employment and income, standards in education and housing and the quality of essential services available. Each of these is a more realistic indicator of how far the law has actually impacted upon the lives of people with disabilities than a simple count of the laws or social security benefits in operation. For unfortunately, if the UK experience of people with disabilities is typical, entrenched rights and benefits cannot be relied upon to counter entrenched poverty. The challenge for legal reform in favour of poor sections of society is likely to revolve around how to prioritise making paper rights real for the citizens concerned, rather than short-term economic considerations in the interests of governing bodies or other groups already in positions of greater power.

REFERENCES

Bachrach, Peter and Baratz, Morton (1970), *Power and Poverty*, New York: Oxford University Press

Banting, Keith (1979), *Poverty, Politics and Policy*, London: Macmillan

Barnes, C. (1991), *Disabled People in Britain and Discrimination: A Case for Anti-Discrimination Legislation*, London: Hurst Calgary and JRF Social Policy Research Findings 39

—— (1993), *Making Our Own Choices: Independent Living, Personal Assistance and Disabled People*, Derby: BCODP

—— (1995), *From National to Local*. Derby: BCODP

Barton, L. (1993), "The Struggle for Citizenship: The Case of Disabled People", in *Disability, Handicap and Society 10*, 1

Baxter, C., Poonia, K., Ward, L. and Nadirshaw, Z. (1990), *Double Discrimination: Issues and Services for People with Learning Difficulties from Ethnic Minority Communities*, London: King's Fund Centre

Baylies, C., Law, I. and Mercer, G. (1994), *Aftercare of Black Ethnic Minority People Discharged from Psychiatric Hospitals*, JRF Social Care Research Findings 58

Berthoud, R., Lakey, J. and McKay, S. (1993), *The Economic Problems of Disabled People*, London: Policy Studies Institute and JRF Social Policy Research Findings 39

Bolderson, Helen (1991), *Social Security, Disability and Rehabilitation*, London: Jessica Kingsley

Bradshaw, Jonathan, Ditch, John, Holmes, Hilary and Whiteford, Peter (1993), *Support for Children: A Comparison of Arrangements in Fifteen Countries*, London: HMSO

Brisendon, Simon (1986), *Disability Handicap and Society*, vol. 1, no. 2, 173–8

Bruce, I. (1991), "Employment of People with Disabilities" in G. Dalley, ed., *Disability and Social Policy*, London: Social Policy Studies Institute

Buckle, J.R. (1971), *Handicapped and Impaired in Great Britain*, Part II, *Work and Housing of Impaired Persons in Great Britain*, Office of Population Censuses and Surveys, HMSO

Campbell, Jane and Oliver, Mike (1996), *Disability Politics*, London: Routledge

Care With Dignity (1973), Economist Intelligence Unit, National Fund for Research into Crippling Diseases, Sussex

Carson, D. (1972), "National Insurance Attendance Allowance: Appeals", in *New Law Journal*, 2 Nov. 1972, 973–4

Central Council for the Disabled (1976), *Report of the Working Party on Mobility Allowance*, London

Clapham, D., Munro, M. and Kay, H. (1994), *Financing User Choice in Housing and Community Care*, JRF Housing Research Summary 6

Cmnd. 917 (1990), *The Way Ahead: Benefits for Disabled People*, London: HMSO

Cooper, J. and Vernon, S. (1996), *Disability and the Law*, London and Bristol, Pennsylvania: Jessica Kingsley

Daunt, Patrick (1991), *Meeting Disability: A European Response*, London: Cassell
Dawson, C. (1995), *Report of the Independent Living Project (Norfolk)*, HAND: Help Advice and Advocacy for Norfolk Disabled People
Department of Social Security (1990), *Disability, Household Income and Expenditure*, London: HMSO
Disabled Persons Accommodation Agency (1995), *DPAA: The Way Forward for Kent*, Rochester: DPAA
Doyle, Y. (1993), "The Uses of the Independent Living Fund and the Views of Recipients in South East London", Report for the South East London Health Authority
Erens, Bob and Ghate, Deborah (1993), *Invalidity Benefit*, London: HMSO
Evans, Eric (1978), *Social Policy 1830–1914*, London: Routledge & Kegan Paul
Grant, L. (1995), *Debt and Disability*, JRF Social Policy Research Findings 78
Griffiths, S. (1995), *The Relationship between Housing Benefit and Community Care*, JRF Housing Research Findings 148
Guthrie, Duncan (1981), *Disability: Legislation and Practice*, London: Macmillan
Harris, Amelia (1971-), *Handicapped and Impaired in GB, Parts I-III*, Office and Population Censuses and Surveys, 1971 and 1972, London: HMSO
Heywood, F. (1994), *Adaptions: Finding Ways to Say Yes*, School of Advanced Urban Studies and JRF Housing Research Findings 123
HMSO (1989), "Caring for People: Community Care in the Next Decade and Beyond"
Kestenbaum, Ann (1996), *Independent Living*, York: Joseph Rowntree Foundation
King, C. (1994), *Development and Training for Self-Organized Groups of Disabled People*, JRF Social Care Research Findings 45
Lakey, J. (1994), *Caring about Independence: Disabled People and the Independent Living Fund*, London: Policy Studies Institute
—— and Simpkins, R. (1995), *Employment Rehabilitation for Disabled People*, London: Policy Studies Institute
Lamb, B. and Layzell, S. (1994), *Disabled in Britain: A World Apart*, London: SCOPE
Laurie, L. (1991), *Building our Lives: Housing, Independent Living and Disabled People*, London: Shelter
Lewis, B. (1992), "A Home for Life". *Search*, 14 Dec. 1992
Lifetime Homes (1994), JRF video and booklet
Lister, Ruth (1973), *As Man and Wife?* Poverty Research Series 2, Child Poverty Action Group
Lukes, Steven (1972), *Power*, London: Macmillan
Lunt, N. and Thornton, P (1993), *Employment Policies for Disabled People: A Review of Legislation and Services in Fifteen Countries*, ED Research Series No. 16, Sheffield Employment Department
Macgregor, Suzanne (1982), *The Politics of Poverty*, London: Longman
Martin, J. and White. A. (1988), *The Financial Circumstances of Disabled People Living in Private Households*, London: HMSO
McConell, Grant (1966), *Private Power and the American Democracy*, 91–118
Morris, J. (1990), *Our Homes, Our Rights: Housing, Independent Living and Disabled People*, London: Shelter
—— (1993a), *Independent Lives? Community Care and Disabled People*, Basingstoke: Macmillan
—— (1993b), *Community Care or Independent Living?* JRF and JRF Housing Research Findings 76

Muncie, John, McLaughlin, Eugene and Langan, Mary (1996), *Criminological Perspectives*, London: Sage in association with Open University

Murray, Charles (1994), *The Underclass, The Crisis Deepens*, London: IEA

National Consumer Council (1995), *Charging Consumers for Social Services: Local Authority and Practice*, London: NCC

Office of Population Censuses and Surveys, Social Survey Division (1988–), *OPCS Surveys of Disability In Great Britain*, Report 1–6, 1988 and 1989, London: HMSO

Ogus, Anthony, Barendt, Eric and Wikely, Nick (1995), *The Law of Social Security*, London: Butterworths

Phillips, V. (1993), *Caring for Severely Disabled People: Care Providers and their Costs*, Nottingham: Independent Living Fund

Pierson, Paul (1994), *Dismantling the Welfare State*, Cambridge, Cambridge University Press

Piven, Frances Fox and Cloward, Richard (1973), *Regulating the Poor*, London: RKP

Rowlingson, K. and Berthoud, R. (1994), *Evaluating the Disability Working Allowance*, London: Policy Studies Institute

Sainsbury, Roy, Hirst, Michael and Lawton, Dot (1995), *Evaluation of Disability Living Allowance and Attendance Allowance*, London: HMSO

Sainsbury, Sally (1970), *Registered as Disabled*, Occasional Papers in Social Administration, No. 35, Bell

Silburn, R. and Winfield, J. (1993), "Evaluation of Services for Younger Physically Disabled People", Report for the North Derbyshire Joint Planning Group

Simpkins, J. and Tikner, V. (1978), *Whose Benefit?* London: Economist Intelligence Unit

Smith, George, Daly, Michael, Noble, Michael and Barlow, Jane (1996), *The Costs of Disability*, Avebury

Social Security Advisory Committee (1988), *Benefit for Disabled People: A Strategy for Change*, London: HMSO

Social Trends, London: HMSO

Straughair, S. (1992), *The Road Towards Independence*, London: Arthritis Care

Thompson, P., Lavery, M. and Curtice, J. (1990), *Short Changed by Disability*, London: Disablement Income Group

Thornton, P. and Lunt, N. (1995), *Employment for Disabled People: Social Obligation or Individual Responsibility?* Social Policy Research Unit, York University

Topliss, Eda (1979), *Provision for the Disabled*, Oxford and London: Basil Blackwell and Martin Robertson

—— and Gould, Bryan (1981), *A Charter for the Disabled*, London: Basil Blackwell and Martin Robertson

Townsend, Peter (1979), *Poverty in the United Kingdom*, Harmondsworth: Penguin

Walker, Alan and Walker, Carol, eds., (1987), *The Growing Divide*, London: CPAG

Zarb, G. and Nadash, P. (1994), *Cashing in on Independence: Comparing the Costs and Benefits of Cash and Services*, London: Policy Studies Institute

Access to Justice for the Poor

6

The Development of the Notion of Poverty and Equal Protection Clauses: A Comparative Analysis of Italy and the United States

ANTONELLA MAMELI

SUMMARY

THIS CHAPTER ANALYSES the development of the concept of poverty in two countries, Italy and the United States of America, and shows that two groups of poor have emerged since the start of the Industrial Revolution: the deserving poor and the undeserving poor. The processes of differentiation were similar, although the social groups identified with this moral classification were the minorities in the United States and the working class in Italy. Reconstructing, from a comparative perspective, the development of the concept of poverty and scrutinising the problems of social differentiation which characterise the different systems, it emerges that the shape taken by each country's constitutional equal protection clause varies accordingly.

THE DESERVING POOR AND THE UNDESERVING POOR

Ways of dealing with the problem of poverty have changed substantially from the Industrial Revolution onwards. Originally, the notion of poverty focused on the deprivation and hardship of individuals and families. Later, with the advent of industrialisation and urbanisation, it shifted to the plight of groups or classes of individuals whose living conditions were below a standard universally accepted as a minimum. An analysis of the development of the concept of poverty in Italy and the United States shows that two groups of poor have emerged. They differ in identity, but are similar in both their social role and their forced acquiescence to their status. They are the deserving poor (working and therefore respectable) and the undeserving poor (that is, paupers requesting public assistance and therefore morally discredited). The processes of differentiation in the two countries were similar, although the social groups identified by this moral classification were different: ethnic and racial minorities in the United States and the working class in Italy.

The United States

In the United States the moral distinction between the deserving poor and the undeserving poor became an ethnic differentiation when masses of new immigrants moved to the biggest cities of that country, creating tension between them and the established community. Before the Civil War, the heavy influx of immigrants, especially in the 1840s and 1850s, and the consequent problems of unemployment and overpopulation resulted in gross poverty. The general tendency was to categorise these immigrants as the "dangerous classes". A few decades later, the growth of industrialism and of the main cities, with overcrowding in their slums, and the growing wave of European immigrants brought in their wake terrible problems. By the late 1880s many American cities were haunted by a permanent pauper class.

The ethnic and racial heterogeneity of the working class contributed to a widespread rejection of the ideological politics associated with labour unions. In the 1920s foreign immigration slowed down because of the restrictive immigration laws of 1921 and 1924, but the United States experienced an increasing fragmentation which slowly became more racial than ethnic. Blacks from the South started migrating to Northern cities at that time, replacing many foreign-born immigrants in the worst slums.

After World War II, the earlier ethnic connotations of poverty in the United States were changed to convey racial attributes. Poverty had become closely associated with racial status. By the late 1950s the plight of the black population was worsened by their location in urban ghettos and their inability to obtain proportionate political representation. The Civil Rights Movement developed in the late 1950s in reaction to this situation. During the early 1960s poverty was still identified with racial and minority status. Only later did it come to light that there was a split between the public image of poverty and the racial overtones related to it.

Italy

After the beginning of the process of industrialisation, the poor constituted most of the population in Italy. However, there were significant differences among the poorest strata of society. On one hand there were workers and peasants who earned their livelihood, which allowed them barely to survive out of their wages, and on the other there were the paupers who were excluded from the labour market and lived on charity. The members of this group included beggars and the beneficiaries of public welfare or private philanthropy.

These two groups differed, not in their standard of living, which was very low in both cases, but rather in their different feelings of group identity. The perception of their own poverty by members of the working class in terms of class consciousness and solidarity created, by exclusion, the identification of the other category of the poor.

In Italy, the exclusion of the paupers from the labour market generated a process of alienation. Welfare and charity caused disintegration of the grouping. Individuals and their problems were considered as individual cases without taking into account the real and common causes of their impoverishment. Thus, the paupers ended up as a mere aggregate of individuals with no group consciousness. On the contrary, the workers became a social class and, owing to their position within the production process, acquired the power necessary to modify the social and economic conditions of its members, overcoming poverty and transforming the role of the working class with this increasing industrial power.

The cessation of the identification of Italian workers with the concept of "poor" dates back to the beginning of the nineteenth century. This phenomenon was accompanied by the deeper splitting among the social classes involved in the development of capitalism. In a situation where the socialist and other left-wing parties were the main political force opposed to the middle class, the different expectations of the weaker classes were constrained by the political and socio-economic perspective of the strongest section of the workers. Slowly, with the development of the labour-management struggle, the problem of the poor and the underprivileged tended to become secondary.

The parallel development

In both the United States civil rights movement and the Italian labour movement, antidiscrimination strategies of social change have, each in its own milieu, fundamentally transformed public consciousness. The role of legal ideology in reinforcing this consciousness has been extremely important. The protection of group interests—underprotected in various ways by political or economic power—is different in Italy and in the United States. In Italy, the increasing diffusion of forms of organised defence favours classes representing social struggles with a related ideological compromising and spreading of political messages. In the United States, social group legitimation has an ethnic and racial dimension; the related creation of mechanisms for implementation are also political, but reflect a different structure.

The analysis of this evolution with its internal differentiation of the poor is important. First, it shows that the social cohesion deriving from this public consciousness creates a group, i.e. an entity of persons who share common perceptions of their societal position and have a common identification as group identity develops together with a social collectivity. A *social group* so-defined, originating as a defence against the violence of the external world or simply as a way of obtaining the recognition of rights and a position within a specific society, must be distinguished from an *aggregate of individuals*, with no common relationships, and who are, as a whole, characterised by a self-perpetuating weakness. The only common elements characterising these aggregates of individuals are their position among the lowest levels of society, the lack of any actual legal protection and the absence of any group-consciousness. Secondly, the analysis of this evolution reflects how these groupings with their social problems relate to law and to the legal system. One part of the poorer strata of society is excluded from effective access to law in general, and to courts in particular. Other groups have taken advantage, directly or indirectly, of antipoverty policies to achieve substantive social reform using their ability for collective action. There is a long-standing underprotection of certain groups with respect to the tools and services provided by the system for the protection of individuals. New problems constantly appear and are left unsolved by the organisation of groups already existing among those privileged by the legal system (from trade unions to political parties).

THE CONSTITUTIONAL EQUAL PROTECTION CLAUSES

The different forms of the social structure in both Italy and in the United States are reflected at the constitutional level, in the analysis of the changes and developments of each country's equal protection clause.

Each country's constitution fixes beyond question the current values of that society (or of its dominant elites). This reflects the texture of society and the ways in which legal relationships among citizens are regulated. Equality before the law assumes a range of social groups. Theoretically, this constitutional assertion of a general parity of rights may operate in conditions very different from those prevailing when the concept was created. Hence, it has an extremely general character. However, in practice the equality before the law clause is tied to the social reality in which it was adopted and accepted. The constitutional assertion of a general parity of rights stems from a reaction to specific conditions of inequality operating at a particular time.

The United States

Before the enactment of the Fourteenth Amendment,[1] ratified in 1868, no constitutional document in the United States explicitly invoked the concept of

[1] Section 1 of the Fourteenth Amendment of the United States Constitution states: "All persons born or naturalized in the United States and subject to the jurisdiction thereof, are citizens of the United States and of the State wherein they reside. No State shall make or enforce any law which shall abridge the privileges or immunities of the citizens of the Unites States; nor shall any State deprive any person of life, liberty, or property, without the due process of law; nor deny to any person within its jurisdiction the equal protection of the laws."

equality. Nevertheless, no one would have doubted that every white male citizen was entitled to equivalent respect and equality. Nor would there have been any debate about whether the system should ensure effective protection of minorities whose interest differed from the interest of the majority, such as religious groups. The law's focus on equal protection was centred on the creation of constitutional devices, direct or indirect, for the protection of minorities at the pluralist table. In this context, the concept of minority was devoid of a racial connotation.

This situation lasted while slavery could be ignored as a source of inequality and discrimination. The recognition that the institution of slavery was not exempt from constitutional protection was a compromise which made federal union possible. The guarantees against unequal treatment were traditionally formulated as correcting certain kinds of discrimination on the basis of race. The black race in particular needed protection by special constitutional provisions. Race was the basis for systematic governmental and private discrimination. The original intent of the legislators drafting the Equal Protection Clause was merely to safeguard blacks from hostile state action.

After the Civil War, the three important goals of abolishing the institution of slavery, conferring the full benefit of American citizenship upon blacks and enabling them to exercise the franchise were transposed into three amendments to the Constitution. The end of the Civil War, however, did not bring to an end important battles related to slavery and to the rights of black people, which continued long after it. In the South, Federal Reconstruction forces backed the exercise by blacks of their civil rights. The withdrawal of these troops, however, allowed Southern leadership to restore the *status quo ante*. All in all, between 1880 and 1920 there was a massive retreat from protecting black rights. In the subsequent years, much legislation was enacted which severely restricted the legal rights of blacks, together with a number of "black codes". A substantial legal burden was imposed on blacks, and race was frequently invoked as a classification to discriminate against black people in education, in housing and in public accommodation.

On the other hand, the Supreme Court held that the Fourteenth Amendment did not place under federal protection the active domain of civil rights belonging exclusively to the states. In 1896, the Court upheld the concept of "separate but equal" in *Plessy* v. *Ferguson*.[2] Until World War II, the federal government had a limited role in the protection of civil rights at the state level. Only the end of the war brought increasing pressure on the federal government to fight the various manifestations of racial discrimination.

The formulation of a special judicial role with respect to minorities and their rights required a constitutional restructuring, which took place in 1938. The massive increase of federally administered programmes during the New Deal required specific attention to the reciprocal aspects between these programmes

[2] 163 US 537 (1896).

and various racial patterns in different parts of the nation. At that time people perceived the need to conceptualise a minority problem which cut across the contingent experiences of any particular minority. A new path of racial justice and minority rights was created with the *Carolene* case. The new road to minority rights was directed to granting special protection for those who had been deprived of their share of political influence. Prior to this case[3] constitutional categories were historically determined. After 1938, the concept of "minority" grew to include any group, whatever the particular characteristics and history of a given group. Religious, ethnic, national and racial minorities became special objects of judicial protection.

In this case, discrimination against racial minorities is identified as a characteristic voice of majoritarianism in the twentieth century. A discrete and insular minority cannot expect majoritarian politics to protect its members as it protects others, and is therefore entitled to a stricter judicial protection. The special position of blacks as a group under the Equal Protection Clause is due to historical reasons: it dates back first to slavery and then to segregation. The civil rights movement used the plight of blacks to achieve broader social reform.[4] Blacks have been considered the prototype of the protected group, but they are not the only group entitled to protection, which has been slowly extended to others. However, things changed with the proposal to extend the population of beneficiaries of the equal protection clause to the poor, a group which identifies itself in terms of economic position. To make anti-poverty a constitutionally permissible strategy is apparently a concept alien to the American constitutional spirit.[5]

In the pursuit of constitutional values dealing with equality, some values are more fundamental than others. The focus on blacks should be viewed as a question of setting priorities. Poverty is not absolutely unalterable for those afflicted by it and, according to the traditional American ethic, inequality may be tolerated as long as there is economic and social mobility.

In conclusion, the dichotomy found at the social level is reflected in the content and implications of the Fourteenth Amendment. This clause is used to

[3] *United States* v. *Carolene Prods Co.* 304 U.S. 144, 152 n. 4 (1938). The entire text of the footnote is as follows: "There may be narrower scope for operation of the presumption of constitutionality when legislation appears on its face to be within a specific prohibition of the Constitution, such as those of the first ten amendments, which are deemed equally specific when held to be embraced within the Fourteenth. See *Stromberg* v. *California* 283 US 359, 369–70; *Lovell* v. *Griffin* 303 US 444, 452."

[4] One of the most significant examples is *Brown* v. *Board of Education* 347 US 483 (1954).

[5] In *Dandbridge* v. *Williams* 397 US 471 (1970), the Supreme Court stated that welfare classifications are not subject to strict scrutiny under the Equal Protection Clause, saying that "in the area of economics and social welfare, a State does not violate (equal protection) merely because the classification made by its laws are imperfect. If the classification has some 'reasonable basis', it does not offend the Constitution." The Court added that "the Constitution may impose certain procedural safeguards upon systems of welfare administration. But the Constitution does not empower this to second-guess state official charged with the difficult responsibility of allocating limited public welfare funds among the myriad of potential recipient."

protect important interests of disadvantaged groups in the legislative arena, but only if these groups have certain characteristics and a predetermined historical background. This shows that interpretations of the Equal Protection Clause are shaped according to the societal structure.

Italy

In Italy, social antagonism characterised by class relationships and dominated by the middle class gave birth to a constitutional history based on class division and on the prejudicial exclusion of the working class from power.

In the present Italian Constitution, the emphasis has shifted away from the previous system, which was characterised by liberalism and *laissez-faire* doctrines and dominated by a regime of free competition. It guaranteed as a fundamental value the protection of property, ownership of which brought the power of political participation. Workers were subjected to a subhuman wage system as a consequence of the excess of supply of labour over demand. The result was the development of a class consciousness directed towards gaining the right to associate as a weapon to overcome their situation of inferiority. Over time this process slowly brought about several modifications of the system of political and social relationships and resulted in conflict between social groups. However, open social ferment was frozen by repression during the Fascist period. The decisive contribution to the restoration of democracy also came from the political parties which have historically represented the working class in the fight against Fascism.

The 1948 Constitution resulted from a political process which started at the end of the Fascist regime and developed through the assertion of the prime role of anti-Fascist political parties joined together in the *Comitato di Liberazione Nazionale* (National Liberation Committee). The constitutional document was created mainly by the efforts of the representatives of political forces which were majoritarian in the new society, with the participation (sometimes significant) of minor forces and intellectuals operating independently of the sphere of action of political parties. The Constitutional Assembly was dominated by deeply different forces (Christian Democrats (35%), Socialists (20%) and Communists (19%)) who had the common intention of founding a state clearly opposed to the Fascist one, but also profoundly different from the pre-Fascist one. Therefore, the Constitution is not the expression of the views of a majority, but the outcome of a compromise between various forces, representing a meeting point of people with deeply different ideological and cultural backgrounds (i.e. the political parties) present in the Constitutional Assembly. The Constitution is the result of agreement and reconciliation going beyond ideological divergences.

Some important new principles found a place in the constitutional text: the recognition of work as a relevant value in the economic and political organisation of the country; the assertion of the state's responsibility to overcome the subordinate position of workers as a class in the liberal state, and the explicit formulation of objectives to transform the socio-economic system. This involved public intervention and regulation as well as limiting the economic system based on the market and on free enterprise.

As a result of intervention by left-wing forces, the Constitutional Assembly gave a special qualification to the democratic form of government, as appears in Article 1 of the Constitution.[6] Democracy is based on work: work is a necessary factor for progressive homogenisation of societal strata, and work has the function of highlighting a different type of social order from that characterised by the ownership of wealth. The working class became aware of the injustice of its own plight of inferiority and became the protagonist of a social movement directed towards accomplishing a new balance based on the predominance of the working forces over the other social forces. The working class came to assume the role of the general class because its activities were directed to protectioning the interests which transcend those more immediately pertaining to the working class itself. It became the centre of attraction of other social interests.

Article 3 of the Constitution[7] proclaims the principles of equal social dignity and legal parity among all individuals, irrespective of their different personal and social conditions. The equal protection clause is understood both as a prohibition against unjustifiable privilege and discrimination (paragraph one), and also as a substantive means to accomplish equality through active intervention of public power in the socio-economic system (paragraph two). The state is responsible for removing the economic and social obstacles (not merely the legal ones) which in fact limit freedom and equality, and for abolishing those obstacles which impede the full development of the human person. This Article is an explicit admission that Italian society is based on a *de facto* inequality. The element which distinguishes this Constitution from its predecessors can be found in this very explicit proclamation of the contrast between the general principle of social organisation which is an intrinsic feature of the new state and the existing social reality. It might be said that Article 3, paragraph 2 repudiates the historical experience of liberal and democratic roots from which the Constitution originated.

The working class represents the prototype, not only historically but also constitutionally, of the underprotected social categories of citizens, i.e. those

[6] Article 1 of the Italian Constitution states: "Italy is a democratic republic founded on work. Sovereignty is vested in the people and shall be exercised in the forms and in the limits of the Constitution".

[7] Article 3 of the Italian Constitution reads as follows: "All citizens have equal social standing and are equal before the law, without distinction of sex, race, language, religion, political opinion or social and personal conditions.

It shall be the task of the Republic to remove the obstacles of an economic or social nature that, by restricting in practice the freedom and equality of the citizens, impede the full development of the human personality and the effective participation of all workers in the political, economic and social organization of the country".

affected by the implicit workings of the capitalistic society. The range of underprivileged groups includes those workers who are not represented and who remain at the margins of the industrial world in conditions of underemployment or of precarious employment. The working class is riven with factions caused by inequalities, often unacceptable, between the various sectors of the national economy and between different geographical areas (such as North and South).

The Italian Constitutional Court considered formal equality as tempered by substantive equality, even if its interest decreased, from the beginning of the 1960s, due to self-restraint caused by practical legislative conditions. For several years the trend was for the active protection of less privileged classes and in general of the weakest in the social structure, in the sense of their relationships with the labour market. Equality is intended to embrace two objectives: the development of the personality and participation in the organisation of the state, which are part of that historical heritage of values found in the depths of the collective conscience, and which are for the most part reflected in the constitutional document. These objectives are to be achieved at the legislative and the judicial level.

The central contents of constitutionally protected equality are related to the concept of the underprotected social group. This group is identified within Italian culture with the workers, the direct members of the labour movement, and only indirectly with other underprivileged persons who do not belong to the labour market but who can be indirectly identified in relation to it (the unemployed, the underemployed, etc.).

CONCLUSIONS

Reconstructing, under a comparative perspective, the development of the concept of poverty and the differential access of the various groups to the legal system granted by the USA and the Italian equal protection clauses reveals the processes of discrimination and exclusion of two particular societies and the different ways in which those two systems control conflicts.

A constitution becomes an expression of the assumptions which are firmly rooted in a culture, shaped by the history of that particular society. It is also an expression of the people's attitudes toward each other. An equal protection clause reflects the texture of society and the ways in which legal relationships between citizens are regulated. If we scrutinise the problems of social antagonism which characterise the different systems, we will see that the shape taken by the equal protection clause varies accordingly, not only in the formulation of the constitutional text, but also, and principally, in the moulding of case-law. In every system the equal protection clause, considered in the formal sense of the term, refers to identical values and has a constant fundamental nucleus. In this formal meaning, constitutional provisions may represent a solemn bond to future legislatures and may have, in certain parts, a programmatic value.

However, the various ways in which systems react to this principle, as well as the dissimilar reconstructions it receives, both in legal doctrine and in case-law, work in such a way that equality before the law fulfils functions and assumes configurations which are very different. In this substantial sense, the constitutional assertion of a general parity of rights originates from a reaction to precise and effective conditions of inequality. Although in theory this constitutional assertion may be extended to cover situations beyond those giving rise to the constitutional protection, to strike all privilege, thus assuming an extremely general character, in fact the clause is tied to the social reality in which it is adopted and accepted.

The different configurations of the societal structure are also apparent in the analysis, at the constitutional level, of the developments of an equal protection clause. The above social analysis of the legal systems of the USA and Italy shows that the evolution of the concept of poverty centred in Italy on the concept of class, and in the United Stated on the concept of minority. Legal analysis at the constitutional level in these two systems reveals the same differentiation. The roots of constitutionally protected equality are related to the concept of the underprotected social group. In Italy this group is identified with the workers and with other underprivileged individuals indirectly identified in relation to the labour market. In the United States the focus is on minorities: not only racial minorities but also religious, ethnic and national minorities have been found to be in need of protection.

In both systems the outcome of the social analysis perfectly matches the outcome of the legal analysis. In each country the plight of the deserving poor has shaped the equal protection clause: when dealing with the problems of the deserving poor, poverty came to be seen as an element in the network of social relations and to be studied as a social phenomenon. The dynamics of social classes bring the problems of this kind of poverty within a more general debate about the process which gave rise to it and, to a certain extent, about finding a way to eliminate or at least to mitigate it. This means inclusion in the societal structure and, indirectly, inclusion in the legal system. As a consequence, by the mere fact of being included, the fight for the rights of the deserving poor and the struggle against any possible deprivation of these rights once granted, is carried out not only by the deserving poor but also—and sometimes mainly—by other social forces or groups.

In both countries, the analysis of the undeserving poor concentrates on how poverty manifests itself. The focus is on the individual history of the indigent. Such individuals are often considered responsible for their own plight and must be helped only to the extent which avoids them becoming socially dangerous. The underprotection (or rather lack of protection) of certain groups within the legal system is remarkable, particularly in practice. Merely belonging to an aggregation of individuals results in legal protection only in theory, in the ringing exhortations of the constitutional text. The implementation of those exhortations is far from the reality for excluded groups.

The undeniable conclusion from the analysis carried out for this chapter is that the undeserving poor are left out of the social arena. They do not have the ability to intervene as a group, even less so as individuals, due to their isolation and alienation from society. Other social forces or strata do not act on their behalf to achieve the recognition of their rights. They are deprived of any hope of improving their social position and depend entirely on the charitable process operating in their society.

Needs in general, and in particular access to a legal system and to justice, cannot be separated from the system of social relationships. The needs of a group are, to a significant extent, a cultural product. Where poverty exists without support from any social organisation, or without any kind of common identification, poverty ultimately creates and strengthens social disaggregation.

REFERENCES

Abraham, H.J. (1982), *Freedom and the Court: Civil Rights and Liberties in the United States*, 4th ed., New York: Oxford University Press, esp. ch. 8

Barile, P. (1984), *Diritti dell'uomo e liberta' fondamentali*, Bologna: Il Mulino

Basso, L. (1971), "Giustizia e potere: la lunga via al socialismo", in *Quale giustizia*, 654

Bell, D. (1980), *Race, Racism and American Law*, Boston: Little Brown, 492

Braces, C.L. (1872), *The Dangerous Classes of New York*, New York

Branca, G. ed., (1975), *Commentario della Costituzione*, vol. 1, "Principi fondametali" (arts. 1–12), Bologna: Zanichelli, esp. U. Romagnoli, art. 3, part 2, 162–98

Calamandrei, P. (1950), "Introduzione storica alla Costituente", in *Comm. Sist. alla Costituzione Italiana*, I, CXXXV.V

Cerri (1974), *L'equaglianza nella giurisprudenza della Corte costituzionale*, Bologna: Il Mulino

Cover, R. (1982), "The Origins of Judicial Activism in the Protection of Minorities" 91 *Yale Law Journal*

Ely, J.H. (1980), *Democracy and Distrust*, Cambridge, Mass.: Harvard University Press, 79

Fiss, O., "Groups and the Equal Protection Clause", in *Philosophy and Public Affairs*, 5, 107–77

Friedman, L.M. (1985), *A History of American Law*, New York: Simon & Schuster

Himmelfarb, G. (1983), *The Idea of Poverty*, New York: Random House, Vintage Books

Katz J. (1985), "Caste, Class, and Counsel for the Poor" in *American Bar Foundation Resarch Journal*, 2, 259

Mortati (1954), "Il lavoro nella costituzione", in *Diritto del lavoro*, 153

Myrdal, G. (1944), *An American Dilemma: The Negro Problem and Modern Democracy*, New York: McGraw-Hill

Onida, V. (1984), "I principi fondamentali della Costituzione italiana", in *Manuale di diritto pubblico*, Amato e Barbera, eds. Bologna: Il Mulino

Paladin, L. (1965), Eguaglianza (dir. cost.), in *Enciclopedia del diritto*, 519 (551), Milano: Giuffrè

Palombara, J. La (1964), *Interest Groups in Italian Politics*, Princeton, New Jersey: Princeton University Press, 103–6
—— (1987), *Democracy Italian Style*, New Haven: Yale University Press
de Tocqueville, A. (1848), *Democracy in America*, Garden City: Anchor Books
Winter, R. K. Jr (1972), "Poverty, Economic Equality, and the Equal Protection Clause", in *Supreme Court Review*

7

Substantive Justice and Procedural Fairness in Social Security: The UK Experience[1]

MICHAEL ADLER

SUMMARY

THIS CHAPTER EXAMINES the relationship between substantive justice and procedural fairness in social security. After considering whether this is a theoretical or an empirical issue, and concluding that it is an empirical matter, it reviews developments in the UK social security system since 1979. It provides a critical assessment of the adequacy of benefit levels and of the proposals contained in the UK government's Green Paper *Improving Decision Making and Appeals* (DSS 1996). It then explores the implications of substantive justice and procedural fairness for different theories of citizenship and contrasts the different positions of social democratic and "new right" thinkers on the status of social rights and their relationship to civil and political rights. It concludes with an examination of the relationship between poverty, justice and citizenship in the UK.

The chapter has four parts. Part 1 analyses the concept of justice; part 2 reviews the recent evidence relating to substantive justice in the UK social security system; part 3 does likewise with procedural fairness; and part 4 discusses the implications of recent developments for citizenship. Part 2 draws extensively on the CPAG publication *Poverty: the Facts* (Oppenheim and Harker 1996) and the Joseph Rowntree Foundation's *Inquiry into Income and Wealth* (Barclay 1995, Hills 1995), while part 3 draws on the Richard Titmuss Memorial Lecture

[1] This paper is dedicated to the memory of Matthew Walsh, whose Ph.D. thesis on "The Concept of 'Quality' as a Possible Means of Evaluating the Social Security System" would have addressed many of the issues raised here, in particular the relationship between process and outcome, albeit in a rather different way. Tragically, Matthew died in a climbing accident on Mont Blanc in 1992, at the end of his first year in Edinburgh, by which time he had developed a novel theoretical framework and produced a detailed research proposal (Walsh 1992) but had not yet embarked on any empirical research. In writing this paper, I have been reminded of how much I learned from Matthew's imaginative and iconoclastic approach and of how much he might have contributed to the problems I have sought to address.

(Adler 1997a) which this author delivered in Jerusalem in November 1996 and subsequently published (Adler 1997b, Adler and Sainsbury 1988a and b).

THE CONCEPT OF JUSTICE

The meaning of justice

According to the American social philosopher John Rawls:

> "justice is the basic structure of society, or more exactly, the way in which the major social institutions distribute fundamental rights and duties and determine the distribution of advantages from social co-operation" (1972, 7).

For Rawls justice is the primary criterion by which the basic structure of society should be judged, "the first virtue of social institutions, just as truth is of systems of thought" (ibid., 3).

Rawls distinguishes between the *concept* of justice, which refers to "a proper balance between competing claims", and competing *conceptions* of justice, each of which expresses a different set of "principles for identifying those considerations which determine the balance" (ibid., 10). The coexistence of a single concept and several competing conceptions suggests that justice, like many other important social and political ideals, is essentially contested (Gallie 1964). As such, it can be defined in a relatively uncontroversial or uncontentious way (in this case as "a proper balance between competing claims") but the terms in which it is defined (i.e. what constitutes "a proper balance" and even what are to count as "claims") are the subject of considerable disagreement.

Put another way, justice entails "ensuring that everyone receives their due" (Miller 1976, 20) and a just state of affairs is one in which individuals receive exactly what is due to them in terms of their personal characteristics and circumstances. Although it is clear that there is considerable disagreement about what is due to an individual and how this should be determined, there is general agreement that justice is concerned with the ways in which items are distributed among persons or groups whose characteristics and circumstances are open to inspection. Thus justice refers to the share of an item which individual members of a group receive rather than to the total amount of an item that is enjoyed by the group as a whole; it is threfore a *distributive* rather than an *aggregative* principle.

Legal justice and social justice

It has become commonplace to distinguish between different subdivisions of justice in terms of their fields of application. Thus, Honoré (1970) points out that while *restorative justice* is concerned with compensation for harm or injury (in civil matters), *punitive justice* is concerned with the punishment of wrongdoing (in criminal matters). Together they comprise *legal justice* and are largely, but not exclusively, the concern of the legal system, i.e. of lawyers and the courts. *Social justice*, on the other hand, is concerned with the distribution of benefits and burdens among individuals and groups in society. As such, social justice refers to matters such as the distribution of income, wealth and other "primary goods" such as health, education, social security etc. However, two caveats should be noted:

- because punishments have been included in the domain of legal justice, the burdens included here refer to disadvantages other than punishments, e.g. to taxes or unpleasant work;
- although social justice usually refers to the allocation of material benefits and burdens, it can also refer to intangible (non-material) resources, e.g. praise and blame.

Although social justice has been distinguished from legal justice, some of the same moral considerations apply to them both. Likewise, although legal justice is obviously bound up with the law as an institution, so too is social justice: legal justice and social justice are merely concerned with different aspects or areas of law.

Substantive justice and procedural fairness

A distinction can also be made between *substantive justice*, which is concerned with outcomes, and *procedural justice* (which we shall refer to as *procedural fairness*), which is concerned with process. Substantive justice is perhaps more straightforward and is therefore considered first.

There are at least two dimensions to substantive justice. In his seminal analysis of the choices confronting policy makers in social security, Richard Titmuss (1970) distinguishes *adequacy* (defined in terms of sufficiency and referring to the absolute amount received) from *equity* (defined in terms of fairness and referring to the relative treatment of one person or group in relation to others). Titmuss' insight that concepts of adequacy are increasingly entangled with concepts of equity is not only important but clearly also of wide and general application to fields far removed from social security.

One view of procedural fairness, to which Rawls amongst others subscribes, ties it to substantive justice by equating it with those procedures which lead to just outcomes. Galligan (1986, 138) likewise argues that "the object of procedures is to realise a given object, and so in this sense procedures are instrumental to outcomes". However, another view suggests that substantively just outcomes are not necessarily enhanced by increasing procedural fairness. Indeed, Prosser (1981) even suggested that enhanced procedural fairness may provide a degree of legitimacy to unjust substantive outcomes, thereby deflecting criticism and making them impervious to change.

There have been various attempts to specify the requirements of procedural justice. Thus, in legal justice, we refer to a fair trial (in the case of criminal prosecutions) and to fair proceedings (in civil matters). In a criminal prosecution, the procedural requirements reflect the rights and duties of the accused and the state. However, there is wide agreement that accused persons should be entitled to know the case against them and to be legally represented, to plead not guilty and, if they do so, to be deemed innocent until proven guilty. The evidence against them must stand up and the case for the prosecution must be established "beyond reasonable doubt". Similarly, in a civil action, there are procedural requirements which reflect the rights and duties of the parties in dispute.

Procedural considerations are also an important component of social justice. Thus, for example, it is widely held that like cases should be dealt with alike; policies should not be applied retrospectively; people should be shown respect, their circumstances should be investigated thoroughly, and their claims should be decided impartially and expeditiously irrespective of the outcome. There have been a number of attempts to specify what procedural fairness involves. Mashaw (1983, 24) defines *administrative justice* (the procedural justice inherent in administrative decision-making) in terms of "those qualities of a decision process that provide arguments for the acceptability of its decisions", i.e. the principles which can be invoked in seeking legitimation for the justice of the decision-making process.

In his study of the American Disability Insurance (DI) scheme, Mashaw identified three broad strands of criticism levelled against it: that it produced inconsistent decisions, that it failed to provide a good service, and that it failed to ensure "due process" and respect claimants' rights. He argued that each strand of criticism is based on a different normative conception of the DI scheme, i.e. a different model of what the scheme could and should be like. These three models are *bureaucracy* (Mashaw refers to this as "bureaucratic rationality"), *the professions* (Mashaw calls this "professional treatment") and the *legal system* (Mashaw's term is "moral judgement").

Each model is associated with a different set of principles. Based on Mashaw's approach, we can associate a different mode of decision making, a different legitimating goal, a different mechanism of accountability and a different type of remedy with each of the three models. The characteristics of each of these models are set out in Table 7.1.

According to Mashaw, each of the models is also associated with a different conception of administrative justice. This is because, in each case, different principles are invoked to assess the acceptability of decisions. Thus one conception of administrative justice is based on the model of an organisation as a bureaucracy, another is based on the model of the organisation as a profession, and a third is based on the model of the organisation as a legal system. Mashaw argues that each of the three models is "coherent and attractive" and that, in his terminology, they are *highly competitive* rather than *mutually exclusive* (ibid., 23). Thus, these models can and do co-exist with each other. However, other things

Table 7.1: The Characteristics of Different Models of Administrative Justice

Model	Mode of decision making	Legitimating goal	Nature of accountability	Characteristic remedy
bureaucracy	applying rules	accuracy	hierarchical	administrative review
profession	applying knowledge	service	interpersonal	complaint to a professional body
legal system	weighing up arguments	fairness	independent	appeal to a court or tribunal

being equal, the greater the influence of one, the less will be the influence of the others. It follows that overall administrative justice, i.e. the justice inherent in day-to-day decision making, can be understood as a "trade-off" between the different conceptions of administrative justice associated with each of the three models, i.e. with bureaucracy, professionalism and the legal system.

The trade-offs which are made, and likewise those that could be made, reflect the concerns and the bargaining strengths of the institutional actors who have an interest in promoting each of the models, typically civil servants and officials in case of the bureaucratic model; doctors, social workers, police officers, other professionals and "street level bureaucrats" (Lipsky 1980, 1991) in the case of the professional model; and lawyers, court and tribunal personnel and groups representing clients' interests in the case of the legal model. Thus, these trade-offs vary from one organisation to another and, within a given organisation, from one area of activity to another.

Developing a constructive critique of Mashaw's approach, Sainsbury (1992) puts forward a much less relativistic conception of administrative justice, suggesting first that it comprises accuracy and fairness, and secondly that fairness consists of promptness, impartiality, participation and accountability. Galligan (1996, 95) is, like Mashaw, more relativistic and equates procedural fairness with those "procedures which lead to fair treatment according to authoritative standards".

Although Mashaw's approach is attractive, it can be criticised on a number of grounds. It is extremely prescriptive since it holds that the three models of administrative justice referred to above, and only these three models, must always be taken into account. This is not necessarily correct: for example, a strong argument can be made that the new emphasis on managerialism in public administration represents an additional model which is in competition with the other three (Adler 1997a and b). It is also very relativistic in that it implies that the administrative justice of an organisation necessarily depends on what kind of organisation it is.

A more fundamental criticism of Mashaw's approach is that it assumes a high degree of consensus on the values underlying programmes like the DI scheme and a correspondingly high level of agreement on the goals which such programmes should aim to achieve (Boyer 1984, Maranville 1984). Consensus on values and agreement on goals may exist, but on the other hand it may not. However, as Adler and Longhurst (1994) demonstrated in their analysis of decisions relating to the management of long-term prisoners, Mashaw's approach can also be applied to competing models of what programmes are for as well as to competing models of how programmes should be run, i.e. to competing models of substantive justice as well as to competing models of procedural fairness. Each of the models of substantive justice may, in theory, be combined with each of the models of procedural fairness, and each of the paired combinations can be associated with a different group of institutional actors.

The resulting two-dimensional model of justice is necessarily more complex but its characteristics are still the same, in that it not only enables us to see what trade-offs are made between different combinations of substantive and procedural justice in particular cases, but also to consider what different sets of trade-offs might be more desirable. What is desirable is, of course, not necessarily feasible.

The relationship between substantive justice and procedural fairness

At this point it is appropriate to ask whether there is a relationship between substantive justice and procedural fairness. Before doing so, however, it is important to determine what kind of question this is and whether it is theoretical or empirical. If there were a causal relationship between substantive justice and procedural fairness, i.e. between procedures and outcomes, it would follow that the question were theoretical, but if, on the other hand, the relationship between them was purely contingent, then the question would be empirical.

By considering social security, it should be clear that there is no causal relationship between substantive justice and procedural fairness. This is because fair procedures do not necessarily lead to just outcomes: scrupulously fair procedures can result in manifestly unjust outcomes, while outcomes which are, at least in the aggregate, accepted as just may be arrived at rather arbitrarily. Similarly, low levels of entitlement can be given a high degree of procedural protection whereas high levels of entitlement can receive very little protection at all. It therefore follows that the relationship between procedural justice and substantive justice in social security is an empirical one which can only be investigated by reviewing the empirical evidence.

SUBSTANTIVE JUSTICE IN THE UK SOCIAL SECURITY SYSTEM

The goals of social security

Three of the main goals of social security are *the provision of income support, the reduction of inequality* and *the promotion of social integration.* The provision of income support refers to poverty relief, the protection of customary living standards and the smoothing out of income over the life cycle. The reduction of inequality involves redistribution from individuals and families on higher incomes to those on lower incomes through vertical transfers and from individuals and families with lesser needs to those with greater needs through horizontal transfers. Social integration implies that benefits should not be stigmatising or socially divisive but, on the contrary, should foster social solidarity (Barr and Coulter 1990).

Substantive justice refers to the extent to which these aims have been realised in practice and policy can be evaluated in terms of its success in achieving these goals. Providing a comprehensive assessment of the UK social security system in terms of all of these goals and each of the measures they refer to is clearly beyond the scope of this paper and I therefore focus here on two of the most important measures: poverty relief and the extent of redistribution from rich to poor. This will be done by looking first at social security policy in the period up to 1979 under a succession of Conservative and Labour governments and then at social security policy in the period after 1979 when the Conservatives were returned to office under Margaret Thatcher.

The aims of social security policy

During the 1960s and 1970s the main aim of social security policy was to move away from means testing by raising the level of national insurance and other categorical benefits above that of supplementary benefit, the national scheme of social assistance. Thus, during the 1970s, real spending on national insurance and other non-means tested benefits rose by about 25 per cent. Other important aims were to protect benefits against inflation, to make more benefits earnings-related and to increase public expenditure on social security.

The main aims of social security during the 1980s and 1990s could hardly have been more different. The primary aims of social security policy were: to increase incentives in order to encourage people to remain in or to rejoin the labour market; to introduce greater targeting by increasing the reliance on means testing; and to reduce public expenditure on social security. However, because of the large rise in unemployment, expenditure on social security rose. Within the larger total, the proportion of expenditure on means-tested benefits increased substantially.

Poverty relief

The definition and measurement of poverty are both highly controversial. A key issue is whether poverty should be regarded as absolute or relative, i.e. whether it should be defined in relation to a fixed subsistence level uprated only in line with price inflation or in terms of the living standards of society as a whole, being uprated broadly in line with increases in earnings or income. Poverty can be defined in terms of an insufficiency of income (and/or other disposable resources) but the existence of these two apparently irreconcilable conceptions of insufficiency suggests that, like justice, poverty is also an *essentially contested concept* (Gallie 1964). However, this conclusion has been contested by Sen (1983) who argues that poverty has absolute as well as relative features. His approach involves distinguishing those *capabilities*, or basic needs, whose satisfaction is a condition of effective social functioning, from the bundle of *commodities*, and the income required to obtain them, which make effective social functioning possible in practice. Sen argues that, whereas basic capabilities (which include the need to meet nutritional requirements, to escape avoidable diseases, to be sheltered, to be clothed, to be able to travel, to be educated, to live without shame, to participate in the activities of the community and to have self-respect) can be defined absolutely, their commodity requirements are clearly variable and can only be defined in relation to the society in question.

Accepting Sen's conclusion that the commodities required for effective social functioning will vary across time and space still leaves us with the problem of deciding what, in a given society at a given time, these commodities are and what level of income is required to purchase them. Ongoing empirical research on this issue is called for but, needless to say, it does not exist in the United Kingdom and it is therefore necessary to make the best of the available survey data.

Measures of poverty

Unlike some other countries, there is no official poverty line in the United Kingdom, i.e. no government-sanctioned marker which admits the existence of poverty. However, two sets of official statistics are routinely used to provide proxy measures. The first of these is based on the *Low Income Families (LIF) Statistics* which were published by the Department of Social Security (DSS) from 1972 until a decision was taken to cease publication in 1985. Subsequently, they were produced by the independent Institute of Fiscal Studies and are now published under the auspices of the House of Commons Social Security Committee. This statistical series gives the number of people living on, below or just above supplementary benefit/income support, i.e. social assistance, levels. The second poverty line is based on the *Household Below Average Income (HBAI) Statistics* with which the government replaced LIF. The measure of poverty most commonly used gives the number of people living at or below 50 per cent of average income net of housing costs and adjusted for family size.

Both sets of statistics are derived from the *Family Expenditure Survey* (*FES*), an annual government survey of a representative sample of around 7,000 households in the UK. Neither is perfect and each has its strengths and weaknesses (Oppenheim and Harker 1996, Appendix 1). The first approach allows us to assess how many people are living on or below what the state deems to constitute a minimum level of income for people who are not in full-time work and is an important way of assessing the extent to which, on the government's own terms, social security provides an effective means of poverty relief. The second approach is an explicitly relative measure and looks at how people at the bottom end of the income distribution have fared in relation to the average. In spite of the differences between them, the two measures give similar results.

The extent of poverty

The LIF statistics show that 13.7m people in the UK (24 per cent of the population) were living at or below income support levels in 1992. Of these, 4.7m people (8 per cent of the population) were actually living below the "official" poverty line. In addition, 18.5m people (33 per cent of the population) were living in or on the margins of poverty with incomes of up to 140 per cent of income support levels.

Table 7.2 shows the increase in the number of people living at below or just above Income Support levels between 1979 and 1992. Due to recent changes in the way in which figures are calculated, two sets of figures are given for 1989 (reflecting the old and the new methods). In 1979, 7.7m people (14 per cent of the UK population) were living in poverty but, by 1992, this had risen to 13.7m people (24 per cent of the population). The bulk of this increase occurred in the early 1980s and was due to the sharp rise in unemployment. Since 1989, there has been an increase in the number of people receiving Income Support and in the number of people below Income Support levels. However, while the proportion of people living on Income Support has increased, the proportion of people living below this level has remained fairly constant. One of the most important things that the LIF Statistics reveal is the large number of people who, for whatever reason, fall through the "safety net" of Income Support.

The HBAI statistics show that in 1992/93 14.1m people (25 per cent of the population) were living in households with incomes, net of housing costs, below 50 per cent of the average. Table 7.3 shows that this was almost three times the number in 1979 when 5.0m (9.0 per cent of the population) were living below this poverty line.

Tables 7.4 and 7.5 show how poverty is related to economic and family status. The groups most likely to experience poverty are the unemployed (75 per

Table 7.2: Numbers and proportion of children living in poverty, on or below supplementary benefit/income support in 1979, 1989 and 1992 by family type

Notes: The percentages show the proportion of children in each family type living in poverty—*e.g.*, in 1979. 47% of children in lone-parent families were living in poverty. Two sets of figures are given for 1989 because of methodological changes in the way the figures were calculated. 1989[1] relates to the method used for the 1979 figure also. 1989[2] relates to the method used for the 1992 figure also. Comparisons between 1979 and 1992 should be drawn with caution.

Source: DSS, *Households below Average Income, a statistical analysis, 1979–1992/93*, and revised edition, HMSO, 1995.

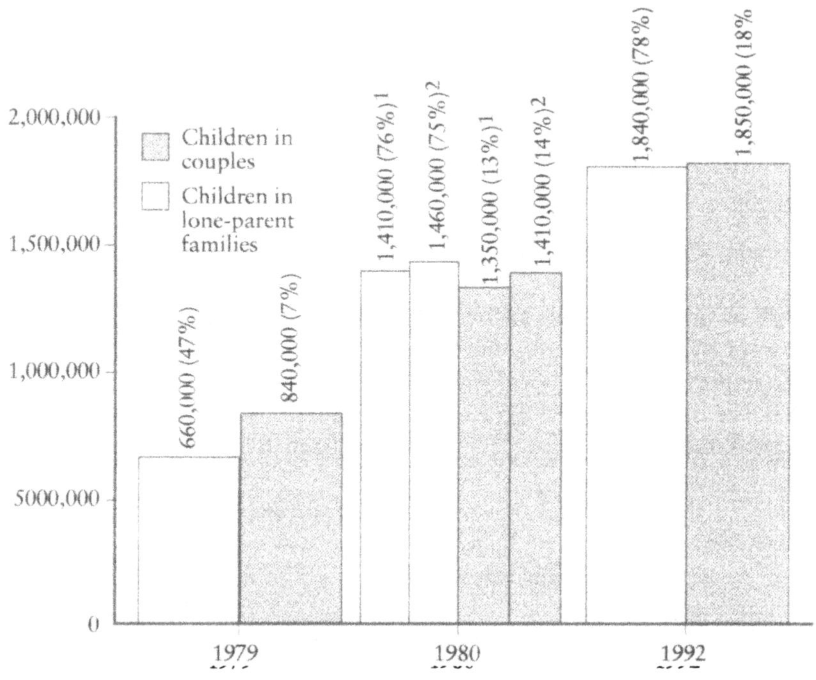

cent of whom were in poverty) and lone parent households (58 per cent of whom were in poverty in 1992/93). Table 7.2 also shows that children were more vulnerable to poverty than society as a whole throughout the period from 1979 to 1992/93. Thus in 1979 10 per cent of all children and 9 per cent of children were in poverty, while in 1992/93 the corresponding figures were 33 per cent of all children compared to 25 per cent of the population.

Redistribution from rich to poor

The HBAI statistics only go back as far as 1979 and cannot be used to make comparisons over a longer period. However, the Joseph Rowntree Foundation's *Inquiry into Income and Wealth* (Barclay 1995, Hills 1995) analysed changes in the distribution of income over a longer period.

Table 7.3: Proportion of children and population living in poverty between 1979–1992/93 (living below 50% average income after housing costs)

Source: DSS, *Households below Average Income, a statistical analysis, 1979–1988/89*, and revised edition, HMSO, 1992 and 1995.

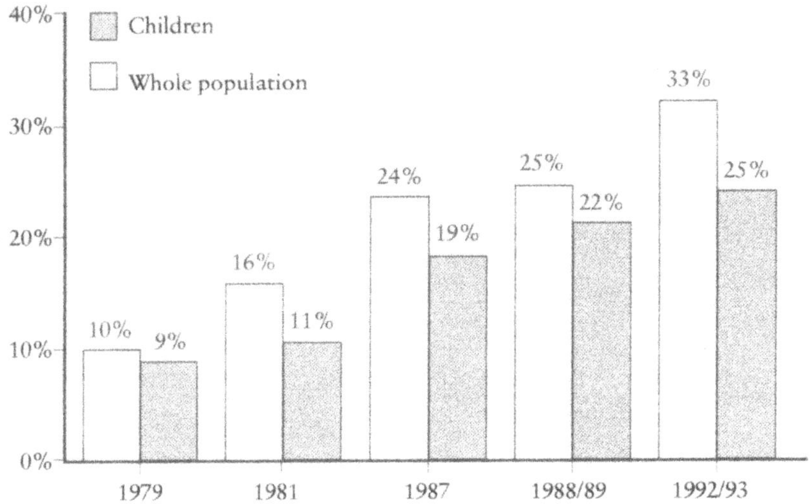

Table 7.4: The risk of poverty by economic status in 1992/93 (defined as living below 50% of average income after housing costs)

* *Note*: Other = all those not included in previous groups

Source: DSS, *Households below Average Income, a statistical analysis, 1979–1992/93*, and revised edition, HMSO, 1995.

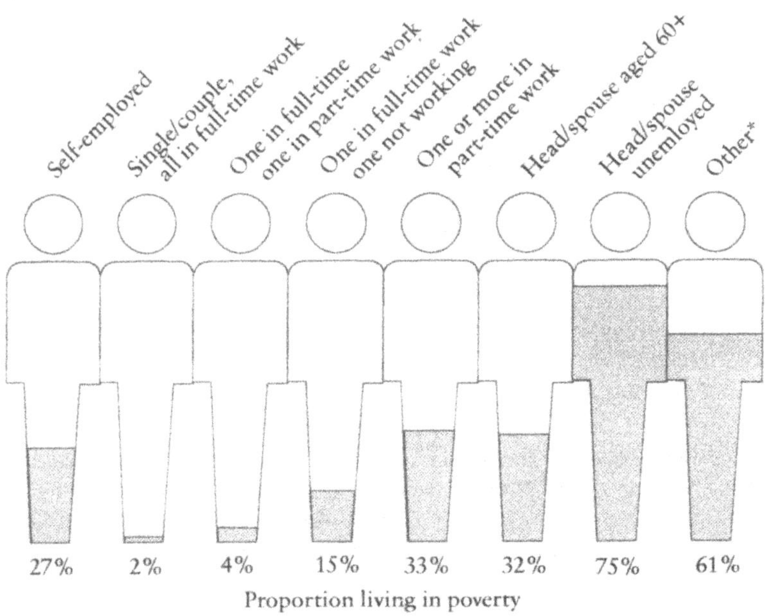

Table 7.5: The risk of poverty by family status in 1992/93 (defined as living below 50% of average income after housing costs)

Source: DSS, *Households below Average Income, a statistical analysis, 1979–1992/93*, and revised edition, HMSO, 1995.

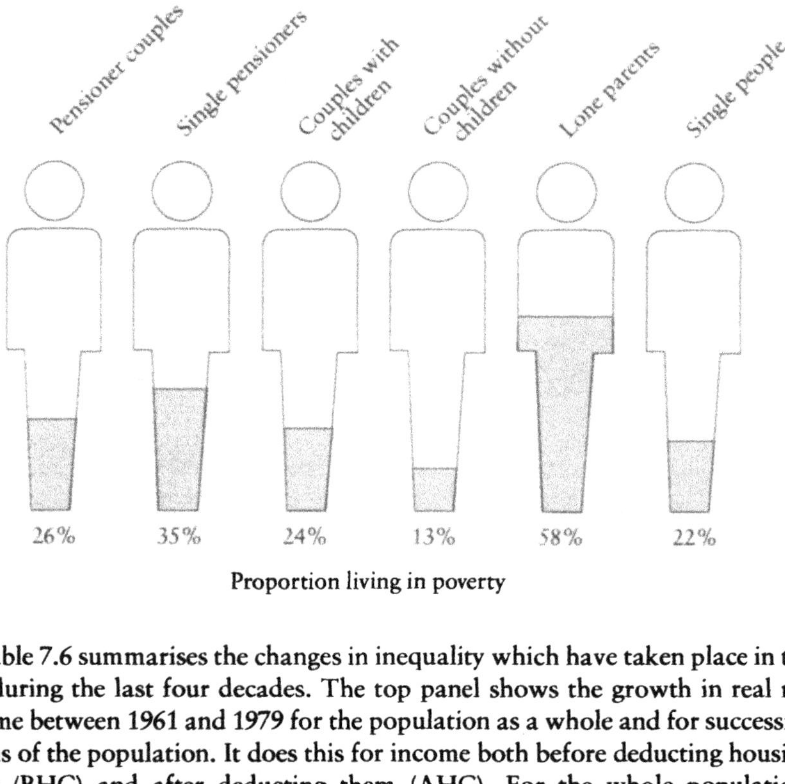

Table 7.6 summarises the changes in inequality which have taken place in the UK during the last four decades. The top panel shows the growth in real net income between 1961 and 1979 for the population as a whole and for successive tenths of the population. It does this for income both before deducting housing costs (BHC) and after deducting them (AHC). For the whole population, incomes grew by 35 per cent (BHC) and 33 per cent (AHC). But at 55 per cent (BHC) and 51 per cent (AHC), the growth was about 50 per cent greater than this "average" for the lowest decile group. The bottom panel shows what happened between 1979 and 1991/92. For the whole population, incomes grew by 36 per cent (BHC and AHC), slightly faster over this twelve to thirteen-year period than over the previous eighteen years. But the growth was smaller than this "average" for the bottom seven-tenths of the distribution. In the lowest decile group, BHC incomes were no higher in 1991/92 than they had been in 1979 and AHC incomes actually fell by 17 per cent. By comparison, incomes grew by more than the average for the top three-tenths of the income distribution. In the highest decile group AHC incomes rose by 62 per cent and BHC incomes by 57 per cent, substantially more than for any of the lower income groups.

Table 7.7 shows the annual rate of change in inequality over the most recent period for which a generally consistent trend can be identified in the UK and

Table 7.6: Change in real net income, 1961–79 and 1979–91/92

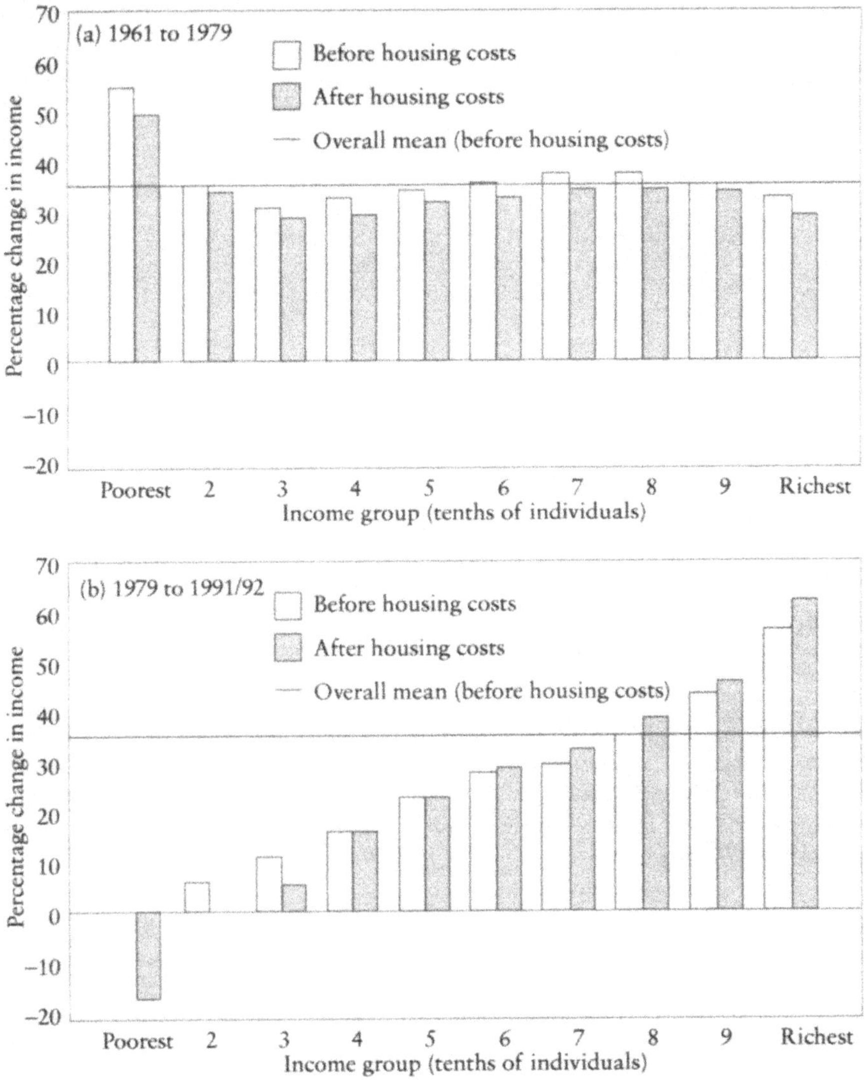

Source: *The Joseph Rowntree Inquiry into Income and Wealth* (Chairman: Peter Barclay) Vol. 1, Fig. 3 (1995).

seventeen other countries. While the data do not make exact comparisons possible, their implications are clear. There has not been a universal trend towards greater inequality in recent years, although this has been the case in the majority of other countries shown. However, inequality increased faster in the UK

Table 7.7: International trends in income inequality

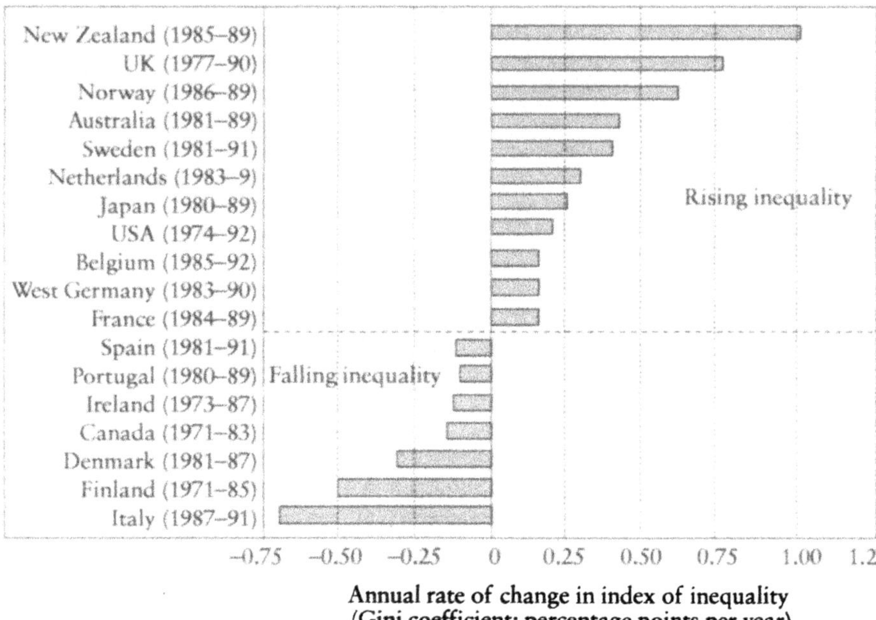

Source: *The Joseph Rowntree Foundation Inquiry into Income and Wealth* (Chairman: Peter Barclay) Vol. 1, Fig. 2 (1995).

between 1977 and 1990 (with the index of inequality increasing at 0.75 percentage points each year) than in any of the other countries listed with the single exception of New Zealand over the four years to 1989. In most of the other countries where inequality was increasing, this was at less than half the rate of the increase in the UK.

Summary: changes in substantive justice

A more recent study (Hills 1998), which updates the 1995 study with data available at the end of 1997, suggests that, for a variety of reasons, the post-1979 trend towards increased poverty and greater inequality may have been halted, and possibly even put into reverse, in the three years since 1991/92. Moreover, for the first time in many years the 1998 Budget brought about a redistribution of income from rich to poor (Clark and Giles 1998). Nevertheless, the incidence of poverty and the extent of inequality in the UK were at unprecedentedly high levels. During the 1960s roughly 10 per cent of the population had incomes below half the mean income level. This fell to 7 per cent in 1977 before increasing to 20 per cent in 1991/92. Although it fell back somewhat in the next three years, it was still 18 per cent in 1994/95. Likewise, although income inequality may have become less unequal in the three years since 1991/92, it was greater than at any time in the fifty-year period since the end of World War II and near the top of the international range.

Seventy per cent of the two poorest decile groups comprise households with no earnings, and 70 per cent of the gross income of these two groups comes from social security benefits. Since 1979 the substantive entitlements provided by social security have not kept up with the higher living standards enjoyed by the rest of the population and social security has provided increasingly less adequate protection to those unable to support themselves through employment. As to the future, the number of people with relatively low incomes will reflect the balance between the positive effects of "welfare to work" measures, which are intended to get those who can work into work, and the negative effects of falling relative incomes for those who cannot work and remain dependent on benefits.

PROCEDURAL FAIRNESS IN THE UK SOCIAL SECURITY SYSTEM

A dual system of adjudication

Until 1980 there were two parallel systems of adjudication in social security (Bradley 1985, Wikeley 1994, Adler 1995). Under arrangements which can be traced back to the introduction of Unemployment Insurance in 1911, there was a three-tier system—or more accurately, a "three-tier plus" system (Bradley 1985)—of adjudication for social insurance and related benefits. At the first tier, all non-medical, i.e. lay, questions were dealt with by National Insurance Officers (the forerunners of the present Adjudication Officers) while medical questions (most of which arose in relation to sickness/invalidity and disability benefits) were dealt with by general medical practitioners. Appeals against first-tier decisions were heard by National Insurance Local Tribunals (NILTs) and Medical Appeal Tribunals (MATs). The former dealt with lay questions and the latter with medical questions. There was a further appeal from NILTs and MATs on a point of law to the National Insurance Commissioners.

Although National Insurance Officers (NIOs) were civil servants, as far as adjudication was concerned they were expected to act independently in applying the law (statute law and case-law) to the facts of the case. Thus they were not answerable to management or to the Minister in Parliament for their decisions. NILTs comprised a legally qualified chairman and two lay members (one representing employers and the other trade unions) while the Commissioners were all experienced lawyers of at least ten years' standing. Their decisions constituted a set of precedents which had to be followed by NILTs and NIOs. Thus, they were in effect specialised administrative law judges. Finally, since all tribunals are supervised by the courts, there was the possibility of a further appeal, on a point of law, from the Commissioners to the Court of Appeal (in England

and Wales) or the Court of Session (in Scotland) and ultimately to the House of Lords.

A wholly different model of adjudication applied to social assistance benefits. Under arrangements which can be traced back to the introduction of unemployment assistance in 1934, there was a simpler (and more attenuated) two-tier system of adjudication. At the first tier, decisions were taken by Supplementary Benefit Officers (SBOs). There was then a right of appeal to a Supplementary Benefit Appeal Tribunal (SBAT) whose decisions were final. SBOs were also civil servants and were expected to apply statute law and Commission policy (there was very little case-law) to the facts of the case. SBATs also comprised three members but they had a lay chairman and could override Commission policy by substituting their own discretion for that of the SBO.

The contrast between the two systems was striking. In the case of supplementary benefits, the law gave considerable discretion to the Supplementary Benefits Commission. Although Commission policy was expressed in endless rules and codes, officials nevertheless had a considerable amount of discretion in implementing policy. There were no precedents to be followed and SBATs functioned rather like case conferences. In the case of national insurance, officials had much less discretion to apply the law, tribunals were more like courts and Commissioners' decisions constituted a body of case-law.

Rights (associated with a legal model of decision making) were much stronger in national insurance, while discretion (associated, perhaps somewhat incongruously, with a professional model of decision making) was much greater in supplementary benefit. However, rules and regulations (associated with a bureaucratic model of decision making) were even more important in both cases. The fact that first-instance decision makers were all generalist civil servants (and as such were trained neither as lawyers nor as welfare professionals) and the limited availability of specialist advice and representation which are needed to enable claimants to challenge bureaucratic procedures, guaranteed their pre-eminent position (Adler 1997a and b).

The emergence of a single system

As far as supplementary benefit was concerned, legislation in 1980 changed the position completely. The model of adjudication in supplementary benefit was subjected to sustained attack by the welfare rights movement for failing to protect claimants' entitlement to benefit, while the Supplementary Benefits Commission, and subsequently the government, concluded that the model was no longer viable. This was partly due to changes in the size and composition of the claimant population and to pressure from welfare rights activists, but also reflected a lack of trust by claimants in officials who were being asked to exercise discretionary powers more suited to professionals. This model of adjudication was eventually abandoned in favour of the national insurance model, which for some years applied to all social security benefits administered by central government. The status of the first-tier decision makers in supplementary benefit cases became the same as that of first-tier decision makers in national insurance cases, the composition and powers of SBATs became the same as those of NILTs, and in 1983 the two tribunals were merged into Social Security Appeal Tribunals (SSATs).

In 1984 all Adjudication Officers (AOs) were made accountable to the Chief Adjudication Officer, whose roles include advising AOs on the performance of their functions, discharging certain responsibilities relating to appeals to the Commissioners, and monitoring standards of adjudication (Sainsbury 1989). In the same year, responsibility for appeal tribunals was transferred from the Department of Social Security to an independent statutory body (known as the Independent Tribunal Service) under a President (appointed by the Lord Chancellor after consultation with the Lord Advocate) who is responsible for the appointment and training of all tribunal personnel, and all tribunal chairmen were required to be lawyers of five years' standing. Commissioners' decisions in supplementary benefits cases constituted a body of case-law with the force of precedent in exactly the same way as in other social security benefits (Baldwin, Wikeley and Young 1992; Adler 1995).

The extent of discretion available to AOs and SSATs (whose responsibilities now embraced all social security benefits) in supplementary benefit cases had clearly declined while the rights of those claiming supplementary benefit had been brought into line with national insurance and related benefits.

The re-emergence of two systems

In 1986 the pattern of adjudication changed again. Supplementary benefit was replaced by a simplified income support scheme and a cash-limited, discretionary Social Fund. In addition to providing grants and loans as one-off extras on a discretionary basis, the Social Fund is also responsible for a number of non-discretionary social security benefits, e.g. maternity and funeral payments. However, since decisions about entitlement to these benefits are made by AOs and there is a right of appeal to a SSAT, there is no need to say more about this here. In the case of income support, the pattern of adjudication which had formerly applied to all social security benefits administered by central government continued to apply. In addition, a new requirement, that appeals to a tribunal had to be preceded, as a first stage, by internal administrative review, was introduced for a number of new benefits (Sainsbury 1994). The effect of this was to reduce the number of decisions which were reversed on appeal.

The case of the Social Fund is altogether different (Drabble and Lynes 1989). First-tier decisions are made by Social Fund Officers acting under the direction and guidance of the Minister. There is no right of appeal as such (if there had been, tribunals could have made decisions which would have breached the cash-limits) although dissatisfied claimants can obtain a review of the decision in question (Dalley and Berthoud 1992). This is carried out first by the official who made the original decision and subsequently, after an interview with the claimant, by a senior member of the local office. Claimants who are still dissatisfied may request a further review by a Social Fund Inspector whose decisions are monitored by the Social Fund Commissioner. Although the arrangements are rather complex, the important point is that there is no appeal from an initial decision to an independent appeal tribunal, or from there to a body such as the Social Security Commissioners, no body of case-law and no mechanism that is in any way analogous to the review by Chief Adjudication Officer. Thus the resulting balance between rules, discretion and rights is similar to that which applied in supplementary benefits before the 1980 reforms. The trade-offs between bureaucratic rules, administrative discretion and procedural (welfare) rights in each of the periods referred to are set out in Table 7.8.

Table 7.8: Trade-offs between bureaucratic rules, administrative discretion and procedural rights in social security legislation over the last 25 years

	Bureaucratic rules	Administrative discretion	Procedural rights
1971–80			
Nat. Ins.	very strong	very weak	strong
Sup. Ben.	very strong	quite strong	weak
1980–1986			
Nat. Ins.	very strong	very weak	strong
Sup. Ben.	very strong	weak	strong
1986-present			
Soc. Sec. (inc. IS)	very strong	very weak	quite strong
Social Fund	very strong	quite strong	weak

The latest changes

I shall next summarise the latest set of proposals for "improving" decision making and appeals in social security, which have now been implemented, and then to subject them to critical scrutiny. These proposals were first put forward by the (previous) Conservative government in a Consultation Paper (DSS 1996) and most of them appeared again in the 1998 Social Security Bill introduced by the (present) Labour government and now enacted as the Social Security Act 1998. Although few of the proposals put forward in the Consultation Paper received much support (Sainsbury 1997) the new government determined to press ahead with them.

The aims of the "new" approach set out in the Consultation Paper were inoffensive enough. They were:

> "[t]o improve the processes for decisions and appeals; to produce a less complex, more accurate and cost-effective system for making and changing decisions; and to preserve customers' rights to an independent review of decisions in appropriate cases" (ibid., para. 1.2).

It was the detailed proposals which were so worrying. In regard to first-tier decision making, the Consultation Paper favoured the use of simpler and better designed claim forms; clearer rules and guidance about the evidence needed to support claims to benefit; an increased emphasis on direct contact with claimants: better explanations for decisions and improved computer support (ibid., para. 1.3). However, in the light of the likely cuts in expenditure on the administration on benefits (referred to below) it was hard to see how some of these worthwhile reforms, in particular more direct contacts with claimants (now known as "customers") would be paid for.

The Consultation Paper also recommended that claimants who do not provide the evidence which can reasonably be sought from them should be penalised, e.g. by postponing the start of the entitlement until they produce it (para. 4.8). Such a measure is bound to hit the most vulnerable claimants, e.g. those with learning difficulties or mental health problems, and those who are socially disadvantaged or have a poor command of English.

In place of the dual system of accountability, the Consultation Paper proposed that first-tier decision makers, who are managerially accountable to the Minister and accountable to the Chief Adjudication Officer in respect of adjudication, should be accountable to the Minister alone (para. 4.9). Their status would not be prescribed in law and the system of dual accountability, which appears to have worked well since it was established in 1911, would be ended. Moreover, in transferring the functions of the Chief Adjudication Officer to the Chief Executive of the Benefits Agency, which is now responsible for the delivery of social security benefits (para. 4.14) all the advantages of an independent check on the standards of adjudication would be lost.

Finally, the Consultation Paper proposed a series of reforms to the appeals process. Only cases which need to proceed to appeal would do so; the appeal would cover only the issue in dispute rather than the whole decision, and would refer to the date on which the decision appealed against was made rather than the date of the appeal hearing as at present (para. 5.4). Cases would be sifted to decide how they should be handled; the range of expertise available to tribunals and their composition would not be prescribed; legal expertise would be reserved for "appropriate" appeals with others being heard by non-legal decision makers; single decision makers would hear most cases, with two or more decision makers sitting "only as necessary" (para. 5.5). Finally, and this is one of the provisions swiftly put into effect in 1997, there would be a specific statutory provision for *paper hearings*, i.e. hearings dealt with on the papers alone, where appellants did not opt for an oral hearing (para. 5.6).

The Consultation Paper ended by inviting comments on an appropriate model for decision making and appeals in social security for the future. Waiting in the wings was the alternative model of internal (administrative) review found in the Social Fund where there is no appeal to an independent appeal tribunal. This was commended for achieving "independence" and "public accountability" (para. 6.14) and it is no secret that this was former Secretary of State Peter Lilley's preferred option for the entire social security system.

The case for reform set out in the body of the Consultation Paper was not particularly compelling in that the arrangements which it sought to change had existed for many years and have neither been regarded as problematic nor in need for reform. The real case was to be found in Appendix G which reproduces the speech in which the Conservative Secretary of State Peter Lilley announced the Department's "Change Programme". Although administrative costs only accounted for 4–5 per cent of the total social security budget, the sums involved (£3–4bn. per year) were very substantial and, in an attempt to rein them in, he announced measures designed to achieve administrative savings of 25 per cent over three years. Standards of adjudication, which currently leave a great deal to be desired (the Consultation Paper acknowledged that 22 per cent of income support decisions were inaccurate in 1994/95) are bound to deteriorate further as the result of these "efficiency savings". However, instead of recognising that this constituted a strong argument for strengthening appeal procedures, the Government decided that the Independent Tribunal Service, which in spite of its independence from the Department of Social Security was financed by it, should bear its share of the cuts.

Submissions were received from 437 individuals and organisations and subjected to a detailed analysis (Sainsbury 1997). Although there was general support for the government's stated aims, there was considerable opposition to most of the detailed proposals. However, instead of producing a White Paper which responded to and took account of these criticisms and would have been particularly appropriate in light of the change of government, the Labour government introduced a Bill which adopted nearly all the proposals put forward by the Conservatives and ignored the results of extensive public consultation. Thus, Part I of the Bill: abolished the status of independent adjudication officers, all decisions henceforth being taken by civil servants (or computers) acting on behalf of the Secretary of State; did away with the Chief Adjudication Officer and made agency Chief Executives responsible for issuing guidance, monitoring the quality of decisions and reporting on standards; removed statutory time-limits on Agency staff but imposed tougher time-limits on claimants, e.g. by reducing the time-limit for appeals from three months to one month; restricted the backdating of valid claims to a maximum of one month before the date of claim; allowed for all appeals to be sifted to identify the nature and type of expertise needed to deal with them; removed the requirements that all cases must be heard by a three-person tribunal and that tribunal chairman must be legally qualified; undermined the inquisitorial role of the tribunal by allowing them to ignore "any issue that is not raised by the claimant" in the letter of appeal, even if it is unlawful; and extended the anti-test case rule to limit the extent to which others can benefit from successful test cases. Why the new government chose to do this is both unclear and beyond the scope of this article (for some possible explanations, see Adler and Sainsbury 1998a and b).

The trade-offs entailed by the government's proposals are set out in Table 7.9.

Table 7.9: Trade-offs between bureaucratic rules, administrative discretion and procedural rights entailed by the proposed reform of decision making and appeals in social security

	Bureaucratic rules	Administrative discretion	Procedural rights
Soc. Sec. (inc. IS)	stronger still *(previously very strong)*	very weak	weak *(previously quite strong)*
Social Fund	very strong	quite strong	weak *(unchanged)*

What is at risk?

One of the major virtues of the pre-1998 arrangements for decision making and appeals was that the system of independent adjudication provided a measure of protection for those dependent on social security comparable to that provided by lawyers and the courts for private forms of property (Reich 1964, 1965). This is not to suggest that everything in the garden was rosy—far from it—or that there was no scope for improvements which would enhance the justice inherent in the administration of social security. However, far from enhancing procedural fairness, the government's policy is virtually certain to diminish it, and to do so significantly. Although the influence of administrative discretion had been squeezed out of most social security benefits, it still existed in the Social Fund. However, with the Bill passed and the proposals implemented, claimants' rights have been weakened across the board.

Summary: changes in procedural fairness

Prior to the 1980 reforms, applicants for and recipients of social assistance were largely dependent on the discretion of officials and received little protection from appeal tribunals. However, as a result of these and other reforms, supplementary benefit was brought into line with other social security benefits and the rights of applicants and recipients greatly enhanced through the establishment of the office of the Chief Adjudication Officer to monitor the standards of initial decision making and the strengthening of appeal tribunals which resulted from the establishment of the Independent Tribunal Service. Some of these gains were subsequently lost in the 1986 reforms by the establishment of a discretionary Social Fund, which discarded the model of independent adjudication in favour of a model of bureaucratic decision making in which, among other things, internal review has been emphasised at the expense of an appeal to an external tribunal. Similar developments in other areas of social security have likewise weakened the rights of claimants but are trivial in comparison to the proposals for "improving" decision making and appeals which the British government introduced in 1998. These changes will have the effect of abolishing the system of independent adjudication and severely curtailing the degree of procedural protection which appeal tribunals would be able to provide. With the legislation passed and the proposals implemented, procedural fairness has been substantially diminished in much the same way as occurred with substantive justice. Until recently, it could be argued that gains in procedural fairness had accompanied losses in substantive justice, i.e. that claimants had secured stronger rights albeit to lower levels of benefit. However, this "trade off" has now been seriously threatened.

THE IMPLICATIONS FOR CITIZENSHIP

The concept of citizenship

T.H. Marshall (1963) defines citizenship as "a status which is bestowed on everyone who is a full member of a community" and refers to the rights (and duties) which people have in common as citizens. Marshall argues that citizenship comprises *three clusters of rights*: civil rights, political rights and social rights.

- *Civil rights* refer to rights which are necessary for individual freedom (freedom of movement, freedom of assembly, freedom of speech and freedom of religion), the right to own property and conclude valid contracts, the right to work and the right to justice (*habeus corpus*, i.e. freedom from arbitrary arrest, the assumption of innocence until proven guilty, and the right to a fair trial).
- *Political rights* comprise rights to participate in the exercise of political power both as a voter and as a candidate.
- *Social rights* embrace the right to "a modicum of economic welfare and security and to live the life of a civilised person according to the standards of society".

The reference in the elucidation of social rights to "the standards of society" makes it clear that the content of each of the three components of citizenship is, to a degree, *open-textured*. Their meaning cannot be completely specified in advance and can only be determined in the light of changing circumstances.

According to Marshall, each of these clusters of rights is associated with a different set of institutions. Thus, civil rights are intimately bound up with, and in theory protected by, the *courts*, political rights are linked to *parliament* and, in the United Kingdom, social rights are associated with what came to be known, in a generic sense, as the *social services*, i.e. the public provision of benefits and services and the regulation of those that are privately provided (Cranston 1985).

In so far as citizenship refers to what people have in common as citizens, e.g. the right to make and enforce contracts, to vote and to receive treatment from the National Health Service, it is an egalitarian concept and can be contrasted with all those attributes and characteristics which are unequally distributed in society, e.g. intelligence, strength, health, income, wealth etc.

One consequence of citizenship is that it reduces the significance of economic and social inequalities. This applies to each of the clusters of rights which make up citizenship. In the absence of civil, political and social rights, the ability to make and enforce contracts, to vote and to obtain health care will all be distributed unequally and determined by the pattern of economic and social inequalities in society. Where men and women have civil, political and social rights, however, the right to make and enforce contracts, vote and obtain health care will be available to everyone. Although economic and social inequalities still exist, they are of less significance. In this sense we can say that citizenship ameliorates social and economic inequalities. It can also legitimate such inequalities: since they are of less significance, they may be seen as more acceptable.

However, although citizenship may be equal in form, it does not follow that it is equal in content. That is why the weakening of procedural rights and substantive entitlements for those who are dependent on social security in the United Kingdom is of such great concern. Marshall defined social rights in terms of a level of economic welfare and security that enabled people "to live the life of a civilised person according to the standards of society" but, for an increasing number of poor people in Britain, it is not clear that they can still do so.

Social democratic and "new right" perspectives on social rights as a component of citizenship

Social democrats like Marshall and Plant (1993) argue that social rights are an essential component of citizenship. This is because, in the absence of rights to minimum levels of income, health care, education etc., people will be unable to participate fully in the life of society or to exercise their civil and political rights. On the other hand, classical liberals like Hayek (1982) and Barry (1993) assert that social rights are not a component of citizenship at all. They argue that social rights are positive rights (unlike civil and political rights, which are negative rights and embody absolute standards) and that positive rights reflect normative judgements. Social rights are positive because they can only be achieved at the expense of other rights. Thus, it is claimed that the "right" to social security pre-supposes agreement on how much social security a person should receive and the existence of a social security system paid for out of taxation to ensure that they receive their entitlment. However, the level of social security payments necessarily reflects political judgements and the compulsory nature of taxation is, they argue, inconsistent with respect for property rights.

In fact, these robust arguments are not as overwhelming as they might initially appear. This is because social rights cannot be distinguished from civil and political rights in this way. The extensiveness of civil and political rights is also a matter of judgement, and taxation is also required to finance the legal system and parliamentary institutions. Thus, the difference between social rights on one hand and civil and political rights on the other is one of degree rather than of kind.

In an important article, Ignatieff (1989) contrasts a rights-based citizenship of entitlement (based on Marshall's conception of citizenship) with a duty-based citizenship of empowerment (as championed during the 1980s and 1990s in the UK and the USA). The former is described as *passive* and was formerly championed by governments of the centre left (mainly by Labour governments in Britain and by Democratic administrations in the USA) in order to counter and compensate for unacceptable inequalities generated by the market. The latter is described as *active* and was subsequently championed by governments of the right (by a string of radical Conservative governments in Britain and Republican administrations in the USA) in order to deal with the "despotism" and "dreariness" of public provision and the state of dependency which it is said to have generated. While governments of the left argued that a generous structure of universal social entitlements was a precondition for the exercise of liberty in a capitalist society and that the economy actually required a citizenship of entitlement for its efficient functioning, governments of the right claimed that this approach destroyed the liberty it was intended to enhance and effectively throttled the market.

Like justice, citizenship appears to have all the characteristics of an essentially contested concept (Gallie 1964). The concept of citizenship can be defined relatively uncontentiously as "a status which bestows equal rights and duties on those who are full members of a community", but this is interpreted in very different ways by those with competing conceptions of what rights and duties it should entail. Thus, a citizenship of entitlement and a citizenship of empowerment can be understood as two competing conceptions of citizenship, each resting on a different set of value assumptions but each coherent, attractive and compelling in its own way. However, according to Ignatieff, the active (duty-based) and the passive (rights-based) conceptions of citizenship are not wholly independent. On the contrary, they are quite closely bound up with one another. Moreover, the failure of politicians on the right as well as the left to realise this had created serious and, at the time when he wrote, unresolved problems.

Governments of the centre, e.g. "New" Labour under Tony Blair in the UK and the second Clinton Administration in the USA, need to recognise both that entitlement is a means to an end rather than an end in itself, and that empowerment requires a basic infrastructure of entitlement for its own realisation. If Ignatieff's argument is correct, it follows that empowerment and entitlement are two facets of citizenship (just as absolute and relative deprivation are two facets of poverty). The same argument applies to rights and duties. In their attempts to redress the balance between rights and responsibilities, Blair and Clinton also need to recognise that a duty-based citizenship for those able to work should not be emphasised at the expense of a rights-based citizenship for those who cannot work and must therefore remain dependent on social security (Plant 1998).

Social justice, citizenship and poverty in the UK

As demonstrated above, social justice has substantive and procedural components, both of which are in jeopardy. Benefit levels have been allowed to fall with the result that there has been a substantial increase in the extent of poverty and inequality in the United Kingdom. The Blair government, acting on proposals put forward by the previous government, has reduced the degree of procedural protection for those dependent on social security and has reversed a series of reforms which, over the last twenty to thirty years, had considerably strengthened their procedural rights. Both these developments diminish the meaning and significance of citizenship for the poor. The reduction in the level of social security benefits has already reduced their social rights, had knock-on effects for civil and political rights and made it considerably harder for them to participate in the life of society as full citizens while the reduction in the level of procedural protection afforded to them reduces their civil rights still further and ensures that they are doubly disadvantaged.

REFERENCES

Adler, Michael (1995), "The Judicial Protection of Social Security in the United Kingdom", *East-West Review of Social Policy* 1 (1): 127–46

—— (1997a), "Welfare Rights, Rules and Discretion: All for One or One for All?" (*Richard Titmuss Memorial Lecture*). Jerusalem: Hebrew University, Paul Baerwald School of Social Work (published simultaneously as *New Waverley Paper SP 12*, Edinburgh: University of Edinburgh, Department of Social Policy)

—— (1997b), "Decision Making And Appeals In Social Security: In Need of Reform?", *Political Quarterly* 68 (4): 388–405

—— and Longhurst, Brian (1994), *Discourse, Power and Justice: Towards a New Sociology of Imprisonment*, London: Routledge

—— and Sainsbury, Roy, eds., (1998a), *Adjudication Matters: Reforming Decision*

Making And Appeals in Social Security (New Waverley Paper SP14), Edinburgh: University of Edinburgh, Department of Social Policy
—— and Sainsbury, Roy (1998b), "Downgrading Decision Making and Appeals", *Benefits*, 22: 26–8
Baldwin, John, Wikeley, Nick and Young, Richard (1992), *Judging Social Security: the Adjudication of Claims for Benefit in Britain*, Oxford: Clarendon Press
Barclay, Peter (Chairman) (1995), *The Joseph Rowntree Foundation Inquiry into Income and Wealth*, Volume 1, York: Joseph Rowntree Foundation
Barr, Nicholas and Coulter, Fiona (1990), "Social Security: Solution or Problem?", In *The State of Welfare*, ed. John Hills, Oxford: Clarendon Press
Barry, Norman (1990), "Markets, Citizenship and the Welfare State: Some Critical Reflections", in *Citizenship and Rights in Thatcher's Britain: Two Views*, ed. Raymond Plant and Norman Barry, London: IEA Health and Welfare Unit
Boyer, Barry (1984), "Review of Mashaw (1983)", *Michigan Law Review* 82: 971–80
Bradley, A.W. (1985), "Recent Reform of Social Security Adjudication in Great Britain", *Les Cahiers du Droit* 26: 403–49
Clark, Tom and Giles, Christopher (1998), "It's the Poor what Gets the Gain", *Guardian*, 25 March, 18
Cranston, Ross (1985), *The Legal Foundations of the Welfare State*, London: Weidenfeld and Nicolson
Dalley, Gillian and Berthoud, Richard (1992), *Challenging Discretion: the Social Fund Review Procedures*, London: Policy Studies Institute
Department of Social Security (1996), *Improving Decision Making and Appeals in Social Security* (Cm. 3328), London: HMSO
Drabble, Richard and Lynes, Tony (1989), "The Social Fund: Discretion or Control?" *Public Law*: 297–322
Gallie, W.B. (1964), "Essentially Contested Concepts", in *Philosophy and Historical Understanding*, London: Chatto and Windus
Galligan, D.J. (1986), "Rights, Discretion and Procedures", in *Law, Rights and the Welfare State*, ed. C.J.G. Sampford and D.J. Galligan, London: Croom Helm
—— (1996), *Due Process and Fair Procedures*, Oxford: Clarendon Press
Hayek, F.A. (1982), *Law, Legislation and Liberty*, volume 2: *The Mirage of Social Justice*, London: Routledge and Kegan Paul
Hills, John (1995) *The Joseph Rowntree Foundation Inquiry into Income and Wealth*: Volume 2, York: Joseph Rowntree Foundation
—— (1998), *Income and Wealth: the Latest Evidence*, York: Joseph Rowntree Foundation
Honoré, A.M. (1970), "Social Justice", in *Essays in Legal Philosophy*, ed. R.S. Summers, Oxford: Basil Blackwell
Lipsky, Michael (1980), *Street Level Bureaucracy*, New York: Russell Sage
—— (1991), "The Paradox of Managing Discretionary Workers in Social Welfare Policy", in *The Sociology of Social Security*, ed. Michael Adler, Colin Bell, Jochen Clasen and Adrian Sinfield, Edinburgh: Edinburgh University Press
Maranville, Deborah (1984), "Review of Mashaw (1983)", *Minnesota Law Review* 69: 325–47
Marshall, T.H. (1963), "Sociology at the Crossroads", in *Citizenship and Social Class*, London: Heinemann
Mashaw, Jerry L. (1983), *Bureaucratic Justice: Managing Social Security Disability Claims*, New Haven and London: Yale University Press

Miller, David (1976), *Social Justice*, Oxford: Clarendon Press
Oppenheim, Carey and Harker, Lisa (1996), *Poverty: the Facts* (Poverty Publication 93), 3rd ed., London: Child Poverty Action Group
Plant, Raymond (1990) "Citizenship and Rights", in *Citizenship and Rights in Thatcher's Britain: Two Views* (Choice in Welfare Series No. 3), ed. Raymond Plant and Norman Barry, London, IEA Health and Welfare Unit
—— (1998), "So You Want to be a Citizen?", *New Statesman*, 6 February, 30–2
Prosser, Tony (1981), "The Politics of Discretion: Aspects of Discretionary Powers in the Supplementary Benefits System", in *Discretion and Welfare*, ed. Michael Adler and Stewart Asquith, London: Heinemann
Rawls, John (1972), *A Theory of Justice*, Oxford: Clarendon Press
Reich, Charles (1964), "The New Property", *Yale Law Journal* 73: 733–87
—— (1965), "Individual Rights and Social Welfare: the Emerging Legal Issues", *Yale Law Journal* 74: 1245–57
Sainsbury, Roy (1989), "The Social Security Chief Adjudication Officer: the First Four Years", *Public Law*, Summer: 323–41
—— (1992), "Administrative Justice: Discretion and Procedure in Social Security Decision-Making", in *The Uses of Discretion*, ed. Keith Hawkins, Oxford: Clarendon Press
—— (1994), "Internal Reviews and the Weakening of Social Security Claimants' Rights of Appeal", in *Administrative Law and Government Action*, ed. Hazel Genn and Genevra Richardson, Oxford: Oxford University Press
—— (1997), *Consultation on "Improving Decision Making and Appeals in Social Security": Analysis of Responses*, London: Department of Social Security
Sebatier, Paul (1986), "'Top-down' and 'Bottom-up' Approaches to Implementation Research", *Journal of Public Policy*, 6: 21–48, reprinted in *The Policy Process: a Reader*, ed. Michael Hill, Hemel Hempstead: Harvester Wheatsheaf
Sen, A.K. (1983), "Poor Relatively Speaking", *Oxford Economic Papers*, 35: 153–69
Titmuss, Richard M. (1970), "Equity, Adequacy and Innovation in Social Security", *International Social Security Review*, 23 (2): 259–68
Walsh, Matthew (1992), "The Concept of 'Quality' as a Possible Means of Evaluating the Social Security System" (unpublished Ph.D. proposal), Edinburgh: University of Edinburgh, Department of Social Policy
Wikeley, Nick (1994), "Social Security Appeals in Britain", *Administrative Law Quarterly*, 46 (2): 183–212

Overviews

8

The Rule of Law and Poverty Reduction: Some Issues[1]

HÉLÈNE GRANDVOINNET

SUMMARY

IN WHAT WAYS do legal systems affect the poor? Can they contribute to the alleviation of poverty? Legal rules may overtly discriminate against some categories of people. This discrimination may either worsen poverty or aim to alleviate poverty (positive discrimination). The rule of law in general is often unknown to the poor, who are forced to live outside the protection or opportunities permitted by the law for reasons related to their poverty as well as those pertaining to the legal system itself. A fair legal framework which includes the whole society, even its vulnerable members, is a feature of good governance.

INTRODUCTION

The rule of law is a crucial aspect of good governance. According to North (1990), formal rules and the way they are enforced define, together with informal constraints, the incentive structure of societies, and specifically economies. The power of enacting and enforcing formal rules is a major privilege of governments, and is therefore closely linked with a good governance process.[2]

Studying the links between the rule of law and the reduction of poverty means studying in which ways legal systems and their operation affect situations of poverty. By enacting and implementing rules, governments may either increase the overall participation of the whole population, and therefore of the poor, or hinder it. The legal obstacles to reducing poverty may be more or less direct. A legal decision, either positive or negative, is the consequence of a political decision and has a direct effect targeted on certain groups. In the first section of this

[1] This chapter was prepared in the context of the OECD's Development Centre's research programme on "Good Governance and Poverty Alleviation". The Development Centre does not necessarily share the views expressed in this chapter.

[2] Governance means the use of political authority and exercise of control in a society in relation to the management of its resources for social and economic development.

chapter, we assess its effect on poverty. In the second section, we study the ways in which the rule of law in general may hinder or enable the poor to take advantage of economic opportunities, by allowing them access to the legal system and the protection it affords.

DIRECT LEGAL DISCRIMINATION AND POVERTY

Direct legal discrimination may be negative or positive: it may discriminate against people in some areas, or it may be part of a policy intended to promote more effective equality. It involves using legal instruments deliberately to change the socio-economic circumstances (positive discrimination).

We first consider how direct negative discrimination increases or creates poverty, before studying how some "positive discrimination" intended to benefit the poor aims to alleviate poverty, with mixed results.

Direct discrimination which creates or increases poverty

Direct discrimination involves open and targeted discrimination against some categories of people. Certain rules increase poverty, by explicitly preventing people suffering poverty from involvement in some activities. Other rules discriminate against all those with a particular characteristic or origin, thus creating or reinforcing poverty: this is often the case with ethnic minorities, and even more frequently with women.

Discrimination based on economic factors

Such direct discrimination may be based on economic factors: for instance on the value of assets. Some rules are "specifically biased against the smallholders who are, more often than not, the poor" (World Bank, 1996). For instance, in Malawi smallholders have not been allowed to grow burley tobacco for many years, which has had an adverse effect on their levels of income.[3]

Discrimination may be less obvious: for instance, rules restricting rural– urban migration. This usually involves an attempt by the poor to find a decent income in town. Restricting migration affects particularly the poor. The Rwandan government implemented this kind of control, resulting in an increasing demand on the already degraded land; and landless people were particularly affected.[4]

[3] According to Tony Killick (1995: 319) Malawi is an example of "a country in which the government showed little concern with the interests of the 55 per cent of the population living in absolute poverty, with policies and institutions systematically discriminating against poor smallholders in favour of the owners of large estates".

[4] These restrictions are considered to be one of the factors which led to the civil conflict in 1994, cf. Andre, C., J.P. Platteau (1996), *Land Tenure Under Unendurable Stress: Rwanda Caught in the Malthusian Trap*, Cahiers de la Faculté des Sciences Economiques et Sociales No.164, Namur, January.

Ethnic discrimination

However, direct discrimination is most commonly linked with an inherent characteristic of the persons discriminated against. Hence, ethnic minorities suffer from legal discrimination which limits their rights in the economic or political arenas.[5] Such stigmatisation occurs when a particular ethnic group (e.g. characterised by a different religion, a different language, different customs) is defined in opposition to a more powerful or more numerous group, at least politically. The process is likely to increase or create poverty in the ethnic group relative to the majority group.[6] Groups discriminated against tend to lack rights to exercise control over their own economic, social and cultural development. Their resources may be exploited for the benefit of other groups in society. They may be excluded from public sector employment. They may be subject to arbitrary expropriation. Consequently, their capacity for economic development is hindered, and sometimes prevented.

Discrimination against women

The main and most dramatic example of direct legal discrimination is the existing legal discrimination against women. It is particularly damaging because it currently operates in many societies and potentially involves one human being out of two. In global terms, of 1.3 billion people in poverty in 1995, 70 per cent were women (UNDP, 1995). This situation is not due solely to legal discrimination, but to a whole range of factors involving discrimination against women in different spheres of activity. Discrimination may be social or economic and is often deeply embedded in the culture through religion or custom. However, discrimination may also be part of the law: discriminatory laws often mirror especially strong social stigmatisation of women. This is of particular concern since such legal discrimination is both blatant and broadly criticised in international forums.

The concept of "heads of household" who are assumed to be men is the commonly and widely stated basis for differential treatment both within households and, by extension in society large. Many aspects of discrimination are built upon this notion. Husbands are supposed to be the breadwinners and the persons responsible for the well-being of the whole family; therefore they own the assets and are granted, socially as well as legally, decision-making power within the family. Consequently, the estimated one-third of the world's households which are headed by women—widows, wives whose husbands have migrated to find a job, refugees—are particularly vulnerable to poverty. Given the limited access to jobs or credit for women, such households often fall below the poverty

[5] The Kurds in Iran, Iraq and Turkey, the Oromo and Somalis in Ethiopia, the Southern Sudanese, among others, suffered economic and legal discrimination in the 1980s.

[6] In some cases the group discriminated against is numerically more important than the other group(s), but is weaker e.g. because of economic backwardness, or lack of political representation.

line. This threat is of course always present. In the case of the death or departure of the husband, or after a divorce, women have no fallback position and are left alone to contribute to the well-being of their families, and their restricted legal capacity often does not allow them to meet the basic needs of their dependants.

Property rights

Women are disadvantaged by the law in several crucial areas of their economic life, the most significant, according to Agarwal (1994), being their access to property.

> "The gender gap in the ownership and control of property is the single most critical contributor to the gender gap in economic well-being, social status and empowerment" (ibid., 1455).

In some circumstances equality of rights, even over property, does exist. When ownership is not legally but traditionally forbidden, however, the social reality and lack of awareness of their property rights often prevent women from claiming their due. Property laws often limit women's inheritance rights and prohibit married women from holding property in their own names. For instance, in the Koran the inheritance shares of female heirs are half those allotted to males, and the precepts of the Koran are the basis for family law in most countries of which Islam is the state religion. Hence, in almost every Muslim country, the legal position of the wife is inferior to that of the husband, and in many cases is precarious.

Legal obstacles to female ownership are particularly strong in the case of land ownership, given the symbolic value of such property. In rural areas married women are often only granted the right to use land during their lifetime, by virtue of their position as wives in their husband's clan or social group. In the case of land reform, even in countries where progressive gender legislation was enacted in the 1950s asserting women's independent rights to land, gender biases still occur. Property is frequently registered in the name of male household members. Thus, even when women are legally entitled to land, customary rights and practices generally lead to the control of their land by male relatives.

Ownership may also be accompanied by legal restrictions on disposal. For instance, among the Jaffna Tamils in Sri Lanka, under the *Thesawalami* legal code a married woman needs her husband's consent to dispose of land which she legally owns:

> "The full advantages of land ownership cannot be derived by women if they continue to be excluded from managerial control and jural authority" (Agarwal, 1994: 1466).

As for rights to manage property, married women are under the permanent guardianship of their husband and have no right to manage property in several countries, including Botswana, Chile, Lesotho, Namibia, and Swaziland (Le Courrier Acp-Ue, 1995: 57). Formal banking procedures or regulations often require a husband or other male relative to act as cosignatory if a woman applies for a loan. Regulations restricting credit to one single loan per household, although less discriminatory in theory, are often highly detrimental to women, given the assumption, that the "head of the household" is the husband.

Discrimination in economic activities

Many rules or regulations prevent women from participating fully in economic activities by stigmatising their presence in many sectors. For instance, in the commercial dairy sector in India, the National Dairy Development Board has created a nation-wide grid of village co-operatives in charge of collecting and testing the milk, but in many areas women are not granted membership of these co-operatives (Chen, 1989). Other rules discriminate against women in a more indirect way: for instance, where zoning legislation prevents the selling or making of goods from the home, and particularly in countries where their freedom of movement is socially restricted, women have no possibility of earning an income other than illegally (Moser, 1989).

The labour market may also legally discriminate against women. This discrimination may be particularly damaging in some areas. In the Indian context the negative association between female labour force participation and excess female mortality operates, even when allowing for regional variables (Kabeer, 1996). A husbands can restrict his wife's employment outside the home in Bolivia, Guatemala and Syria (Le Courrier Acp-Ue, 1995). Discrimination in access to jobs also exists but is usually not the consequence of a legal provision. Husbands or employers prevent women from obtaining waged labour for women, or confine them to circumscribed areas: for example, in rural Tanzania men forbid their wives from taking any waged labour (Kabeer, 1996). In addition, there may be a wide difference between the right to work and the control over one's work and its income. As Sen pointed out, not only laws but also deep-seated notions of "legitimacy" (however specious) and formal restrictions operate in intrahousehold relationships (1990).

As regards wage discrimination,[7] this tends also to be indirect, and to relate to differences in jobs and qualifications. However:

> "if legislation or public opinion exerts pressure to eliminate traditional wage differentials by sex, the employer is most likely to react by making all operations sex-specific and continue to pay lower wages to women" (Tinker, 1990: 22).

Discrepancies between legal provisions and their implementation

Legal gender discrimination is still a reality in various areas of life and in many countries. Legal discrimination contributes to the unequal situation of the woman, and must be eradicated as a first step towards equality of rights between

[7] On average, women throughout the world receive 30 to 40 per cent less pay than men for work of comparable value, whether payment is in cash or kind, in benefits or food (United Nations, 1995: 16).

women and men. There are, however, numerous countries whose customary or domestic laws do not accord with the constitution or the international treaties signed by the state, which often proclaim equality between men and women. For instance, the Pakistani Constitution of 1973 guarantees women fundamental rights and protections, but discrimination of every kind is the common lot of many Pakistani women. In general:

> "legislation providing for equality of rights is only as forceful as the legal institutions of the state make it, and very often those institutions themselves are imbued with traditional values and received wisdom about the respective role of men and women" (McLean and Burrows, 1988).

Formal rules are not self-enforcing, and to be enforced they require a credible commitment toward their implementation from the state. Otherwise, an important discrepancy between *de jure* and *de facto* legal changes is very likely to occur:

> "Property rights, arranged marriages, dowry and child custody rights provide much-cited examples of the highly sensitive strategic gender needs which are often still curtailed by custom, even when amended by law" (Moser, 1989: 1811).

Gender-sensitive legislation is an essential element for the elimination of discrimination. However, the existence of such legislation does not automatically improve women's condition. Even when there is strong political will on the part of the state, social opposition often slows down or even prevents equality from being implemented.

> "It is the admixture of formal rules, informal norms, and enforcement characteristics that shapes economic performance. While the rules may be changed overnight, the informal norms usually change only gradually" (North, 1994: 366).

There is often strong opposition from men where equal rights for women are alien to the dominant cultural values. An improvement in the condition of women is also a threat to men's own power and social position. As regards women's reactions, their low status is deeply integrated in the culture of some societies, and therefore imbues their education. Accordingly, they may not want to change their situation, as this appears to them to be normal and the only one socially recognised. They may be resigned to their lot, or even promote the discrimination which affects their status and well-being, and often transmit that acceptance to their daughters. Even individuals, be they men or women, who perceive the positive aspect of non-discriminatory legislation may be prevented from living by it for fear of social ostracism. As Pankhurstobserved:

> "proposals to outlaw all discriminatory practices against women have enormous symbolic value, but such change has proved extremely difficult to implement where it has been attempted in Africa" (1995: 560).

The fact that such non-discriminatory legislation exists may none the less gradually lessen such fears and slowly change the relative male–female positions. For instance, the Tunisian legal code guarantees equality in inheritance, access to education and the right to work. It recognises women's right to administer property independently of their husbands. All of this has contributed to the advance toward gender equality in this country (UNDP, 1995). In any case, and even if it takes time to change social values, legal provisions are a basis from which women's groups may organise and build decisive action:

> "The 'basic rights' of the poor and the transformation of the institutions that subordinate women are inextricably linked. They can be achieved together through the self-empowerment of women" (Dawn, 1985, 73).

To conclude, it is essential to stress the importance of the removal of direct legal discrimination, without neglecting the fact that it can take many years, and perhaps generations, for practice to catch up with the revised law.

Problems linked with positive discrimination

"The law is the most useful and deliberate instrument of change available to people" (De Soto, 1989: 187). Policies of positive discrimination[8] meet this definition. They entail legal provisions, often including compulsory measures, to promote the interests of specific groups which are being or have been discriminated against in society and are therefore particularly vulnerable. Positive discrimination is specifically aimed at poverty alleviation where there is a relationship between a defined group and poverty (for instance in India with the lower castes[9]). Even if positive discrimination has a broader goal, it is generally closely linked with poverty reduction (for instance, positive discrimination towards equal opportunities for women or ethnic minorities). Making such legal policies voluntary is thought to be more effective than the simple non-discrimination principle, which is likely to remain a pious aspiration. Positive discrimination may entail quotas for jobs in the civil service, admission to higher education, preferential treatment for business contracts and permits, and so on. (See Bardhan, 1997.)

The intrinsic fairness of positive discrimination has been much debated. Our purpose is not to enter into this discussion, but to determine whether such policies have had satisfactory results as regards overall poverty reduction.

An example: India

Indian policy is particularly relevant in this context, since there is an almost perfect connection between poverty and untouchability. Untouchability has been linked with poverty for centuries, while these "scheduled castes" have

[8] Also called "positive action", "affirmative action", or "reverse discrimination".
[9] Which does not mean that poverty is absent from other castes in Indian society.

suffered handicaps and disabilities imposed by other economically and culturally dominant groups. The "scheduled" and other "backward castes" form the majority of the poor population. In order to change this situation, the Indian Constitution states, in Article 17 of Part III, that "untouchability is abolished and its practices in any form forbidden". However, it was clear that to abolish untouchability on paper would not suffice to change such a deeply rooted system. In accordance with the Constitution, therefore, affirmative action was implemented, which has resulted in the

> "reservation of specific proportions of membership in legislatures, public sector jobs and higher education for these groups, as well as development programmes and assistance meant specifically for their benefit" (Rodgers *et al.*, 1995: 239).

However, despite more than fifty years of affirmative action, progress has been slow. Rodgers points out that:

> "there are indications that, while the process of growth along with state intervention (especially affirmative action) has widened the access of disadvantaged groups to assets, public sector jobs and higher education, [but] the extent of disparities between these and the rest of the community remains unacceptably large" (ibid., 240).

Considering the force of social constraints involved in the caste system in India, we should be wary of drawing negative conclusions about the consequences of affirmative action.

Elements of positive discrimination policies

The presence of negative side-effects however reinforces this impression. According to Bardhan (1997) affirmative action is sometimes conceived as a "low-cost" strategy. In the long term, however, it may be very costly:

> "Job quotas for minorities may splinter the labour market, distort the allocation of labour between covert and other sectors, and seriously impede efficiency and morale".

Furthermore, affirmative action may in fact benefit the politically well connected. This kind of policy also creates tensions between the "favoured" people and the others, who are deprived of opportunities that should have been open to them. Finally, "preferential policies, once adopted, are extremely difficult to reverse" (Bardhan, 1997). They may even be extended. In India, "though not mandatory, the scope of positive discrimination in public jobs and education has been extended to cover the 'Other Backward Castes'" (Rodgers *et al.*, 1995: 239).

According to Tom Mullen:

> "the importance of the goal of affirmative action—fair equality of opportunity [. . .]—might permit some loss of social utility. It is also possible to argue that any losses in terms of efficiency may be offset by the gains to society as a whole which affirmative action could achieve" (1988: 254).

This argument[10] has some value. For instance, in Bangladesh 60 per cent of the vacant posts for primary school teachers are reserved for women, thus permitting female schooling (UNDP, 1995). The essential question, however, is whether the goal of affirmative action might not have been achieved by other policies, and with less tensions? For instance:

> "a policy of subsidising workers directly for achieving employment success can generally achieve the elimination of prejudicial views about minorities without the negative side-effects possible under affirmative action" (Coate and Loury, 1993: 1239).

It is thus essential to determine which are the priorities, to try to devise some alternative policies to affirmative action policies, and if such policies are to be implemented, to be conscious of the related costs involved.

Even if affirmative action is useful in a limited form, it is difficult to envisage it as a generally applicable instrument for poverty reduction, considering its results and the adverse side-effects linked with its implementation. The most neutral way of acting on poverty by legal measures seems to involve the legal system operating in a way that does not exclude any citizen, and especially not the poor. Instead of creating barriers within the country, legal systems should ensure the full participation of all the population. The vulnerability of the poor means that we must always keep in mind their particular situation, in order to increase their access to the legal system and the protection it offers. This can be achieved by changing the structures creating *de facto* discrimination.

INDIRECT DISCRIMINATION DUE TO THE IMPERFECTIONS OF LEGAL SYSTEMS

As well as direct discrimination, the operation of legal systems may create indirect discrimination: the exclusion of the poor, particularly the most vulnerable, from the potential benefits of the legal system. This indirect discrimination entails two elements. Access to the law may be impeded or prevented for the poor. And the poor may be exclused from the legally regulated system, i.e. from the benefits of legal protection.

Factors limiting access to the law by the poor

Access to legal information and to the court system is necessary for the reduction of poverty, in that its absence diminishes the poor's vulnerability to exploitation or deception. Such access may enable them to take advantage of economic opportunities. However, access to the law is generally restricted to the educated, and usually urban sectors of the population. The poor tend to be unable to make use of the law, due both to their own poverty and to aspects of

[10] Advanced by Mullen (1988) in respect of affirmative action for women, but in our view it may also be extended to other underprivileged groups.

the legal system. On the whole, these difficulties are linked with an imperfectly functioning legal system, which particularly affects the poor.

Factors related to the main features of poverty

Illiteracy

Contemporary legal systems, as opposed to traditional or customary legal systems, are written systems. Therefore their access is intrinsically difficult for the poor who are likely have a low level of literacy. The poor, unable to read legal provisions, have no knowledge of their rights. When they do acquire some knowledge of them, this is usually indirect and imperfect. They may be insufficiently or wrongly informed, or even deceived, whether deliberately or not.

The poor are particularly disadvantaged in court proceedings. Legal procedures often require literacy. In Latin America trials are conducted almost exclusively on the basis of written documents (Blair and Hansen, 1994). In addition a good knowledge of the specific legal provisions relating to the claim is crucial. The poor often lack both. They may even lack sufficient knowledge for seeking the resolution of disputes or redress for grievances when their rights have been violated.

Another aspect of this problem concerns the language used within the legal system. In countries with many languages, language barriers are a real obstacle. Legal texts are not translated into the local languages, often those spoken by the poor, and official language is used in court cases, thus effectively excluding the poor.

Low income

Lack of money has consequences for access by the poor to the legal system in terms of both direct cost and in the cost of information.

As regards the direct costs of access to the legal system, these deter the poor from taking legal action for obvious reasons. The direct costs of court procedure include both process fees and lawyers' bills. There are additional costs, for example travel to a distant court, or the payment of bribes as a necessary precondition for advancing the proceedings.

Indirect costs also add to the difficulty experienced by the poor in securing access to the legal system. Obtaining information costs money which poor people can rarely afford. Yet access to legal information is a primary problem to be solved: it is a precondition for empowering the poor while creating or increasing their self-reliance. The search for information, however, requires time and money, particularly for a person unfamiliar with the legal system. A lay person undertaking such research is unable to earn their livelihood. The opportunity costs of searching for information may thus be unaffordable, especially considering the aleatory benefits. This creates a situation which disadvantages the poor in comparison with wealthier people. Furthermore, an imbalance of information may be caused by other reasons, for example information may be deliberately retained by some interest groups.

Marginalisation

The poor are marginalized in society. Their general lack of resources weakens them in every respect. They consequently lack power, as well as valuable connections.

The poor are disempowered, and thus unable to challenge "the system". Poverty hinders people from organising themselves to defend common interests. The poor therefore have little or no influence upon the institutional setting which governs their lives, and the existence of laws which theoretically protect them is no guarantee that they will actually enjoy such protection. The poor often lack the means or knowledge to assert their rights. In societies in which personal connections to the upper strata are essential to achieve a successful political, social and economic life, lack of connections considerably reduces the chances of being helped through legal means. There is thus differential access to courts for different legal claimants. In practice this adversely affects the poor. As regards women, who typically lack education and financial resources, social factors may further deter the pursuit of their legal rights in court. In certain societies women's relationships outside the home, and with other social institutions whose members are almost exclusively masculine, are restricted. Hence women's rights are denied. Female seclusion prevents women from asserting their rights.

Disempowered, and sometimes already victims of the legal system, the poor may distrust the legal system as a whole, viewing it as unfair or illegitimate. As a result of such marginalisation the legal system often has no credibility for the poor, and can actually contribute to their further marginalization. For example, lack of power may prevent the poor from bringing their cases to justice. In order to claim their rights, the poor must be sure that their case is not hopeless, otherwise they will not risk a claim. They may be afraid of losing the case, or fear physical reprisals. Going to court may jeopardise an already precarious livelihood, especially given the fact that the poorest have learnt that in seeking their due in a given matter it is often preferable not to be in the wrong in some other respect (Council of Europe, 1992). Lack of power entails lack of choice.

These characteristics are all part of the experience of poverty. However, governments can promote good governance to remedy some of the difficulties experienced by the poor, either directly or through co-operation with non-governmental organisations.

Factors related to the characteristics of the legal system

The legal labyrinth

The complexity and proliferation of laws have a particularly dramatic effect upon access to the legal system. According to Mario Vargas Llosa, Peruvians "live in a legal labyrinth in which even a Daedalus would get lost" (De Soto, 1988, xviii). What is true for Peru applies to many developing countries. The rules are often unclear, intrinsically complex and particularly numerous.

Furthermore, legal provisions are not systematically published, and when published they are not always in terms understandable to all citizens. Legal inconsistencies puzzle even the average citizen, and particularly the poor.

The ineffectiveness and arbitrariness of a legal system create a further deterrent influencing access to the legal system.

The ineffectiveness of a legal system may stem from the unpredictability of its rules, their instability, or discrepancies between enacted and implemented laws. To those who lack money and connections, the enforcement of law is as important as its enactment (Swedish International Development Authority, 1996: 61). If governments are satisfied with the mere appearance of action which legislation provides, discrepancies between the enactment of laws and their implementation will continue to frustrate the poor. The existence of "paper laws", including basic rights written into the constitution but not implemented by legislation,[11] is a real problem over which the poor have no influence, lacking the means to tackle this issue.

An example of gaps between a rule and its application: freedom of association

The principle of freedom of association is now recognised world-wide, even if legal obstacles remain which deprive rural workers of this right in some countries (see Egger, 1995). The main problem is the application of the rule. A variety of legal measures is used to deter people from organising themselves, without disputing the principle: "laws requiring licensing of associations and public meetings, or prohibition against 'seditious activities' and 'threats to public order' "(Dembo *et al.*, 1986, 245).

The practical aspects are the most difficult to deal with, especially for the poorest: illiteracy, registration costs, lack of information and training, little spare time for trade-union activities, geographical isolation, and labour mobility. To these must be added political violence, and the fact that organising work is deterred by the relationships of dependence between the poor and local traders, landlords and people of influence. Legal provisions protecting freedom of association do not change the power relations within a society. Furthermore, the situation of the poor is all the more difficult as they usually have casual jobs, sometimes seasonal, almost always for a short period, and migrate from one place to another to find work. It is particularly difficult to unite people in the rural, small-scale and informal sectors. When workers from the informal sector do organise themselves, they encounter difficulties in matching the official trade-union criteria: for instance, it took ten months and a lot of endeavour to register the Self-Employed Women's Association (SEWA) in India,[12] because

[11] While the Indian Constitution calls for compulsory elementary education, the state has not taken any legislative action to make elementary schooling compulsory. In the absence of legal compulsion, economic disincentives for children's schooling (which also involves substantial private expenditure) appear formidable to poor parents in perpetual need for extra income (Rodgers, 1995: 242).

[12] SEWA was registered in 1972.

the Registrar considered that "work" presumes a specific and formal employer–employee relationship (Bhatt, 1989: 1062).

Legal provisions protecting freedom of association benefit only a part of the working population.

The judiciary

There may be inadequate resources for the judicial system in many countries, preventing the courts from fulfilling their proper role. Undertrained court staffs inadequate facilities and budgets,[13] and congestion can prevent courts from settling disputes fairly and speedily. This has further negative consequences for the vulnerable poor.

This situation also has other consequences, in particular on the partiality of the judicial system. Economic deprivation breeds corruption among staff, who favour those financially better off or enjoying political connections; arbitrariness in the enforcement of judiciary decisions tends to benefit the same privileged groups. As stated by Blair and Hansen:

> "these problems are largely an outgrowth of governmental structures and political environment that relegate the judicial system to a minor and deliberately underfunded appendage of the executive or legislative branch of government, thus keeping the courts from making their rightful contribution to good governance" (1994: 6).

The legislature

Arbitrariness also occurs in relation to the legislature, being that part of government which creates most of the rules. Lacking political or organisational power, the poor cannot lobby for their interests. They are thus bound to suffer from rules enacted, not in the general interest, but to promote particular interests.

> "Institutions are not necessarily or even usually created to be socially efficient; rather they, or at least the formal rules, are created to serve the interests of those with the bargaining power to create new rules" (North, 1994: 361).

All these factors prevent the poor from knowing and using the law, and from asserting their rights in court or in society in general. The poor are therefore vulnerable from the start, but the specific requirements of a regulated society add to this vulnerability by restricting their integration in to formal society.

Consequences: Limitation of the benefits and protection of the law

Rules may present the poor from improving their condition. They also may prevent them from benefiting from the protection associated with the law, by confining them in an outlawed environment, due to the lack of funds needed to enter

[13] For instance, in Zimbabwe there is a lack of trained staff, office space and legal texts, and even of typewriters and other office requisites (Gothe, D.R. (1997), "Helping the Poor to Obtain Their Rights", *Development and Cooperation (D+C)*, no. 1, January–February, DSE.)

and remain in formal society. This has various consequences, including lack of protection in the labour market, and disadvantages linked with the absence of secured property rights. (The latter aspect is dealt with below in relation with land reform, as an example of the potentially adverse effects of measures aiming at reducing inequality.

The costs of formality and its consequences

There are direct costs imposed by the law, such as taxes and payments required to comply with bureaucratic procedures. They may discriminate against people according to income. According to De Soto, this kind of discrimination occurs in many sectors:

> "government regulations of varying nature and importance [. . .] give rise to a number of costs which discriminate against people according to income, ensuring that those who are financially better off enjoy the benefits of legal protection more readily, and that those who are poor are forced to engage in (. . .) activities such as building, trade, industry or transport without the protection of the law" (1989: 146).

The costs of formality hinder the poor from entering into the formal economy, while encouraging them to act outside the legal system.

Many children and adults living in poverty are discriminated against from birth. There are obstacles to the civil registration of births. This may be because parents do not know the procedure, or because they do not meet official requirements, as for instance the proof of a legal domicile. This has the effect of depriving them of legal existence and therefore of rights or protection.

> "The fact of not being registered makes it extremely difficult to obtain the papers necessary to prove parentage, to marry, to exercise political rights, to be able to travel freely within and outside national frontiers, to stand surety before the courts, to obtain employment, to benefit from social services, to avoid being imprisoned, etc." (Commission on Human Rights, 1996: 32).

More generally, pricing and licensing policies neglect labour-intensive, small-scale informal activities, because the resources required to take advantage of these policies put the opportunities beyond the reach of producers in the sector (Berger, 1989: 1027).

On the whole, these costs are a consequence of a bureaucratic system ignoring the particular situation of the poor. This also has consequences for the working conditions of the poor, and on their access to ownership, two areas of particular concern for the poor. The labour market is important because the capacity to work is often the only thing possessed by the poor. Access to secured ownership is significant because it gives them a fallback position and is a way of getting out of poverty.

Absence of labour standards for the poor

Labour regulations are of particular importance for the poor. The importance of protecting measures such as age limit and minimum wages has been stressed. The absence of minimum age limits is especially damaging to the poor, since the poorest families have to use their children's labour to survive. If children enter the labour market their future is likely to be prejudiced as they are more likely to suffer from physical weakness and are prevented from acquiring education. Thus poverty perpetuates itself. However, in this area as in many others, even the existence of protective legislation does not prevent this occurring. One out of eight children between the ages of ten and fourteen works, whereas almost all national governments have signed the Convention on the Rights of Children, recognising that children must be protected from economic exploitation and not deprived of their chances of education.

However, age limits and minimum wage regulations are unlikely to reach all the poor. As stated by Lipton:

> "nor are the poor of Asia or Africa much helped by nineeenth-century European styles of labour law reforms -limits on the working week, conditions of work, dismissals and so on—in a context where demand for labour grows more slowly than supply, and where the laws are either used mainly to protect a small, privileged urban labour aristocracy against competition by the poor, or not enforceable at all because the labour's market position is so weak" (1995: 9).

Similarly, Rodgers wrote:

> "Labour market regulation is unlikely to be a primary instrument in reducing poverty, for it is liable to be ineffective in the situations where poverty is most extreme" (1995: 52).

Many of the poorest are employed in the casual labour sector, and are therefore deprived of the benefits of existing labour laws and labour standards. For example, between 70 and 90 per cent of women in developing countries work in businesses that are unregistered and largely unregulated, and under conditions that frequently threaten their health (United Nations, 1995).

There are two interrelated problems with legislation: its enactment, and its implementation. Either there is no law to refer to, or the problems caused by unregulated activities occur where, theoretically, formal protective rules apply. It would be unrealistic to try to apply immediately to the casual sector all existing labour legislation. "However, if action in the informal sector is to contribute to reduce poverty, it is essential to ensure that at least minimum levels of income and protection be attained" (Rodgers, 1995).

Similarly, where social security schemes exist, they are inaccessible to many of the poor who do not belong to the formal society. Therefore, the poor do not belong to any institutionalised system of insurance against risks. The poor are the most likely to lack fallback positions or to lack support from friends or relatives, and this perpetuates poverty.

Problems associated with property rights and land reform

Daily insecurity is one of the worst problems experienced by the poor. The security of rights to property is therefore of the utmost importance for them. The absence of secure and enforceable property rights, due either to the complexity and cost of the formalities required to gain exclusive entitlement to property, or to the non-existence of formal property rights, has three main disadvantages. 1) It is a disincentive to invest, thus lowering potential productivity; 2) it is a hindrance to the use of the property, which cannot be easily transferred or used as collateral; and 3) it forces *de facto* owners to defend their property without legal protection, and creates a climate of insecurity. This kind of situation typically affects the poor who live in informal settlements or cultivate land without any legal title.[14] Furthermore, there may be numerous problems associated with the lack of a legal residence: without a residence certificate, for example, a child may be prevented from going to public school (Commission on Human Rights, 1996).

It is important to stress the problems associated with legal measures aimed at increasing access by the poor to secure ownership. In this connection, land reform is particularly relevant, especially considering the number of poor people affected by such policies. Land reform is generally thought to be a measure in favour of the poor, whose effects will change the distribution of assets in favour of the poorest. However, it is important to note the difficulties, from a legal point of view, in the design and implementation of such reforms, and their potentially adverse effects.

It is estimated that approximately 80 per cent of the poor live in rural areas (Swedish International Development Authority, 1996). Land reform is therefore particularly relevant to the many who depend on land for their home and livelihood. A negative relationship between absolute poverty and access to land (owned or operated) is noted in several studies (Agarwal, 1994). The role of land as a social asset enabling people to acquire some economic and political power is of particular importance in the process of empowerment of the poor. It is important to note, however, that economically, the distribution of assets is necessarily only a first step. It is insufficient unless accompanied by skills training, investment and appropriate pricing policies (Lieten, 1996). Land reform may entail redistribution, the regulation of tenancy contracts, and land titles. Land reforms tend to individualise property rights, and therefore to allow holders to use their assets without the economic or social constraints linked to the insecurity of tenure and tenancy relationships, and to increase their income and standard of living. Individualising land titles, thus securing ownership rights, should allow better access to credit, improvement of the land through incentive and capacity to invest and an increase of such investment, leading to higher produc-

[14] For instance, available statistics for Peru show that 37 per cent of the peasantry had no legal title to their land in 1984, and 43 per cent of people living in shanty towns had no legal title on their urban plots in 1991 (Rodgers, 1995: 20).

tivity. It should reduce "the oligopsonistic influence of large landholders in rural labour markets, resulting in lower wages and employment" (Gaiha, 1995: 299). The legal role of the state in relation to access to land is therefore crucial. Useful changes may occur through carefully managed legal rules.

Some land reforms aim at promoting the commercial farm sector, ignoring the particular needs of the poorest. However, some reforms whose aim was redistributive or whose main purpose was to increase small tenants' security have failed, at least partially, to do so. Rules which should theoretically alleviate poverty, once enforced, may have adverse effects, leading to even more extreme poverty. This does not mean that land reform (for instance in Brazil, where 1 per cent of the landholders were estimated to own 44 per cent of the land in 1991) is antagonistic to the poor. It only means that rules which should theoretically help people to escape poverty may entail biases against the poor or some of the poor, or may be implemented in a context where powerful interests take advantage of them in their own favour or prevent them from operating efficiently.

Biases may occur which principally concern the redistribution of land and land registration processes.

The redistribution of land

The redistribution of large private properties (often in the case of major social and political upheaval), or of state-owned or communal land is intended to provide a broad range of people with the advantages of individual ownership. However, this purpose may be subverted from the beginning if the enabling provisions do not take into all relevant factors, or if there is no consideration of the social significance of some of these regulations. Two main types of problem can occur. First, if previously landless people are merely provided with permits to use the land, while ownership of the resettled land is retained by state, this severely restricts the benefits of the distribution. This has been the case in Bolivia and Zimbabwe. Secondly, there may be a detrimental effect for a particular group of people, such as women, who are not likely to be accorded legal ownership rights.

The redistribution may also have adverse effects in its application. The authorities, whether local, regional or national, in selecting beneficiaries may favour specific groups or families, and probably not those whose situation would be aggravated by the individualisation of communal land. If customary rules regulating use of common land disappear, the situation of those people who remain landless is worse than before. Hence, women who traditionally enjoyed subsidiary or derived rights to use land can be deprived of their livelihood. Research indicates that,unlike men, women use the major part of their income for the care and well-being of their children and the improvement of the family's livelihood, Accordingly, women's income is more important to the well-being of the whole family. Lowering it may have dramatic consequences. The specific situation of pastoralists is also at stake.

The land registration process

Land titling processes, facilitating land transfer mechanisms and inheritance, may prejudice the poor, whose access to information about land laws or administrative procedures is very limited. There is a risk of manipulation of the registration process to the advantage of an elite. The poor may even not realise the benefit of the registration procedures, especially where there is no such tradition or precedent. There is therefore a risk of the more vulnerable part of the population being denied recognition of its customary rights to land. Land registration may require a long and complex administrative procedure in order to register all title deeds. Delays and inaccuracies are likely to be frequent, and to produce numerous conflicts. The extent of litigation over land is likely to increase. In litigation about a piece of land, the wealthier and better connected claimants are likely to win.

As a result of these ambiguities, it is essential to stress the "importance of governance infrastructures for policies directed at property rights institutions" (Field, 1989: 340). Too often, land reform has no beneficial effect, or negative, effects. The law remains disconnected from reality. The system in practice ignores or manipulates. Title deeds do not provide the anticipated security. The result may well be an increase in inequality. A precondition for the success of a redistributive and pro-poor land reform is wide and effective promotion of its terms, and the existence of supporting institutions. Also essential is the participation of the population affected by the reform. As stated by Hans-H. Munkner:

> "if land reform laws are to have any real effect, they are to be developed in a dialogue with the population, be couched in a language which the lay person can understand, and include simple, practicable procedures" (1996: 14).

CONCLUDING REMARKS ON THE SCOPE FOR IMPROVING ACCESS BY THE POOR TO THE LAW WITHIN THE EXISTING SYSTEM AND WITHIN A REFORMED SYSTEM

As indicated above, two main problems affect the poor in relation to the legal system. Direct legal discrimination, and *de facto* legal discrimination, i.e. an overall lack of access for the poor to knowledge of their rights, to the way the system functions, and to the prerequisites for coping with the requirements of this system.

Good governance implies the elimination of legal discrimination which creates or increases poverty, and allowing easy access for the poor to the legal system:

> "It is not always a question of needing new legislation. There is often also considerable need for the communication and enforcement of existing rights" (Thorp *et al.*, 1995: 108).

The poor need to be able to assert their rights, to enter into a legally protected society and to defend their particular interests within society. This implies that society is governed by the rule of law: there are strategies aimed at supporting rule of law, including comprehensive legal reform. Our concern is to determine which changes will allow the poor to secure access to the law. This may be possible by encouraging legal access strategies and by empowering of the poor. If the rights of the poor are to be protected, they must be:

> "helped to develop 'legal resources'—a functional knowledge of relevant law and the skills to use, and develop, law in order to promote and protect shared group interests and rights" (Dembo *et al.*, 1986: 4).

To encourage legal access, strategies led by governments may entail reform of the existing legal system (see Blair and Hansen, 1994; and Deutsche Stiftung für Internationale Entwicklung, 1995) and involve:

- clear communication of the rules, including the elimination of language barriers;
- the decentralisation and deconcentration of the justice system to allow geographical access to the law;
- free legal advice and free legal representation before the courts for the poor;
- introduction of alternative dispute resolution mechanisms (ombudsmen and ombudswomen) as a low-cost and rapid measure for settling disputes.[15]

They may also entail specific measures targeting the poor:

- legal literacy campaigns;
- paralegal campaigns targeting specific constituencies.

In order to increase access to the law for the poor, the work of legal advocacy NGOs should be facilitated and promoted. Legal advocacy NGOs:

> "seek, through legal means, to reform structures perpetuating poverty and oppression, to empower communities to take action in defence of their rights, and to break the bonds of passivity or dependency" (CAD, 1996, 30).

Their work is highly effective because it is done at grassroots level and is highly participatory. Special treatment may be afforded to these NGOs in order to enhance their ability to assist the poor. For instance, the Indian Supreme Court, under the banner of Social Action Litigation (SAL), allows legal-resource NGOs to file cases on behalf of groups, such as bonded labourers, whose rights have been violated (CAD, 1996).

Legal-advocacy NGOs are an essential intermediary between the law and the poor. The abstract of change, when expressed by the poor, is not likely to take the form of legal action. This is as much a question of unfamiliarity with

[15] However, this process has to be carefully monitored, as there is a risk of it being perceived as less legitimate or even as representing a counter-legal system.

the legal system as a question of distrust due either to personal experience or to general beliefs preventing the poor from seeing the legal system as an ally. Legal changes favouring poverty reduction may be enacted and implemented, and even if they cannot provide the only solution to poverty reduction, they may be helpful and this must not be overlooked. Empowering the poor to enable them to become familiar with and then challenge the legal system is likely to be an effective way of reducing poverty through legal means. In practice, however, a top-down approach to reducing poverty through legal means entails a risk of enacting provisions which do not meet the actual needs of the poor.

A good governance approach to the rule of law implies a particular concern of the government for the most vulnerable part of the population. It is important to consider the power relationships within a society. At the national level, the interests of the poor are likely to be ignored or mismanaged. Who will be interested in identifying legal provisions disadvantaging the poor and in taking steps to eliminate them? Who will be able to identify these provisions, some of them being *a priori* neutral, or at least meant to be so? A bottom-up approach is required to make the system operate in a way which is less unfavourable for the poor. A participatory approach is needed to allow the poor to speak out for their rights and their needs.

Once asserted, the rights of the poor must not only be implemented, but also be socially recognised. This may be a lengthy process, but the mere existence of legally recognised rights is a basis from which advances may be made.

Legal rules are not self-enforcing. They need a strong commitment from government and bureaucracy, particularly for the rules benefiting the poor, whose endeavours to put lobby for effective implementation require considerable time and energy. The crucial question may be, the recognition, not but the effective exercise of the rights and consequent opportunities by the poor. However, "a lack of financial and human capital means that the poor do not respond to changes in [. . .] incentives" (Sverisson, 1996: 131). In order to tackle poverty, law may be of real importance, but it is only one of the many dimensions required.

Some rules, particularly rules abolishing deep-rooted discrimination, may not be accepted initially. "The informal constraints that are culturally derived will not change immediately in reaction to changes in the formal rules" (North, 1990: 45). Social and cultural patterns are pervasive, and likely to remain so, whatever the legal changes. A change of law must be accompanied by changes in social values, which may be initiated through overall education programmes, or wide publicity campaigns. Such changes are likely to take time, maybe generations. In some cases social pressure is so high that even if a social feature, is almost universally rejected as undesirable. The caste system in India maintained by society as a whole, has persisted because each member of the society fears being penalised (by ostracism or otherwise) for not adhering to this rule (Lin and Nugent, 1995). It is important to take into account each society as a whole.

There is no simple common legal recipe.[16] Each society has its own ways and varied reactions to policies. Legal instruments must be viewed in relation to the functioning of each society, whose opportunities must not be overstated but do need to be recognised.

We have stated some of the problems faced by the poor in their relationship with the legal system. A good governance approach to development should promote a legal framework which is conducive to the development of the whole society, without excluding its vulnerable members. It means always taking into account the particular situation of the poor, in relation to general legal measures as well as to those targeting the poor.

REFERENCES

Agarwal, B. (1994), "Gender and Command Over Property: A Critical Gap in Economic Analysis and Policy in South Asia", *World Development*, vol. 22, no. 10

Bardhan, P. (1997), *The Role of Governance in Economic Development: A Political Economy Approach*, OECD

Bell, C. (1990), "Reforming Property Rights in Land and Tenancy", *World Bank Research Observer*, 2 July, 5

Berger, M. (1989), "Giving Women Credit: The Strengths and Limitations of Credit as a Tool for Alleviating Poverty", *World Development*, vol. 17, no. 7

Bhatt, E. (1989), "Toward Empowerment", *World Development*, vol. 17, no. 7

Blair, H. and Hansen, G. (1994), "Weighing in on the Scales of Justice. Strategic Approaches for Donor-Supported Rule of Law Programs", USAID Program and Operations, Assessment Report No. 7, February

CAD (1996), *Evaluation of Programs Promoting Participatory Development and Good Governance*, Synthesis Report, Revised Draft, OECD, August

Chen, M. (1989), "A Sectoral Approach to Promoting Women's Work: Lessons from India", *World Development*, vol. 17, no. 7

Coate, S., and Loury, G.C. (1993), "Will Affirmative Action Policies Eliminate Negative Stereotypes?", *American Economic Review*, 1220–40, December

Council of Europe (1992), *Toward Justice Accessible to All: Legal Aid Machinery and Certain Local Initiatives As Seen by Families Affected by Severe Poverty*, Study prepared in December 1989 by the International Movement ATD Fourth World at the Request of the Council of Europe, Directorate of Human Rights, Strasbourg

Dawn (1985) *Development, Crisis and Alternative Visions: Third World Women's Perspectives*, Delhi

Dembo, D., Dias, C., Morehouse, W., and Paul, J. eds., (1986), *The International Context of Rural Poverty in the Third World, Issues for Research and Action by Grassroots Organizations and Legal Activists*, International Center for Law in

[16] "The constitution of the United States is generally credited with facilitating economic development in that country. Although similar constitutions were adopted in many Latin American countries after their independence in the nineteenth century, they have been less effective due to less effective enforcement mechanisms, and both norms of behaviour and world views that are less conducive to innovation and growth" (Lin and Nugent, 1995: 2312).

Development, Series on Law, Social Action and Rural Poverty,New York: Council on International and Public Affairs

De Soto, H. (1989), *The Other Path. The Invisible Revolution in the Third World*, with foreword by Mario Vargas Llosa, New York: Harper & Row

Deutsche Stiftung für Internationale Entwicklung (1995), *Rule of Law, Legal Certainty and Judicial Reforms in Latin America*, Berlin: International Roundtable

Egger, P. (1995), "Freedom of Association, Rural Workers' Organisations and Participatory Development", in Schneider, H., ed., *Participatory Development From Advocacy to Action*, Development Centre Seminars, OECD

Field, Barry C. (1989), "The Evolution of Property Rights", *Kyklos*, 42(3)

Gaiha, R. (1995), "Does Agricultural Growth Matter in Poverty Alleviation?" *Development and Change*, vol. 26

Government of India, Planning Commission, (1952), *The First Five-Year Plan*

Heller, P. (1995), "From Class Struggle to Class Compromise: Redistribution and Growth in a South Indian State", *Journal of Development Studies*, vol. 31, no. 5, June, 645–72

Kabeer, N. (1996), "Agency, Well-Being and Inequality: Reflections on the Gender Dimensions of Poverty", *International Development Studies Bulletin*, vol. 27, no. 1

Killick, T. (1995), "Structural Adjustment and Poverty Alleviation: An Interpretative Survey", *Development and Change*, vol. 26, 305–31

Le Courrier Afrique-Caraibes-Pacifique-Union Européenne (1995), *Femmes*, no. 154, Nov.-Dec.

Lieten, G.K. (1996), "Land Reforms at Centre Stage: the Evidence on West Bengal", *Development and Change*, vol. 27, no. 1, January

Lin, Y. and Nugent, J.B. (1995), "Institutions and Economic Development", in Behrman and Srinivasan, eds., *Handbook of Development Economics*, vol. III

Lipton, M. (1995), "Market, Redistribution and Proto-Reform: Can Liberalization Help the Poor?", *Asian Development Review*, vol. 13, no. 1, 1–35

Moser, C. (1989), "Gender Planning in the Third World: Meeting Practical and Strategic Gender Needs", *World Development*, vol. 17, no. 11

Moyo, S. (1995), *The Land Question in Zimbabwe*, Harare: SAPES Books

Mullen, T. (1988), "Affirmative Action", in McLean, S. and Burrows, N., eds., *The Legal Relevance of Gender: Some Aspects of Sex-Based Discrimination*, London: Macmillan

Munkner, H.H. (1996), "Land rights in Africa: Collective Use Rights or Private Property?", *Agriculture + Rural Development*, 2/96, 10–14

North, D.C. (1990), *Institutions, Institutional Change and Economic Performance*, Cambridge: Cambridge University Press

—— (1994), "Economic Performance Through Time", *American Economic Review*, vol. 84, no. 3, June, 359–68

Pankhurst, D. (1995), "Towards reconciliation of the Land Issue in Namibia: Identifying the Possible, Assessing the Probable", *Development and Change*, vol. 26

Rodgers, G., ed., (1995), *New Approaches to Poverty Analysis and Policy, A Contribution to the World Summit for Social Development, The Poverty Agenda and the ILO. Issues for Research and Action*. Geneva: Institute for Labour Studies

Schneider H. (ed.) (1995), *Participatory Development From Advocacy to Action*, Development Centre Seminars, OECD

Sen A. (1990), "Gender and Co-operative Conflicts", in Tinker, I., ed., *Persistent Inequalities, Women and World Development*, New York: Oxford University Press

Sverisson, A.S. (1996), "The Politics and Governance of Poverty Alleviation Programmes: Comparative Case Studies in Sub-Saharan Africa and Latin America", *The European Journal of Development Research*, vol.28, N.2, December 1996

Swedish International Development Authority (1996), *Promoting Sustainable Livelihoods,* A report from the Task Force on Poverty Reduction

Thorp, R., Angell, A. and Landen, P. (1995), *Challenges for Peace: Towards Sustainable Social Development in Peru,* Report of the Pilot Mission on Socio-Economic Reform of the Inter-American Development Bank, Social Agenda Policy Group, Second and Revised Edition, November

Tinker, I., ed., (1990), *Persistent Inequalities, Women and World Development,* New York: Oxford University Press

United Nations (1995), *The Advancement of Women,* Notes for Speakers, Department of Public Information, January

United Nations Centre for Human Settlements (Habitat) (1993), *Support Measures to Promote Rental Housing for Low-Income Groups,* Nairobi

UNESCO Commission on Human Rights (1996), *The Realization of Economic, Social and Cultural Rights,* Final Report on Human Rights and Extreme Poverty, Submitted by the Special Rapporteur Mr. Leandro Despouy, E/CN.4/Sub.2/1996/13

UNDP (1995), *Human Development Report*

World Bank (1996), Report No. 15575-AFR, *Taking Action for Poverty Reduction in Sub-Saharan Africa,* Report of an African Regional Task Force, 1 May

9

An Army of Ideas: Marginalisation, Indigenous Rights and Civil Society in Mexico since the Zapatista Rebellion

CAMILO PEREZ-BUSTILLO

INTRODUCTION

THE ZAPATISTA REBELLION in Mexico's south-eastern state of Chiapas on 1 January 1994 sent shock waves throughout a post-Cold War world which had been characterized by widespread assumptions that revolution was off the agenda, history had ended, and that Mexico and much of the rest of the "Third World" were happily acquiring "First World" status. The uprising was deeply rooted in the Mayan indigenous communities of Mexico's most impoverished region. It thus posed an especially compelling counterpoint to the country's official incorporation into the "neo-liberal" North American Free Trade Agreement (NAFTA) with the US and Canada, scheduled to take effect on that very same date. Mexico was also poised at that time to join the hitherto exclusive club of the world's richest economies, the Organization for Economic Co-operation and Development (OECD). Mexico's President from 1989 until 1 December 1994 was Carlos Salinas de Gortari, who was campaigning aggressively as the US-backed candidate for designation as the first Director General of the new World Trade Organization (WTO), which had grown out of the Uruguay Round of the GATT successfully concluded in December 1993.

An uneven partial economic recovery began in mid-1996, but continues to be thwarted by the continuing immiseration of Mexico's vast, marginalized majority. According to 1998 World Bank estimates, over 30 per cent of the population is in poverty. This is considered by many independent researchers, such as Julio Boltvinik, to be a vast under-estimation of the true dimensions of poverty in the country. The persistent socio-economic patterns of inequity are especially explosive given the continuing failure by Salinas' hand-picked successor, President Ernesto Zedillo, to undertake a serious process of democratic transition from authoritarian rule by the Institutional Revolutionary Party (PRI), which has been in power since 1929.

One of the most important elements of Zapatista political discourse since the rebellion began has been the emphasis on the links between Mexico's lack of real democracy, its widespread socio-economic inequalities, and the systematic violation of the internationally recognised human rights of the country's indigenous peoples, the largest indigenous population in the Americas. This chapter focuses on the inter-relationship between these factors from the standpoint of both international and Mexican law, and in the light of parallel experiences from around the world.

The chapter title comes from the 1987 call issued by the now deceased Puerto Rican writer, pro-independence activist, and former political prisoner Clemente Soto Velez for the formation of an international "army of ideas" to wage battle against the injustices of late twentieth-century globalised capitalism. The Zapatistas remain an armed insurgent group but are distinguished from most of their Latin American predecessors by their development of a singularly innovative variant of traditional left-wing revolutionary discourse through their communiqués, which have been widely published in several languages throughout the world, and distributed via the Internet. At the heart of this new discourse is their arrival at universalistic demands for social justice from their initial focus on the particular needs of Mexico's indigenous peoples. (See generally Bardacke and Lopez, eds., 1995; Barry 1995; Cleaver, ed., 1994; Collier 1994; Katzenberger, ed., 1995; Ross 1995, *inter alia*).

The Chiapas-based Zapatista National Liberation Army (EZLN) and a new insurgent group, the People's Revolutionary Army (EPR), apparently based in Guerrero, another very poor state with a large indigenous population, along the Pacific coast west of Mexico City, are still in rebellion against the central government at the time of writing, but significant political differences prevent the two groups from forging an alliance at present. One of these differences concerns the EPR's refusal thus far to engage in the kind of peace negotiations with the government in which the EZLN has participated intermittently since the uprising in January 1994. A significant portion of this chapter is devoted to an exploration of the agreements which have arisen from these talks dedicated to indigenous rights issues, and an examination of their current status, and their relationship to comparative issues of poverty and international law.

POVERTY AND INDIGENOUS STATUS IN MEXICO

To be indigenous in Mexico—and in Latin America in general—is almost by definition to be poor. There is no way to disentangle the legal resolution of demands for indigenous human rights in Mexico, or throughout the continent, from the transformation of generalised conditions of socio-economic and political marginalisation in which they are immersed. These conditions have been exacerbated by the kind of "neo-liberal" economic policies targeted by the

Zapatistas in Mexico. The conditions were summarised in the description of NAFTA as a "death sentence" for the country's indigenous peoples in the first public statements by the Zapatistas' principal military strategist and spokesperson, known as Subcomandante Marcos, in early January 1994 and reiterated on subsequent occasions. The Zapatista emphasis on these links between neo-liberalism and the deprivation of indigenous peoples' rights has been further developed in the international forums "Against Neo-Liberalism and For Humanity" organised by the EZLN in their base communities in Chiapas in April and July–August 1996, and again at several sites in Spain in July–August 1997.

However, it is important to stress that to recognise this link between patterns of socio-economic marginalisation and indigenous status is not necessarily to fall into primitive economic determinism. Such a recognition can form the basis for an ethical mandate to reflect, act upon, and develop strategies of legal transformation on the basis of addressing the unavoidable underlying relationship between two complementary, interactive domains of oppression and exclusion which impede the exercise and enjoyment of fundamental human rights by the continent's indigenous peoples.

The 1990 Mexican national census documents the extent to which the country's indigenous peoples are characterised by their disproportionate rates of illiteracy, low educational levels, overcrowded housing, lack of access to basic public services (houses without plumbing, drainage, drinkable water, and/or electricity) and by low levels of employment and low pay for those who are employed, in comparison with Mexico's non-indigenous population. (For example, 42.5% of all Mexicans over the age of fourteen have six or more years of formal education against only 12.3% of indigenous persons; 66.5% of all Mexican households have more than 2 rooms against 38.2% of indigenous homes; 36.4% of Mexican homes lack drainage against 72.2% of indigenous households; only 7.8% of all Mexican homes lack electricity, drinkable water and drainage against 25.5% of all indigenous homes. (See e.g. Diaz Polanco 1997; Barry 1995; "For Mexico's Indians, Promises Not Kept" by Anthony de Palma 1994).

The Mexican government has constructed an Index of Marginalization, by state and by municipality, based on a weighted series of socio-economic indicators which include educational levels, illiteracy, access to plumbing, sewerage, drinkable water, electricity, overcrowded housing conditions, unemployment and low pay, plus two additional factors: the percentage of each state or municipal population living in communities of less than 5,000 inhabitants, and the percentage of populations in housing with dirt floors. The country's states and municipalities were then ranked into "very high", "high", "medium", "low" and "very low" marginalisation strata in the Index. The 1990 census figures also indicate that 6 of the country's 32 federal governmental units (31 states and the Federal District of Mexico City) are characterised by "very high" levels of socio-economic marginalisation according to this Index (Chiapas, Guerrero, Hidalgo,

Oaxaca, Puebla and Veracruz) and 9 by "high" levels (Campeche, Durango, Guanajuato, Michoacan, Queretaro, San Luis Potosi, Tabasco, Yucatan and Zacatecas). (Huchim 1994; Vidal 1996).

Chiapas, the cradle of the Zapatista rebellion, is in fact the state with the highest levels of overall marginalisation in the 1990 Index, although it may recently have been overtaken by Guerrero, the apparent base of the EPR. It is worth noting here that the devastation wrought by Hurricane "Paulina" in October 1997 hit both Guerrero and the other most important bastion of the EPR, Oaxaca, most heavily, especially in the remotest regions where those states' already impoverished indigenous populations are most concentrated.

All the six states classified as having "very high" levels of marginalisation in 1990 are among the ten with the highest proportionate indigenous populations, together with three of the states (Campeche, San Luis Potosi and Yucatan) classified as having "high" levels of marginalisation. In the states with the lowest levels of ranked marginalisation, it is the indigenous populations who are the most marginalised (Raramuri or Tarahumaras in Chihuahua, Wirrarika or Huicholes and Coras in Nayarit and Jalisco, Mayas in Quintana Roo, indigenous migrants in the Federal District). Two of the states with the smallest indigenous populations (Nuevo Leon and Baja California Norte) are the only two states with "very low" ranked levels of marginalisation.

The above figures are based on a 1990 census estimate of a an indigenous population of 6.4 million out of a total population of about 70 million, approximately 7.9% of the total. The estimates for both indigenous people and for the total population are considered to be a significant under-representation by most independent analysts. It is worth noting that if the kinds of criteria for racial identification legally mandated as remedies for institutionalised discrimination in the United States as the result of the 1960s civil rights movement (primarily colour and ancestry) were applied in Mexico, at least 90% of the population would be classified by most accounts as of indigenous origin due to skin colour and/or ancestry, regardless of their level of self-identification with indigenous cultural attributes, such as language, or participation in traditional rituals. Most analysts estimate that the current total population of Mexico is over 90 million, with an indigenous population of about 10%, based on some mixture of self-identification and specific attributes such as language or culture, but not "race" in the colour-bound sense in which the term is usually employed in Western social science and media. Indigenous activists and anthropologists critical of the official Mexican census criteria for determining who is indigenous agree in their critique of its underestimate, although often differing as to how to fix it, and argue for a true indigenous population of between 10 and 20 million.

Both the census figures and some of the latter estimates, however, assume a restrictive definition of who counts as indigenous, based on the number of speakers of indigenous languages. The validity of this assumption is undermined by the fact that the census process does not employ any independent measure of relative proficiency in indigenous languages and Spanish, and as a result its totals for the category of speakers of indigenous languages is almost wholly subjective, based either on self-identification or on the perception and judgement of census-takers, who are unlikely to have the specialised ethnographic and socio-linguistic training necessary for such a task. This is especially problematic from a socio-linguistic perspective in any situation (such as Mexico's) where speakers of minority languages are likely to be stigmatised for public use of their languages, since speaking an indigenous language in this case is a "marker" of a marginalised status which is the object of patterns and practices of social discrimination. A similar dynamic occurs, for example, with estimates of Spanish speakers in the United States. (Lomnitz Adler 1995.)

Any efforts to vindicate internationally protected language rights for indigenous persons in Mexico are complicated by the lack of the necessary basic information about the actual current numbers of speakers of indigenous minority languages, and their relative linguistic proficiencies, and levels of comparable literacy in both their mother tongue and Spanish. New protections for indigenous language rights in Mexico must therefore be accompanied by mandates for the accurate gathering of data necessary for adequate language planning and language policy development. A systematic effort must be made to identify, classify and determine the possible applicability of models for such approaches in the legislation, policies and practices of countries around the world facing similar kinds of challenges, e.g. Canada, Belgium, Spain, the US, South Africa, India, Russia, and China. (Phillipson and Skutnabb-Kangas 1995.)

THE SAN ANDRES ACCORDS

The second round of these talks culminated in the only negotiated agreement which has emerged from the intermittent, and currently stalled, peace process between the government and the Zapatistas, signed on 16 February 1996, and focusing on issues relating to indigenous rights and culture. But the government has refused to follow through with the constitutional and other reforms necessary to translate the commitments it made in the San Andres Accords (*Acuerdos de San Andres*, named for the highland Mayan community where the talks were held during 1995 and 1996) into reality. Further talks on issues of democratic reform, development and women's rights are still pending and new negotiation sessions have been suspended indefinitely by the EZLN until the government takes steps to comply fully with the 1996 Accords. The derailment of the Accords became evident in December 1996 and January 1997 when the government backed off from introducing the constitutional amendments called for by the Accords, which had been drafted by a multi-party special commission of the national congress (which includes representatives of the ruling PRI as well as of the most important opposition parties and is known as the *Comision de Concordia y Pacificacion*, COCOPA).

In the last few months of 1997 and the first half of 1998 the deadlock between the government and the Zapatistas deepened. The absence of a shared understanding of the implications of the broad language of the San Andres Accords led the government to introduce its own unilateral version of necessary constitutional reforms. These proposals have been rejected by the Zapatistas and the increasingly influential National Indigenous People's Congress (*Congreso Nacional Indigena*, CNI) made up of the sectors of the country's newly revitalised indigenous communities which sympathise with the EZLN, as well as by the centre-left opposition Party of the Democratic Revolution (PRD). Meanwhile human rights violations have intensified in the regions of Chiapas with most conflict, and in other primarily indigenous regions of the country, as the presence of the Mexican military becomes more generalised. Most recent human rights violations are attributed by independent international human rights monitors such as Amnesty International and Human Rights Watch to the increasingly overt activities of pro-government paramilitary forces made up of local members of the ruling PRI party, which act with virtual impunity against those perceived to be supporters or leaders of the Zapatistas, or in other regions of the EPR. The most dramatic expression of such patterns of complicity was the massacre of forty-five indigenous *campesinos* or peasants (thirty-six of them women and children) belonging to a non-violent, lay Catholic social movement in the village of Acteal in the highlands of Chiapas on 22 December 1997 by local paramilitary forces linked to the PRI.

International human rights observers were targeted by the Mexican government for summary expulsion from the country when they have got too close to military operations against the new *de facto* Zapatista indigenous autonomous governments, which have been established throughout the conflict zone in Chiapas.

The COCOPA was set up pursuant to a law passed in March 1995 which enabled a renewed process of dialogue with the EZLN after an abortive government military offensive in February of that year. The botched attempt to crush the EZLN and concomitant failure to secure the capture of key Zapatista leaders sparked widespread protests both nationally and internationally. This in turn had complicated the Zedillo government's efforts to be "rescued" from the economic crisis unleashed by the sudden devaluation in December 1994, by an emergency $51 billion loan guarantee package from the US Treasury, the International Monetary Fund (IMF), the Bank of International Settlements and the World Bank. In this sense the peace talks were at least in part a government public relations exercise directed at international public opinion or "international civil society", which the EZLN had courted with significant success through Internet and other means since the inception of the rebellion.

By December 1996, however, the worst of the 1994–95 devaluation crisis had passed in orthodox macro-economic terms (which tend to relegate persistent phenomena in Mexico such as devastating losses of purchasing power, structural unemployment and deepening impoverishment, to the category of unaccountable externalities). Significant, if still tentative and easily destabilised, foreign investor confidence has been restored in the Zedillo regime, and the government's pantomime of a meaningful peace process is less important to its international image (although the recent conclusion of an agreement to initiate free trade talks with the European Union, which incorporate a "democratic rights clause", may revive the government's perception of its need to satisfy the formalities of Western liberal democracy, with possible favourable consequences for putting the Chiapas talks back on track). The tense confrontation in Paris in September 1997 between several international non-governmental organisations active in France and President Zedillo during a state visit exemplifies the complexity of this situation.

Meanwhile both the US and the Mexican military establishments have become increasingly prominent in US–Mexican relationships, with unprecedented levels of co-operation and intervention by the Pentagon, and intelligence agencies being structured around the crucial bilateral issues of the so-called "war against drugs" and immigration control. There are increasing reports within Mexico of US military aid and material ostensibly targeted for the drug war, in fact being used in counter-insurgency operations by the Mexican armed forces, especially in Chiapas and Guerrero, as in Colombia and Peru. At the same time it has become clear that the militarisation of the anti-drug effort in Mexico has resulted in widespread high-level corruption of the armed forces, and in the generalised application of US-promoted "national security" doctrines in their "low-intensity warfare" version.

The government has so far persisted in its claim that the proposed constitutional amendments growing out of the San Andres Accords went too far, and has specifically objected to the formal recognition of aspects of the exercise of indigenous rights to "autonomy" which it alleges were not explicitly included in the Accords. The net effect of the government's retreat has been to undermine, if not abort, the Accords themselves, and to reopen them for public debate, especially among elites whose pro-US and or Eurocentric orientation makes them uncomfortable with the idea of a new vigour in government indigenous policy.

Several of the country's most prominent pro-government jurists, academics and writers have spoken out not only against the COCOPA constitutional proposals, but against what they claimed were the implications of the San Andres Accords on their own terms. At the heart of their expressed concerns is the assumption that the recognition of indigenous rights to self-determination through autonomy might undermine Mexican national sovereignty and unity, and create disloyal "statelets" exempt from the "rule of law" supposedly prevalent in the country. Often ignored in this debate is the repeated assertion by indigenous rights activists that what they seek most fundamentally is recognition of the rightful, central place of indigenous peoples within a multicultural Mexican nation, rather than the marginalisation which currently prevails. Ironically, experience elsewhere in the world indicates that it is precisely when such demands for recognition of the rights of racial, ethnic, indigenous, linguistic, cultural and/or religious minorities are resisted that movements for separatism and secession tend to arise.

The government's retreat from the San Andres Accords has re-ignited a long-standing debate in Mexican society about its own character and definition, and about the status of indigenous peoples, culture and languages within that framework. This debate has traditionally been waged primarily in terms of contending visions of history, anthropology, politics and educational policy, but it has now become more than ever a debate about fundamental notions of constitutionalism, legality and democracy.

This debate about the place of the country's indigenous peoples in its constitution, laws, polity and society is inextricably linked to their disproportionate socio-economic marginalisation. As the San Andres Accords themselves note :

> "the conditions of poverty and marginalization which affect indigenous peoples demonstrate the unequal character of the development of Mexican society, and define the extent of the demands for social justice which the State must attend to" (translation by this author paper of Point 2 of the Joint Declaration by the government and the EZLN, one of the five jointly drafted documents which constitute the San Andres Accords, ed. Juan Pablos, 1996).

These issues have their particular Mexican character and content, but they also have resonance, on one hand, in international law on the rights of indigenous peoples, and on the other, in terms of the rights of racial, ethnic, religious, cultural and linguistic minorities (sometimes all subsumed into one category as "national" minorities, especially in Marxist-Leninist parlance and political practice). The contemporary descendants of Mexico's original inhabitants (defined by renowned Mexican historian Miguel Leon Portilla as the country's *pueblos originarios*—aboriginal or original inhabitants—rather than as *indigenas* or *indios*, since those are both are problematic terms from multiple points of view) fit both the standard definitions of "indigenous" peoples under international law and those regarding the latter kinds of minorities.

THE CONTEMPORARY DEBATE OVER INDIGENOUS RIGHTS IN MEXICO, CIVIL SOCIETY, AND INTERNATIONAL HUMAN RIGHTS LAW

Mexico is a signatory of both the International Labor Organization (ILO) Convention 169 regarding the rights of indigenous and "tribal" peoples (the latter term presumably including Hutus and Tutsis, but not Serbs and Croats, for example) and the UN Convention on the Elimination of All Forms of Racial Discrimination. As a result Mexico reports regularly to the UN Committee (known by the initials of its English name as the CERD) set up pursuant to the latter, regarding its measures to overcome "racial" discrimination against a group—its indigenous peoples—which is not normally considered to be racially identifiable in Mexican social or official discourse. This generalised refusal to speak in openly racial terms about the country's population—except generically as a (presumably mixed or *mestizo*) *raza*, a term encompassing all Mexicans as opposed to all foreigners, especially Spaniards and North Americans, and whose holiday is observed on 12 October—is contradicted by official practices such as prescribed specifications of skin colour on passports and drivers' licences.

Mexico is also a signatory to the International Covenant on Civil and Political Rights, whose Article 27 has been interpreted by the UN Human Rights Committee (which oversees compliance with the Covenant through its Optional Protocol, to which Mexico is not a signatory) in at least one instance (the *Lovelace* v. *Canada* communication in 1981) to encompass the rights of indigenous peoples in Canada (Steiner and Alston 1996). Nonetheless unprecedented attention and analysis has been devoted to Mexico's own variants of racism since the Zapatista uprising, and the shift in discourse has been picked up by the international media (see *New York Times* references above).

However, this whole discussion is complicated by the fact that there is no generally accepted social, legal or political definition of who is "indigenous" in Mexico. This fundamental issue of definition would not be settled by the enactment of either the San Andres Accords or of the COCOPA constitutional proposals which are their closest equivalent, since both downplay the need for such a definition, and give great weight to indigenous people's rights to self-definition, together with an emphasis on Leon Portilla's conception of contemporary indigenous groups as "successor" peoples.

One of the few things which is clear about the working definition of indigenous peoples in Mexico is that there is a generalised acceptance (as reflected in the dominant discourses of the government, mass media, academic analysis, public opinion polls and the country's diverse indigenous movements themselves, and as reflected in the census figures described above) of virtual equivalence between indigenous status and poverty, increasingly accompanied by a recognition of Mexican racism. Indeed it has often been alleged by Western-oriented Mexican intellectuals, critical of supposed governmental paternalism towards the country's indigenous communities, that indigenous identity in Mexico is an artifact of entrenched patterns of socio-economic marginalisation and that the best way to define its indigenous peoples out of existence would be through their accelerated modernisation and "development". Both the official ruling PRI's *indigenista* policy and significant sectors of opposition thought, heavily influenced by pseudo-Marxist variants of economic determinism, have fallen into this kind of reasoning at various times during the period since the Mexican Revolution.

The Zapatista uprising, however, has given prominence to a neo-*indigenista* (or *indianista*) critique of the official *indigenismo* implemented by the PRI which emerged from the social and ideological process of the Mexican Revolution. This tendency can be traced back to roots among 1) indigenous activists and scholars long critical of the limitations, abuses and perversities of official policy and linked both to left opposition and *campesino* movements, and their university-based allies; 2) exponents of liberation theology both among the Catholic Church hierarchy (a small minority of bishops, exemplified by Sergio Mendez Arceo of Cuernavaca, Jose Llaguno of the Tarahumara region in Chihuahua, Arturo Lona and Bartolome Carrasco of Oaxaca, and of course Samuel Ruiz of the Diocese of San Cristobal in Chiapas, as well as key Dominican and Jesuit priests such as Fathers Miguel Concha and David Fernandez, respectively) and at the grassroots level (individual priests, nuns and laypersons); and 3) human rights activists and researchers grouped into an increasingly influential sector of national, regional and local non-governmental organizations (NGOs) with international funding and links to international support networks.

The overlap between these three sectors formed the basis for the loosely knit citizens' movement for peace in Chiapas which emerged in the immediate aftermath of the uprising, was activated again in February 1995, and which called for a process of "national dialogue" in the wake of the emergence of the EPR and the breakdown of the talks with the Zapatistas. It is also from the confluence of these three sectors that the EZLN drew its corps of several hundred publicly named citizen and academic advisers (*asesores*) and invited guests to the various different phases and sessions of the now suspended peace talks between April 1995 and September 1996, as well as the most prominent activists in the recently founded Zapatista National Liberation Front (FZLN), the putative political vehicle for the movement's transition away from armed struggle.

Among the most significant intellectual sources of the neo-Zapatista critique of official government policy towards indigenous issues is the work of one of Mexico's most influential anthropologists, Guillermo Bonfil Batalla, whose 1989 book *Mexico Profundo* (Bonfil 1996) is probably the best single summation of an indigenous-centred diagnosis of Mexico's history and present, and vision for its future. The San Andres Accords and the COCOPA proposal for constitutional reform rejected by the government are in effect the translation of this vision into legal terms.

The first step towards this end actually preceded the Zapatista uprising, in the form of a 1991 amendment to Article 4 of the Mexican Constitution, ironically promoted by President Salinas, which for the first time explicitly recognised indigenous peoples as part of the country's constitutional reality. The text of the amendment proposed by a blue ribbon interdisciplinary commission (including Bonfil) was, however, significantly watered down during congressional debates evidencing concerns about maintaining supposedly undivided national sovereignty and the allegedly divisive implications of autonomy, foreshadowing those expressed about the San Andres Accords.

The reform ultimately adopted is essentially a formulaic recitation that the Mexican nation has a "multicultural character rooted in its indigenous peoples", and providing that legislation should assure that the "development of indigenous languages, cultures, usages, traditions, resources, and specific forms of social organisation" be guaranteed, along with "effective access" to the national legal and administrative law system. The 1991 constitutional amendment also specifically provides that indigenous law and custom should be "taken into account" in agrarian law proceedings (without specifying how and to what extent). All these provisions lack binding effect under Mexican constitutional law in the absence of specific implementing legislation: no such legislation has yet been adopted.

Ironically, the pro-government critics of the San Andres Accords and COCOPA reform proposal argue that the most viable route to indigenous rights reform is to adopt (belatedly) such implementing legislation instead of making more constitutional amendments. This is a crucial point of divergence between the EZLN and its supporters and the government, because the COCOPA proposal in fact calls for further modifications to Article 4 of the Constitution itself in order to strengthen and make more explicit its mandate for a new era in indigenous rights. The vigour of any implementing legislation of course depends entirely on the underlying sweep of the constitutional language in Article 4.

Prior to the Zapatista uprising most indigenous rights advocates independent of the government agreed that the way forward was to push for Article 4 implementing legislation, which it was hoped would at least clarify the generalities of the amendments to Article 4 as finally adopted. The impact of the uprising on the reactivation of an independent indigenous movement led to a change in strategy, which bore apparent fruit in the San Andres Accords and then in the COCOPA proposals. Now things have come full circle again as the EZLN has been increasingly boxed into a corner, and with it the nation's newly reborn grassroots indigenous movement centred around the Zapatista-aligned, but multi-tendency, *Congreso Nacional Indigena* (CNI) (National Indigenous Peoples' Congress).

The Congress recently demonstrated its grassroots strength by mobilising the presence of 1,111 masked representatives of Zapatista base communities in Mexico City during the September 1997 Independence Day celebrations. They were joined en route by several thousand supporters from each of the country's most important indigenous groups, who accompanied the caravan on a whistle-stop tour throughout the regions where the country's indigenous population is most heavily concentrated (Chiapas, Oaxaca, Veracruz and Morelos). The motorised march concluded by following the path taken by Emiliano Zapata's forces into Mexico City in 1914, during the Mexican Revolution. The mobilisation's principal demand was for government compliance with the San Andres Accords. It succeeded in filling the capital city's principal public square (known as the Zocalo) with Zapatista supporters for the first time since massive pro-peace demonstrations during Zedillo's failed military offensive in Chiapas in February 1995, but the government's position continues to be that specific legislation to implement the Accords requires a new round of talks with the EZLN. The EZLN insists that no new talks are possible until the substance of the San Andres agreements becomes law. No easy unravelling of this tangled knot is currently foreseeable.

If no meaningful reforms emerge from the current deadlock there is nothing to prevent further radicalisation of the indigenous demands made thus far, including a transition from the claim of autonomy to a demand for sovereignty or even separatism, probably the government's worst nightmare. Indigenous expressions of such "fundamentalism" have emerged with some strength in neighbouring Guatemala over the last decade, and to a more limited extent in Peru, Bolivia and Ecuador. Renewed combat is also possible given the government's continuing reliance on a provocative intensification of direct military pressure on Zapatista strongholds backed up against the green wall of the Lacandon jungle.

The limits of the amended Article 4, in the light of all this, are further highlighted by exploring the impact of the Mexican ratification of ILO Convention 169 in 1990. The Convention clearly goes far beyond the 1991 amendments to Article 4 in its substantive recognition of indigenous rights (such as those to equitable and non-discriminatory treatment, recognition of indigenous legal and customary systems of dispute resolution, and to consultation regarding governmental actions which might affect their interests) but falls short of those proposed to be recognised in both the draft Universal and the American Declarations of Indigenous Rights (such as rights to self-determination and autonomy) which have still not been finalised, much less adopted by the UN and OAS respectively, which would then still have to be signed and ratified by member states.

ILO Convention 169 also offers less protective of indigenous rights than indigenous peoples would have if they were considered to be encompassed by the UN Declaration on the Rights of Persons Belonging to National or Ethnic, Religious, or Linguistic Minorities, adopted by General Assembly Resolution 47/135 on 18 December 1992. The UN Declaration's greater substantive strength is, however, undermined by the fact taht it has a lesser international legal standing than the ILO Convention, since UN resolutions voted on by delegates have significantly less weight under international law than conventions ratified by national parliaments.

In any case ILO Convention 169 goes much further than (and preceded) the amended version of Article 4 of the Mexican Constitution, creating a framework under Mexican law (because of the standing of international agreements of this kind under Article 133 of the Mexican Constitution as "supreme law" of the land) which would mandate the strengthening of Article 4 and/or the passage of implementing legislation reinvigorated by the advances contained in the San Andres Accords and the COCOPA proposals. This would be necessary in order for Mexican domestic law on indigenous rights under Article 4 to comply with the requirements of international law binding on Mexico. The most rational, good-faith and least circuitous way to comply with this international law-derived "duty to legislate" would be by enacting of the San Andres Accords through the COCOPA proposals as constitutional reforms (of Article 4 among others) together with the additional necessary implementing legislation.

The other principal source of positive international law bearing on the issue of indigenous rights in Mexico (aside from the generalities of the Universal Declaration of Human Rights and American Convention on Human Rights) is

Article 27 of the International Covenant on Civil and Political Rights (ICCPR), also ratified by Mexico. Article 27 provides that:

> "in those states in which ethnic, religious, or linguistic minorities exist, persons belonging to such minorities shall not be denied the right, in community with other members of their group, to enjoy their own culture, to profess and practice their own religion, or to use their own language".

This Article of the ICCPR is the basis of the December 1992 UN General Assembly Declaration on the Rights of Minorities, referred to above. Arguably the best way to put into effect and protect these rights from infringement in the case of an indigenous minority group is to recognise their right to autonomy as an expression of their underlying entitlement to self-determination, precisely the route taken not only by the San Andres Accords and COCOPA proposals, but also by the current draft versions of the proposed Universal and American Declarations of Indigenous Rights.

Interestingly, given this book's focus on issues of law and poverty, both ILO Convention 169 and the 1992 UN General Assembly Declaration on the Rights of Minorities stress the link between the affirmative recognition of indigenous minority rights and the need to overcome these groups' socio-economic marginalisation. ILO Convention 169 states in its Article 2 that state parties must affirmatively protect the rights of indigenous peoples within their territory by (among other things) ensuring their enjoyment of equal social, economic and cultural opportunities (subsection b) and by eliminating socio-economic differences between such indigenous groups and the general population (subsection 3), pursuing both goals with due respect for the group's identity, interests and traditions. The 1992 Declaration's Preamble stresses that "the promotion and protection of the rights of persons" belonging to minority groups "contribute to the political and social stability of States in which they live".

CONCLUSION

The unspoken corollary of the language in the UN Declaration is worth noting: Mexico's continued failure to recognise positively, to protect, and to promote indigenous rights in a manner consistent with international law and the mandates of its own heritage is destabilising the country, and threatens to plunge it into (avoidable) prolonged political and even ethnic strife. Varying but parallel experiences in Guatemala, Peru, Canada, Spain, Northern Ireland, Yugoslavia, South Africa, Ethiopia, Nigeria, Rwanda, Russia, India and Sri Lanka, among others, suggest the possible dimensions of the disasters which may lie ahead, and of the downward spiral which may already have begun. Clearly the fault-lines are deepest where, as in Mexico, socio-economic marginalisation has a disproportionate racial, ethnic and culturally identifiable impact, and where its centre of gravity lies in the most meaningful continuous source of the country's very identity.

Since this chapter first went to press, Mexico has a newly elected government led by President Vicente Fox of the center-right Partido Accion Nacional which took office on 1 December 2000. His campaign pledges included taking concrete steps towards the peaceful resolution of the Chiapas conflict. Early actions included sending the COCOPA constitutional reform proposal based on the San Andres Accords to Congress for debate and partial demilitarisation of the Chiapas region. But leading sectors of his own party and of the former ruling PRI pledge to block their enactment. Meanwhile the Zapatistas have organised an indigenous peoples' march on the capital from Chiapas (some 1,100 kms.) in early March 2001 to lobby congress and mobilise public opinion in support of the needed reforms.Their most dramatic peaceful mobilisation thus far will be led personally by their spokesperson and military chief, Subcommander Marcos.

REFERENCES

Bardacke, Frank; Lopez, Leslie, and the Watsonville, California Human Rights Committee, eds., (1995), *Shadows of Tender Fury: The Letters and Communiques of Subcomandante Marcos and the Zapatista Army of National Liberation*, New York: Monthly Review Press

Barry, Tom (1995), *Zapata's Revenge: Free Trade and the Farm Crisis in Mexico*, Boston: South End Press

Cleaver, Harry, and Autonomedia, eds., (1995), *Zapatistas: Documents of the New Mexican Revolution*, Brooklyn: Autonomedia

Collier, George A., with Lowery Quaratiello, Elizabeth (1994), *Basta: Land and the Zapatista Revolution in Chiapas*, San Francisco: Food First Books, Institute for Food and Development Policy

DePalma, Anthony (1995), and (1994), "Racism? Mexico's in Denial" and "For Mexico's Indians, Promises Not Kept", *New York Times*; 11 June 1995 and 15 June 1994; pp. 4 and A1, A6, respectively

Diaz-Polanco, Hector (1997), *La Rebelion Zapatista y la Autonomia*, Mexico: siglo XXI, 73–87

Huchim, Eduardo (1994), *Mexico 1994: La Rebelion y El Magnicidio*, Appendix XV (non-paginated), Mexico: Nueva Imagen

Katzenberger, Elaine, ed., (1995), *First World Ha Ha Ha: The Zapatista Challenge*, San Francisco: City Lights

Lomnitz-Adler, Claudio (1995), *Las salidas del laberinto*, Mexico: Joaquin Mortiz/Planeta, 359

Juan Pablos, ed., (1996), "Nunca Mas Sin Nosotros: Acuerdos de la Mesa de Derechos y Cultura Indigena entre el Ejercito Zapatista de Liberacion Nacional y el Gobierno Federal', *San Andres Sacamch'en de los Pobres*, Mexico, DF

Phillipson, Robert and Skutnabb-Kangas, Tove (1995), "Linguistic Rights and Wrongs", *Applied Linguistics*, vol. 16, no. 4, 483–504

Steiner, Henry J., and Alston, Philip (1996), *International Human Rights in Context: Law, Politics, Morals*, Oxford: Clarendon Press, 1017–19

Vidal, Francisco (1996), "Geografia de la Rebelion", *Reforma*, Mexico City, 8 Sep., 16A

Appendix

CROP *Publications*

1. **Poverty: Research Projects, Institutes, Persons,** Tinka Ewoldt-Leicher and Arnaud F. Marks, (eds.), Tilburg, Bergen, Amsterdam 1995, 248 pp.
2. **Urban Poverty: Characteristics, Causes and Consequences,** David Satterthwaite (ed.), special issue of *Environment and Urbanization*, Volume 7 No. 1 April 1995, 283 pp.
3. **Urban Poverty: From Understanding to Action,** David Satterthwaite (ed.), special issue of *Environment and Urbanization*, Volume 7 No. 1 October 1995, 283 pp.
4. **Women and Poverty: The Feminization of Poverty,** Ingrid Eide (ed.), The Norwegian National Commission for UNESCO and CROP: Oslo and Bergen 1995 (published in Norwegian only), 56 pp.
5. **Poverty: A Global Review. Handbook on International Poverty Research,** Else Øyen, S.M. Miller, Syed Abdus Samad (eds.), Scandinavian University Press and UNESCO: Oslo and Paris 1996, 620 pp.
6. **Poverty and Participation in Civil Society,** Yogesh Atal and Else Øyen (eds.), UNESCO and Abhinav Publications: Paris and New Delhi, 1997.
7. **Law, Power and Poverty,** Asbjørn Kjønstad and John H. Veit Wilson (eds.), CROP Publications: Bergen 1997, 148 pp.
8. **Poverty and Social Exclusion in the Mediterranean Area,** Karima Korayem and Maria Petmesidou (eds.), CROP Publications: Bergen 1998.
9. **Poverty and the Environment,** Arild Angelsen and Matti Vainio (eds.), CROP Publications: Bergen 1998.
10. **The International Glossary on Poverty,** David Gordon and Paul Spicker (eds.), CROP International Studies in Poverty Research, Zed Books, London 1999.

Index

www.ingramcontent.com/pod-product-compliance
Ingram Content Group UK Ltd.
Pitfield, Milton Keynes, MK11 3LW, UK
UKHW021030041026
15470UKWH00013B/1149

9 781841 131900